TRUST, GLOBALISATION AND MARKET EXPANSION

ECONOMIC ISSUES, PROBLEMS AND PERSPECTIVES SERIES

TARP in the Crosshairs: Accountability in the Troubled Asset Relief Program
Paul W. O'Byrne (Editor)
2009. ISBN 978-1-60741-807-8

Trust, Globalisation and Market Expansion
Jacques-Marie Aurifeille, Christopher Medlin, and Clem Tisdell
2009 ISBN: 978-1-60741-812-2

Trust, Globalisation and Market Expansion

Jacques-Marie Aurifeille,
Christopher J. Medlin and
Clem Tisdell
Editors

Nova Science Publishers, Inc.
New York

LIBRARY OF CONGRESS CATALOGING-IN-PUBLICATION DATA

Trust, globalisation and market expansion / [edited by] Jacques-Marie Aurifeille, Christopher Medlin, Clem Tisdell.
    p. cm.
  Includes index.
   ISBN 978-1-60741-812-2 (hbk.)
   1. Trust--Economic aspects. 2. Interorganizational relations. 3. Organizational behavior. 4. Customer relations. 5. Consumer behavior. I. Aurifeille, Jacques-Marie. II. Medlin, Christopher. III. Tisdell, C. A. (Clement Allan)
   HD58.7.T7438 2009
   302.3'5--dc22
                                    2009020639

Published by Nova Science Publishers, Inc. ✝ *New York*

CONTENTS

Contents

PREFACE

This book developed following the Third Annual Workshop of the FACIREM (Franco-Australian Centre for International Research in Economics and Management) on "Trust and Globalisation". The two day workshop was held in March 2008 at the University of Adelaide. The organising committee included Professors Jacques-Marie Aurifeille, Director of the FACIREM, Dr Christopher J. Medlin of the University of Adelaide and Professor Clem Tisdell of the University of Queensland.

Following the second workshop of the FACIREM on "Globalization and Partnerships" (Aurifeille, Svizzero and Tisdell, 2007, Nova Science Publishers), the third workshop focused on the role of trust, a construct which underpins the interactions of institutions, firms and consumers in a globalising world. A recent search on 'trust' in Google Scholar found almost 600,000 articles for the period 2003-2008.

Trust is a complex psychological and sociological construct and developing our understanding of trust is best undertaken by a variety of disciplines. The third workshop brought together researchers from the Economics, Management and Marketing Sciences to present and discuss theoretical and empirical papers across a range of institutional and global contexts. This diverse group of academics brought a variety of theoretical frameworks to the issue of developing and enhancing trust so as to promote market expansion in a global economic environment. As a result the workshop was comprised of interesting debates and discussions which illuminated the complex nature of trust in a globalising world. These papers have been thoroughly revised for the book and reflect the discussion and debate from the many approaches presented at the FACIREM workshop.

The book will be of considerable interest to academic researchers and business people interested in the role of trust in globalising business opportunities. As is apparent from the present crisis in world markets the importance of trust and of its evolution is an ever more challenging issue. The extension of business across multiple markets in a globalising world requires development of trust in new situations, such as across cultural and institutional boundaries. Trust is also an important construct in managing crisis situations, and these situations are more apparent in an increasingly interdependent business world connected by instantaneous and low cost communication.

We thank all those who helped in making this book possible.

Jacques-Marie Aurifeille, Christopher J. Medlin, and Clem Tisdell

PART I. INTRODUCTION

In: Trust, Globalisation and Market Expansion
Editors: J-M. Aurifeille, C. Medlin and C. Tisdell

ISBN 978-1-60741-812-2
© 2009 Nova Science Publishers, Inc.

Chapter 1

TRUST AND GLOBALISATION: AN OVERVIEW

Jacques-Marie Aurifeille[1], Christopher J. Medlin[2] and Clem Tisdell[3]

[1]University of French Polynesia, France
[2]Business School, University of Adelaide, Australia
[3]School of Economics, The University of Queensland,
Brisbane, 4072, Australia

1. INTRODUCTION

In a time of global economic crisis and turbulence, without equivalent since the great 1929 depression, it is important to revisit and analyse the role of trust in the world economic system. Trust is central to economic exchange and plays an important facilitation role in the global economy, enhancing inter-firm interactions and also exchanges between institutions, firms and consumers. Trust has been defined in a variety of ways and with reference to many contexts (see Chapter 2, 3 and 5).

This book consists of a collection of conceptual and empirical research papers which extend the understanding of the role of trust in a globalising world. The chapters in this book encompass a range of different analytical methods in order to provide new insights into the processes of developing and managing trust between firms and consumers in a global economy.

The contributions have been organised into three parts. The chapters in Part II examine trust across a range of contemporary institutions and settings in a globalising world. These chapters highlight the role and varied quality of trust in many settings from inter-firm relationships to the way groups of firms influence their interactions with consumers across the globe, and the role of trust in times of global economic crisis. In these diverse contexts we see that trust plays a pivotal role in explaining development of economic opportunities for institutions, firms and consumers.

The role of trust in a global market place is shaped by the nature of interactions between firms and consumers. These interactions occur in networks of institutions and inter-firm relationships that form global supply chains. Conversely, consumers and managerial decision-makers through their interactions also shape and change the nature of firms and institutions and the way these entities interact with each other. In Part III the role of trust in developing exchange between entities within larger frameworks is examined across a range of global and inter-organisation contexts. Trust operates in diverse ways in these settings; increasing exchange by harmonising and improving the efficiency and effectiveness of interactions between firms, or between firms and other institutions, and even within firms, trust leads to changes in the interactions between managers and their employees.

In Part IV, the role of trust in consumer decisions is considered in an increasingly global market. Globalisation contributes to the emergence and spreading of lifestyles and needs, supported by products whose origins are becoming less clear. In this context, the globalisation strategies of the firms are not limited to industrial choices. Instead, trust becomes an important issue and managers must account for the specific image resulting from a product or a brand becoming more global (see Chapter 12). Are globalised brands perceived as such and do they influence how much consumers trust them? (See Chapter 12 and 13). Globalisation also means more communication among customers from all over the world, thus providing new ways to cope with uncertainty. Are the resulting forums, blogs and other information sharing ways becoming more trusted and relied upon than classical information sources? (See Chapter 14). The non-profit sector is faced with similar questions, with global problems likely to become more pressing than the localised ones and with adapted volunteering and donation approaches needed (See Chapter 11).

2. AN OVERVIEW OF PART II: THE ROLE OF TRUST IN A CHANGING BUSINESS WORLD

Trust has been defined in different ways as the context shifts, but an essential element is a human one of how people deal with an uncertain and risky future (Blau, 1964; Rotter, 1967, 1971). Economic exchange and business opportunities are fraught with risk and uncertainty and trust operates as a psychological and sociological process that smoothes and eases exchange (Morgan and Hunt, 1994; Richardson, 1972; Zand, 1972). Business researchers have called for explanations of economic production that elaborate the human element (cf Coleman, 1984). However, the variables of interest to business researchers exist across different analytical levels; from the individual to the collective, where the individual-collective pair can be a 'person-firm', 'firm-business relationship', 'customer-firms in a distribution channel' or 'person-society' (cf Aurifeille and Medlin, 2007; Chan, 1998; House, Rousseau, and Thomas-Hunt, 1995; Rousseau, 1985). In a globalising world market, these different levels of analysis add further degrees of complexity and call for increased research.

In Part II, there are four contributions, in which trust is examined across different analytical levels, from the collective to the individual, and by geographic spread. In Chapter 2, Jacques-Marie Aurifeille and Christopher Medlin examine the role of trust within inter-firm strategic partnerships in the development of relationship performance. In past research, credibility and benevolence have mostly been examined within an inter-firm setting as combined dimensions of trust (Geyskens, Steenkamp, and Kumar, 1998). Instead, the authors analyse the importance of the two main dimensions of trust and find that benevolence is associated with the collective outcome of economic performance by partner firms.

In Chapter 3, Clem Tisdell examines trust from an economic perspective, where economic rational man operates on the basis of independent and self-interested action. In this perspective the credibility dimension of trust comes to the fore, as the questions facing the exchanging parties are concerning whether the other can perform; whether this is a firm or customer, countries or investment partners. Clem Tisdell explores the nuances of credibility in many contexts and highlights the importance of confidence in performance for expanding world trade.

In Chapter 4, Clem Tisdell and Jacques-Marie Aurifeille investigate the way trust changes as a crisis unfolds. The dynamic perspective taken in this chapter shows how trust lost at the individual level can lead to a loss of trust across the larger financial system level. The solution is to manage the higher (i.e. collective) level of institutions and so prompt the development of trust at the individual level in a cascading effect.

In the final chapter of this Part, Marilyn Healy considers the problem of "blood diamonds" and how a whole industry can cooperate with governments to develop trust within their many customer groups. This case study analysis effectively highlights the way trust can be created at the collective level and so promote trust at the individual level in a top-down effect.

3. An Overview of Part III: The Role of Trust within Institutional and Network Elements of Globalising Business

In this part of the book, we present chapters that portray many of the different ways that trust is involved in enhancing, and also limiting, economic exchange between firms. Trust is known to influence inter-firm performance (see Chapter 2). In Part 3 the focus moves to the different ways that managers and firms can build and engage in trust development to build the collective, whether that is in a network of firms and organisations or occurs within a specific firm considered as a collective of individuals.

In Chapter 6, Giselle Rampersad introduces the concept of 'harmony', a construct closely related to cooperation, and shows that managers across three different types of organisations working as a networks believe that trust enhances harmony within the network. In Chapter 7, Latif Adam and Clem Tisdell present a study of cooperation between a network of firms in the Indonesian garment industry. Trust is found to both enhance and inhibit aspects of inter-firm cooperation, depending on the linkages between managers, with continuous trade and family connections being the most powerful in building trust.

Chapter 8 presents a descriptive analysis of the Toyota Keiretsu using centrality indexes of cross shareholdings and transactions. Trust and influence are assumed to be associated with cross shareholding and the analysis shows an association to transactions within the network. Whether influence and trust lead to increases in trade remains a moot point with this form of analysis, however there is a strong correlation between these constructs. In Chapter 9, Christopher Medlin and Carolin Plewa present research that links university research teams with their downstream commercialising firms. The research presented in this chapter shows trust and commitment towards the commercialising partner by the university research teams explains, in part, the level of satisfaction with the relationship from the commercialising firm's perspective.

Finally in Chapter 10 of this section, Christine Jaeger examines the interplay between trust and control systems within telephone call centers. The analysis shows the nested and complex connections between trust and control, and the often fine line that separates these constructs.

4. An Overview of Part IV:
The Role of Trust in Consumer Decisions

The contributions in Part IV address issues relating to individual decisions and explore the measurement of trust. In these chapters it is shown the nature of trust can vary according to differences in cultures. In Chapter 11 Patrick Valéau considers the development of trust and commitment by volunteers sent to work in a 'less-developed' economy. The processes of personal change required by individuals as they learn their place in a different culture is explained by changes in trust of themselves, of the volunteer scheme that supports them and of individuals in the host culture.

The 'perceived brand globalness' of a product, whether it is a global product or a locally produced item is considered in Chapters 12 and 13. Globalisation separates geographically the producer and consumer and this can lead to mistrust. However, perceived brand globalness offers a value to customers, for global brands can be of higher quality and so signal a product worthy of trust. In Chapter 12, Jacques-Marie Aurifeille and colleagues empirically examine perceived brand globalness and the concept of global attitude, meaning the degree to which consumers are aware of and appreciate a brand being global. A significant association is found, suggesting consumers are sensitive to the degree of globalness of a brand and that this perception should be accounted for in firms' strategic analysis of globalisation key determinant for.

In Chapter 13, Magali Debat explores the concept of perceived brand globalness on the basis of three components, which are then examined empirically in association with trust. The results presented in this chapter show that the structural and commercial size of a brand is related to the degree of trust customers attribute to a brand, while the degree of internationalisation of the brand is negatively associated with trust. This last result reflects the effect of distance between trustor and trustee, the greater the distance the lower is trust. However, the first result offers a different view; the greater is market share and presence, the greater the degree of trust in the brand. This is a conflicting result in relation to the degree of internationalisation and has challenging managerial implications.

In Chapter 14, Stéphane Manin and Robert Trommsdorff apply an interesting technique to determine if amateurs or professional financial advisors are more likely to be trustworthy in their stock purchase advice. In an empirical study based on the largest financial on-line forum (Boursorama), results suggest that amateurs may provide better quality information.

In the final chapter, Peter Batt examines the understanding of trust across a range of Western and Asian cultural settings, but always involving farmers within agricultural food supply chains. The results presented in this chapter suggest that different contexts result in different ways of dealing with trust in relation to an uncertain future.

CONCLUSION

When the concept of a workshop on Trust and Globalisation was first considered, the world economy was growing and there were no obvious signs of the forthcoming financial crisis. Now while the finishing touches were placed on this book, countries around the world have moved into recession and governments are planning to spend large amounts of money to build confidence and trust in the future of their local economies. In this environment, the chapters of this book take on a new significance, for they offer insights for managers and for policy-makers about the way to create a more secure future.

Each section of this book provides different ways to understand the many facets of trust in a globalising world. In the first part, we see the interplay between the individual and collective levels of analysis as an important element of trust development. In Part II, the role of trust in creating the collective is displayed. This is significant, as building trust between firms and organisations is an important way of developing network structures that can allow business to expand globally. Finally in the last part, the role of trust in the connections between customers and products in a culturally diverse world is displayed and developing trust is shown to be an important way for firms to forecast and manage their customer interactions.

Globalisation will continue, even as some resources become scarcer, because communicating is now faster and cheaper with the Internet and the emerging technologies of the 21st century. Knowledge transfer is faster, and people can change consumption patterns more quickly. Cultural diversity continues to be the norm, even though peoples' knowledge of global events is increasing. In this environment trust, in its many forms, will play an important role in easing the exchange of ideas and products, and also creating business structures that can expand global economic possibilities.

REFERENCES

Aurifeille, J.-M., and Medlin, C. J. (2007). Dyadic Analyses of International Business Relationships. In J.-M. Aurifeille, S. Svizzero and C. Tisdell (Eds.), *Globalization and Partnership: Features of Business Alliances and International Co-operation* (pp. 109-123). New York: Nova Science.

Blau, P. M. (1964). *Exchange and Power in Social Life*. New York: Wiley.

Chan, D. (1998). Functional Relations Among Constructs in the Same Content Domain at Different Levels of Analysis: A Typology of Composition Models. *Journal of Applied Psychology, 83* (2), 234-246.

Coleman, J. S. (1984). Introducing Social Structure into Economic Activity. *American Economic Review, 74* (2), 84-88.

House, R. J., Rousseau, D. M., and Thomas-Hunt, M. (1995). The Meso Paradigm: A Framework for the Integration of Micro and Macro Organizational Behaviour. In L. L. Cummings and B. M. Staw (Eds.), *Research in Organizational Behavior* (Vol. Vol. 17, pp. 71-114). Greenwich, CT: JAI Press.

Morgan, R. M., and Hunt, S. D. (1994). The Commitment-Trust Theory of Relationship Marketing. *Journal of Marketing, 58* (3), 20-38.

Richardson, G. B. (1972). The Organisation of Industry. *Economic Journal, 82* (September), 883-896.

Rotter, J. B. (1967). A New Scale for the Measurement of Interpersonal Trust. *Journal of Personality, 35* (4, 1967), 651-665.

Rotter, J. B. (1971). Generalized Expectancies for Interpersonal Trust. *The American Psychologist, 26* (May), 443-452.

Rousseau, D. M. (1985). Issues of Level in Organizational Research. In L. L. Cummings and B. M. Staw (Eds.), *Research in Organizational Behavior* (Vol. Vol. 7, pp. 1-37). Greenwich, CT: JAI Press.

Zand, D. E. (1972). Trust and Managerial Problem Solving. *Administrative Science Quarterly, 17* (2), 229-239.

PART II. THE ROLE OF TRUST IN A CHANGING BUSINESS WORLD

In: Trust, Globalisation and Market Expansion
Editors: J-M. Aurifeille, C. Medlin and C. Tisdell

ISBN 978-1-60741-812-2
© 2009 Nova Science Publishers, Inc.

Chapter 2

DIMENSIONS OF INTER-FIRM TRUST: BENEVOLENCE AND CREDIBILITY

Jacques-Marie Aurifeille[1] and Christopher J. Medlin[2]
[1]University of French Polynesia, FRANCE
[2]Business School, University of Adelaide, AUSTRALIA 5005

ABSTRACT

Past research on inter-firm trust has noted two dimensions, benevolence and credibility. The credibility dimension of trust has been operationalized variously as a combination of honesty, reliability and expectancy; while benevolence has rarely been examined as a unique dimension. We examine the two trust dimensions with empirical data of inter-firm relationships in the software industry and find that benevolence is strongly associated with relationship performance. No association is found between credibility and relationship performance, when discriminant validity is imposed. This result has important implications, as almost all of the inter-firm empirical research on trust has been based on the credibility dimension or a global measure combining the two dimensions. The research in this chapter suggests that benevolence, where managers perceive the other firm willing to look after their firm's interests and so the collective interests of both firms moving forward, is the key to business relationship performance.

1. INTRODUCTION

Inter-firm business relationships offer an efficient and flexible way for firms to globalise their operations without large resource investments (Mattsson, 2003; Yoshino and Rangan, 1995). However, inter-firm relationships cannot develop without resource commitments based on some degree of trust between the parties (cf Morgan and Hunt, 1994). Trust is a multi-dimensional construct, which in much of the inter-firm research has been conceptualised with two theoretical dimensions (Geyskens, Steenkamp and Kumar, 1998). The dimensions are *credibility* and *benevolence*. The first dimension presents a belief that the other firm has the expertise and ability to perform (Anderson and Narus, 1990; Dwyer, Schurr and Oh, 1987). The second dimension is a belief that the other firm will treat the risking party well, under new business conditions (Andaleeb, 1995; Anderson and Narus, 1990).

Trust is considered one of the main coordinating mechanisms that shape social structure (Bonoma, 1976; Bradach and Eccles, 1989), including the nature of inter-firm relationships (Geyskens, Steenkamp and Kumar, 1998; Seppänen, Blomqvist and Sundqvist, 2007). Trust is associated with satisfaction in studies of business relationships (Anderson and Weitz, 1989). Managers that trust each other are more effective in problem-solving (Zand 1972) and more likely to undertake mutual adaptations (Klein and Kozlowski, 2000). Firms that trust each other also have greater levels of performance (Medlin, Aurifeille and Quester, 2005; Zaheer, McEvily and Perrone, 1998). Trust is an essential construct for describing actor bonds in the relationship and network framework of the Industrial Marketing and Purchasing Group (Håkansson and Snehota, 1995).

Empirical studies have generally not discriminated between the two dimensions of trust (Doney and Cannon, 1997). In most cases trust is operationalized as a uni-dimensional construct (Geyskens, Steenkamp and Kumar, 1998; Seppänen, Blomqvist and Sundqvist, 2007). Larzelere and Houston (1980) have argued that the two trust dimensions are inseparable, as each dimension relies on the other. In this argument, experience of openness and credibility within a business relationship leads a manager to attribute mutuality and benevolence to the other party in a continuing risky situation; and conversely, the attribution of mutuality allows a manager to accept the credibility of the other party and hold expectations of promised actions. This presents an interesting problem, for if the dimensions are interacting how does one conceptualise development of trust within an inter-firm context? Does a firm begin by displaying benevolence and mutuality, or openness and credibility? Alternatively, are benevolence and credibility required simultaneously?

This chapter is structured in the following manner. First, we discuss the dimensions of trust within inter-firm business relationships. Next we define a goal variable that allows an empirical examination of the multi-dimensional conceptualisation of trust. In a third section, empirical data from the computer software industry allows examination of the hypotheses. The last sections of the paper discuss the managerial implications and future research opportunities.

2. TRUST AND INTER-FIRM RELATIONSHIPS

Inter-firm research has always presumed that firms exhibit trusting behaviour based upon the perceptions, attribution and cognition of a management group, or an informed respondent (cf Campbell, 1955; Phillips, 1981). Within inter-firm relationships, managers can trust another firm, or the managers of that other firm, and so coordinate their firms' resources and activities for the purposes of collective performance and so the long-term self-interest of their firm. In this conceptualization of inter-firm relationships, the self-interest of a firm in joining with a partner firm is met by achieving the collective interests of the relationship. This suggests an appropriate dependent variable for inter-firm studies is 'relationship performance' (cf Aurifeille and Medlin 2007; Holm, Eriksson and Johanson, 1996; Medlin, Aurifeille and Quester, 2005). This construct is measured as the perceived economic value created by the coordination of activities and resources of two firms. Relationship performance captures the economic outcome of the two firms' collective interests, in the form of sales and growth of sales and market share for their combined efforts, and so provides a sound dependent variable for examining trust dimensions.

Studies of inter-firm trust have relied directly on social psychology theory, see table one which also shows the sources of trust measures including when a measure is based on a past inter-firm study. Noteworthy in table one is the way trust is composed of two dimensions. The first dimension can be generally termed *credibility*, as there are aspects of honesty, reliability and expectancy brought to the fore. The second dimension can be termed *benevolence*.

According to Corazzini (1977), trust is a multi-dimensional psychological construct composed of factors such as; expectancy, reliance upon others, faith, surrender of control, consistency, mutuality and utility for risk. Each of these factors describes the way trust works as a personal cognitive response, with regard to an object that can exist anywhere in the *future* (cf Luhmann, 1979).

Table 1. Basis of Trust Measurement in Inter-firm Studies

Study	Dimensions *	Source of Measure Social Psychology source / *Previous Inter-firm source***
Schurr and Ozanne 1985	Reliability, honesty and fairness	Blau 1964, Pruit 1981, Rotter 1967
Anderson and Weitz 1989	Expectation/confidence, reliability and risk	Blau 1964, Pruitt 1981, Rotter 1967
Anderson and Narus 1990	Reliability and benevolence	Blau 1964, Rotter 1967
Moorman, Zaltman and Desphande 1992	Reliability, credibility and benevolence	Blau 1964, Pruitt 1981, Rotter 1967, Deutsch 1962, Zand 1972
Morgan and Hunt 1994	Confidence, integrity, reliability	Larzelere and Huston 1980
Ganesan 1994	Credibility/reliability and benevolence	*Moorman, Zaltman and Desphande 1992 **
Kumar, Scheer and Steenkamp 1995	Honesty and benevolence	Deutch 1962, Larzelere and Huston 1980, Rempel, Holmes and Zanna 1985
Andaleeb 1995	Reliability and benevolence	Larzelere and Huston 1980
Aulakh, Kotabe and Sahay 1996	Confidence, integrity, reliability	*Anderson and Narus 1990, Moorman, Zaltman and Desphande 1992*
Geyskens, Steenkamp, Scheer and Kumar 1996	Expectation and benevolence	Larzelere and Huston 1980, Rempel, Holmes and Zanna 1985
Doney and Cannon 1997	Credibility and benevolence	Larzelere and Huston 1980, Lindskold 1978
Zaheer, McEvily and Perrone 1998	Reliability, predictability and benevolence	Rempel, Holmes and Zanna 1985, *Anderson and Weitz 1989, Anderson and Narus 1990*
Liu, Tao, Li and El-Ansary 2008	Honesty and benevolence	*Kumar, Scheer and Steenkamp 1995*

*Note: "and" separates the two dominant dimensions discussed in the studies.

**Note: Italics show reliance on inter-firm study, rather than social psychology literature Table adapted from Medlin and Quester (2002).

Accordingly, the object of trust may be a person (Larzelere and Huston, 1980; Rotter, 1967) or an institution (Lewis and Weigert, 1985; Luhmann, 1979; Shapiro, 1987) and so one can distinguish between inter-personal trust (ie between individuals in buying and selling organizations) and inter-organisational trust (ie between an individual and a firm) (Zaheer, McEvily and Perrone, 1998).

However, trust is more than a psychological construct. Luhmann (1979) argued that to fully understand trust one must accept a combined psychological and sociological perspective. Trust development evolves through cognitive processes that rely upon a social structure and time (Luhmann, 1979). The acceptance of socially generated meaning is an important aspect for trust development in business relationships. Group and collectively accepted meaning provides the social structure that frames interaction (Lewis and Weigert, 1985; Luhmann, 1979). In this sense trust and social structure are involved in 'conditioning' effects on each other through time: both are involved in the generation of the other (Giddens, 1979, 1984).

A number of issues are apparent in past research on trust, within the context of inter-firm relationships, when a joint psychological and sociological construction of trust is accepted. A first issue concerns benevolence in business markets, as separating self and collective interest is a difficult task (Ekeh, 1974). For example, the present benevolence of a partner firm may only reflect their self-interests, even if their current actions are clearly not beneficial to that firm. The ambiguous nature of benevolence in business relationships lends support to Geyskens et al.'s (1998) argument that both credibility and benevolence are necessary for trust to exist, for a firm must rely upon honesty and reliability when accepting trust as the means to undertake a risky future.

A second issue arises concerning the roles of time and benevolence in trust development. Whilst benevolence is an attribution of collective interest and mutuality (Larzelere and Huston, 1980), to trust is to rely upon benevolence in the future. Here benevolence moves beyond fairness, as the act of stepping in to support a partner firm in a risky situation is more than fairness or justice. The act of benevolence does not ask for a reciprocal action. In other words, trust involves a risk concerning the future course of events, simply because no alternative exists but to rely upon benevolence. Importantly, this shows trust is a present psychological state concerning the *future* (Larzelere and Huston, 1980) and that the past only figures in evaluating whether one *might* trust. That is to trust, or not, can be evaluated based upon whether credibility or benevolence was displayed in the past, but to trust is another matter involving reliance upon future performance and benevolence given risk. Following this argument, trust is an *orientation to the future*.

An issue with inter-firm trust is whether a global measure, combining the two key dimensions, is appropriate. Two variations on operationalization of trust exist in the literature (see table 2). Morgan and Hunt (1994) operationalized only the credibility dimension (see table 1), whereas a further three studies developed constructs for the two dimensions of credibility and benevolence and then settled for a global construct when examining their hypotheses (indicated by ** in Table 2).

On the other hand, Kumar, Scheer and Steenkamp (1995a, 1995b), in two papers based on one empirical dataset, prepared separate measures for credibility and benevolence and then combined these with other first order constructs to generate a second order composite construct of 'relationship quality' (labelled 'Composite' in table 2). In these studies, of different samples from the USA and the Netherlands, correlations of 0.72 and 0.62 were found between credibility and benevolence (p<0.001).

Table 2. Inter-firm Trust Operationalized

	Credibilty	Global	Composite	Two Dimensons
Schurr and Ozanne 1985		*		
Anderson and Weitz 1989		*		
Anderson and Narus 1990		*		
Moorman, Zaltman and Desphande 1992		*		
Morgan and Hunt 1994	*			
Ganesan 1994				*
Kumar, Scheer and Steenkamp 1995a,b			*	
Andaleeb 1995		*		
Geyskens, Steenkamp, Scheer and Kumar 1996		**		
Aulakh, Kotabe and Arvind 1996		*		
Doney and Cannon 1997		**		
Zaheer, McEvily and Perrone 1998		**		
Liu, Tao, Li and El-Ansary 2008				*

Note: ** Indicates constructs for two dimensions prepared, but global for hypothesis examination Table adapted from Medlin and Quester (2002).

Only two studies, Ganesan (1994) and Liu, et al. (2008) appear to have provided evidence of a distinction between the two dimensions of trust. However, an examination of the wording in Ganesan's (1994) indicators of benevolence shows operationalization of another construct, rather than benevolence. Table 3 shows Ganesan's (1994) indicators and suggests an alternate attribution of the constructs to be "past/present commitment" (PPC). A re-examination of Ganesan's (1994) results supports this interpretation, with specific investments leading to evidence of PPC for retailers, while for vendors PPC is associated with satisfaction with past outcomes.

Table 3. Ganesan's (1994) Benevolence Measures

Indicator	Attribution
Vendor's benevolence	
This resource's representative has made sacrifices for us in the past	Past commitment
This resource's representative cares for us	Present mutuality
In times of shortage, this resource's representative has gone out on a limb for us	Past commitment
This resource's representative is like a friend	Present mutuality
We feel the resource's representative has been on our side	Past mutuality
Cronbach's alpha 0.88, sample size 124	
Retailer's benevolence	
The buyer representing this retailer has made sacrifices for us in the past	Past commitment
The buyer representing this retailer cares for my welfare	Present mutuality
In times of delivery problems, the buyer representing this retailer has been very understanding	Past commitment
Cronbach's alpha 0.76, sample size 52	

The results of the study by Liu, et al. (2008) are interesting as the two trust dimensions are found to have discriminant validity (chi-square 39.557, p<0.01, with 1 degree of freedom, sample size = 251). Liu, et al. (2008) follow the definitions of honesty and benevolence given by Kumar, Scheer and Steenkamp (1995). The indicators are given in table 4.

Table 4. Honesty and Benevolence Indicators

Honesty trust (Cronbach's alpha = 0.810)
HT1 We believe that the supplier will keep the promises they make to our firm on time
HT2 We believe that the supplier is competent to keep the promises they make to our firm
HT3 We believe in the supplier because it has a good reputation
Benevolence trust (Cronbach's alpha = 0.777)
BT1 Though circumstances change, we believe that the supplier will be ready and willing to offer us assistance and support
BT2 When making important decisions, the supplier is concerned about our welfare
BT3 When we share our problems with the supplier, we know that they will respond with understanding
BT4 In the future, we can count on the supplier to consider how its decisions and actions will affect us
Source: Liu, Tao, Li and El-Ansary, 2008

The results of Liu, et al's, (2008) study show that honesty trust is associated positively with contract control (β = 0.690, p<0.000) and positively with relational norms (β = 0.582, p<0.000), while benevolence trust is associated negatively with contract control (β = - 0.334, p<0.003) and positively with relational norms (β = 0.289, p<0.004). Their structural equation model has a Chi-square to degrees of freedom ratio of 1.349 and a Goodness of Fit Index of 0.946. These results suggest that credibility and benevolence are likely associated with relationship performance.

The next section develops hypotheses to empirically examine the two dimensions of trust.

3. HYPOTHESES

Trust within business relationships is important in the development of mutual and collective interests. Whether firms coordinate their resources and activities efficiently and effectively depends very much on the level of trust exhibited between the managers of the firms. Effective and efficient coordination between the firms requires mutual adaptation of resources and activities to allow economic performance of the relationship. Evidence to date suggests that higher degrees of trust between managers and partner firms lead to greater degrees of coordination, which improves relationship performance (Aulakh, Kotabe and Arvind, 1996; Holm, Eriksson and Johanson, 1996; Medlin, Aurifeille and Quester, 2005). This suggests that each of the two trust dimensions is associated positively with relationship performance:

H1: The higher the levels of credibility of a partner firm in a business relationship the higher the relationship performance.

H2: The greater the levels of perceived benevolence of a partner firm in a business relationship the higher the relationship performance.

The next section provides a discussion of the methodology chosen to examine the hypotheses.

4. EMPIRICAL TESTS

Relationships between business software principals and their distributors were chosen as the empirical setting. The sample frame was prepared from Australian Government web sites listing software firms from a wide variety of vertical markets. Each firm was contacted by telephone and their relationships discussed with a CEO or Marketing Manager. A specific relationship was qualified on the basis of being important to the firm's strategy, being arranged only by the two firms, requiring continuous interaction between the firms, and not being an end client relationship. The business-to-business nature of the relationships and the existence of set market boundaries according to country or region meant that expectations of market performance and competition were easily gauged. This meant that measurement of relationship performance was enhanced by the sample being based on a specific and easily defined 'value net' (Möller, Rajala and Svahn, 2005; Parolini, 1999).

The final convenience sample consisted of software principals for 95 business relationships. Following the two-step approach suggested by Anderson and Gerbing (1988) construct measures were prepared by conducting factor analysis using the Maximum Likelihood method. The measurement approach for the 3 theoretical constructs in the model is described in Appendix I. New indicators were prepared for benevolence in an attempt to gain greater discriminant validity with credibility, however, the correlation between benevolence and credibility remained high at 0.78, indicating an issue with discriminant validity. The Kaiser-Meyer-Olkin Measures of Sampling Adequacy ranged between 0.736 for 'relationship performance' and 0.733 for 'credibility'. The correlation matrix and final measurement model, along with Cronbach's alpha are displayed in appendix II. The t values of the measurement parameters are all significant at the 95% level of confidence (see appendix II).

In a first step, a model was prepared with Maximum Likelihood regression using the Lisrel 8.80 software (Jöreskog and Sörbom, 1996). In this model the correlation between the two trust constructs was constrained to 0.70, so as to achieve discriminant validity. The result was that H1 was not supported (β = - 0.05, t = - 0.36); while H2 was supported (β = 0.65, t = 4.46). The Goodness of Fit Index was 0.90 and the Adjusted Goodness of Fit Index was 0.83. The RMSEA of this model was 0.093 with a 90% confidence interval extending from 0.048 to 0.14. The Chi-square statistic of 45.39 with 25 degrees of freedom was acceptable and significant (p = 0.00754) (Bentler 1990).

Given the lack of support for the association between credibility and relationship performance a final model was prepared with the Maximum Likelihood method (see figure 1). A strong association was found between benevolence and relationship performance (β = 0.64, t = 6.20). The Chi-square statistic for the final model (9.79 with 8 degrees of freedom) is not significant (p = 0.27988) (Bentler 1990). The RMSEA of the final model is 0.049. Steiger (1989) considers any value less than 0.05 as a "very good" fit. These measures suggest that the model has a "correct fit". That is, the hypothesis constraining the parsimonious model complies with the observed phenomenon. H2 was supported (see figure 1).

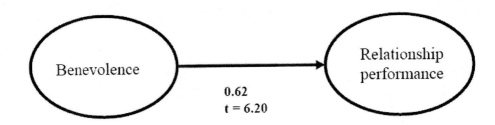

Figure 1. Final Structural Equation Model.

5. DISCUSSION

Benevolence, where managers perceive the other firm willing to look after their firm's interests moving forward, is shown to be strongly associated with perceptions of the performance of inter-firm relationships. This result contributes to the theory on trust within business relationships in at least three ways. First, the results highlight the role of benevolence in achieving relationship performance. The variation in support for the two hypotheses is an interesting result, with only benevolence significantly associated with relationship performance when discriminant validity is preserved. It seems counter intuitive that credibility is not associated with relationship performance. We suggest that managers assess evidence of benevolence to determine whether the partner firm is willing to adapt and change coordination to achieve collective economic outcomes. Presumably when a partner firm is seen to be benevolent managers are willing to adapt their resources and activities to the other firm. This adaptation of the firm's resources and activities towards the needs of the partner firm leads to greater levels of efficiency and effectiveness and so greater economic outcomes.

Second, the association between benevolence and relationship performance indicates how collective interest constructs are important in explaining business relationships. Business relationships are a combination of firm self-interest and collective action: there is individual and coordinated performance by the participating firms and the intent of a collective economic gain leading to private gain. The purpose of business relationships is to achieve a firm's self-interest through the collective interest of the business relationships (Medlin, 2006). Benevolence indicates a collective interest and relationship performance is a collective economic outcome. The role of benevolence in achieving relationship performance highlights this combination of self and collective interest in business relationships.

Third, without a collective outcome, such as relationship performance, the processes and purpose of inter-firm trust and coordinated economic activity have little meaning. In terms of the development processes for trust, the empirical evidence in this chapter suggests that increasing benevolence is associated with greater relationship performance and that over time the meeting of collective outcomes allows the partners to attribute credibility to the other party. This explanation of trust development through time is interesting, for it suggests that benevolence is more future oriented (ie future loaded) than is the credibility dimension.

The explanation also shows credibility to be somewhat more past loaded than the benevolence dimension. There is a reliance on the past to assess credibility, while attributions of benevolence are future oriented.

CONCLUSION

Managerial Implications

The managerial implications of the research presented in this chapter are threefold. First, the positive and strong role of benevolence is now clear with regard to achieving relationship performance in business relationships. However, which actions and commitments of resources are considered acts of benevolence is a contextual issue that deserves careful thought. The issue here is that two firms in a business relationship operate from different network positions and so necessarily have different contexts (cf Halinen, 1998; Medlin, 2003). The research by Malhotra (2004) shows this issue again. Managers of a partner firm do not take the same perspective on the act of benevolence. The resolution of this impasse, so that trust can be built through acts of benevolence, is open communication between the managers from each party. Only in this way can a manager understand the acts and resource commitments that are considered to be supportive of the other firm.

Second, since building trust is based on benevolent acts, managers need to prioritise the strategic importance of their firm's business relationships. Benevolent acts require resources to ensure open communication and also resources for meeting the needs of the partner firm. As a result, benevolent acts necessarily demand making a choice between competing opportunities. Resources are scarce and are likely already in use, so that providing a solution to a partner issue will require adaptation of a resource applied in some other relationships. This means managers will need to understand the strategic importance of each business relationship, and this knowledge and understanding will provide the alternate sources of resources and how a solution can be configured.

Further, for a benevolent act to be understood the adjustments in resources must be applied in a timely fashion according to the agreed needs of the partner firm. Noteworthy, in this discussion is that benevolence is a strategic issue and so the decision will be judged by the giving firm on the basis of self and collective interests.

Finally, managers should note that benevolence is not only about giving resources and time to a business relationship. Benevolence is one act in a series of acts that make up the interactions which build a business relationship. Benevolence today can increase the economic performance of the business relationship and this can lead to both firms increasing their resource base. Importantly, a stronger partner can afford to be benevolent, so that the first firm can free resources for a competing demand in a future time. When business relationships are viewed across time, benevolence can be seen as part of the reason for the flexibility and adaptability of business relationships and the networks they form. Benevolence is one part of how firms remain adaptable in fast changing environments.

Future Research

Future research based on specific measures for benevolence and credibility offers the opportunity to understand more clearly the mediator constructs in the development of business inter-firm relationships. Most research on trust has not applied measures for benevolence, rather measures have tended to be global or of credibility. Given the empirical results presented in this chapter researchers will need to re-consider past research on the basis of specifying benevolence. The more specific construct of benevolence, as compared to the general notion of trust, offers an opportunity to understand more clearly how business relationships develop.

The results in this chapter also suggest interesting future research opportunities concerning the role of credibility within inter-firm relationships. In fact, the evidence from Morgan and Hunt (1994), whose trust indicators are based on credibility, is that commitment is associated with credibility. While Liu, et al. (2008) found that credibility was associated with contract control. There remains considerable research opportunity to understand the role of credibility in developing business relationships.

Finally, trust remains one of the most examined constructs in the area of inter-firm research for as good reason. The shape of the global firm networks that accomplish economic output are partly determined by the decisions of managers who must act without full knowledge of the future. In this context of uncertainty trust remains a required element. Where trust is high and managers are benevolent, rather than opportunistic, the possibility of complex inter-firm arrangements is greater and the quality of economic output is higher and of greater value.

ACKNOWLEDGMENTS

We wish to thank the anonymous reviewers for their detailed comments on an earlier version of this article.

APPENDIX I

Construct Indicators

Construct	Indicators	Source	Response Anchors
Credibility	HT-1 The other firm usually keeps the promises they make to our firm. HT-2 The other party is truly sincere in their promises. HT-3 Our partner is perfectly credible.	Developed for this study. Larzelere and Houston 1980 Rodriguez and Wilson 1995	9 point scale Strongly agree to strongly disagree
Benevolence	BT-1 In the future we can count on the other firm, to consider how its decisions and actions will affect our firm.	All developed for this study	9 point scale Strongly agree to strongly disagree
	BT-2 Though circumstances change, we believe the other firm will be ready and willing to offer us assistance and support. BT-3 When making important decisions, the other firm is concerned about our firm's welfare.		

Appendix I. (Continued)

Construct	Indicators	Source	Response Anchors
Relationship Performance	Consider all of the costs and revenues with the Focus Relationship. Relative to your firm's expectations in the focus market, what has been the performance of the inter-firm relation on the following dimensions? 1. Sales, 2. Sales growth, 3. Market share growth	Holm et al 1996	9 point scale Extremely strong to extremely weak

Appendix II

Correlation Matrix

	HT-1	HT-2	HT-3	BT-1	BT-2	BT-3	Perf-1	Perf-2	Perf-3
HT-1	1.00								
HT-2	0.90	1.00							
HT-3	0.84	0.83	1.00						
BT-1	0.51	0.53	0.42	1.00					
BT-2	0.69	0.70	0.62	0.61	1.00				
BT-3	0.57	0.58	0.43	0.67	0.72	1.00			
Perf-1	0.38	0.31	0.27	0.58	0.47	0.45	1.00		
Perf-2	0.45	0.43	0.38	0.59	0.50	0.48	0.92	1.00	
Perf-3	0.37	0.37	0.28	0.53	0.41	0.43	0.84	0.89	1.00

Measurement Model

Construct	Item	Lambda	t-value	R^2
Credibilityt ($\alpha = 0.946$)	1	0.95	12.29	0.90
	2	0.95	12.20	0.90
	3	0.88	10.72	0.77
Benevolence ($\alpha = 0.851$)	1	0.76	8.34	0.58
	2	0.86	10.06	0.74
	3	0.82	9.33	0.67
Relationship Performance ($\alpha = 0.957$)	1	0.93	11.79	0.86
	2	0.99	13.29	0.98
	3	0.90	11.25	0.81

References

Andaleeb, S. S. (1995). Dependence Relations and the Moderating Role of Trust: Implications for Behavioural Intentions in Marketing Channels. *International Journal of Research in Marketing, 12* (2), 157-172.

Anderson, E., and Weitz, B. (1989). Determinants of Continuity in Conventional Industrial Channel Dyads. *Marketing Science, 8* (4), 310-323.

Anderson, J. C., and Gerbig, D. W. (1988). Structural Equation Modeling in Practice: A Review and Recommended Two-Step Approach. *Psychological Bulletin, 103*, 411-423.

Anderson, J. C., and Narus, J. A. (1990). A Model of Distributor Firm and Manufacturer Firm Working Partnerships. *Journal of Marketing, 54* (1), 42-58.

Aulakh, P. S., Kotabe, M., and Arvind, S. (1996). Trust and Performance in Cross-Border Marketing Partnerships: A Behavioural Approach. *Journal of International Business Studies, 27* (5), 1005-1032.

Aurifeille, J.-M., and Medlin, C. J. (2007). Dyadic Analyses of International Business Relationships. In J.-M. Aurifeille, S. Svizzero and C. Tisdell (Eds.), *Globalization and Partnership: Features of Business Alliances and International Co-operation* (pp. 109-123). London: Nova Science.

Blau, P. M. (1964). *Exchange and Power in Social Life.* New York: Wiley.

Bonoma, T. (1976). Conflict, Cooperation and Trust in Three Power Systems. *Behavioral Science, 21* (November), 499-514.

Bradach, J. L., and Eccles, R. G. (1989). Price, Authority, and Trust: From Ideal Types to Plural Forms. *Annual Review of Sociology, 15*, 97-118.

Campbell, D. T. (1955). The Informant in Quantitative Research. *American Journal of Sociology, 60* (January), 339-343.

Corazzini, J. G. (1977). Trust as a Complex Multi-dimensional Construct. *Psychological Reports, 40*, 75-80.

Deutsch, M. (1962). Cooperation and Trust: Some Theoretical Notes, *Nebraska Symposium on Motivation.*

Doney, P. M., and Cannon, J. P. (1997). An Examination of the Nature of Trust in Buyer-Seller Relationships. *Journal of Marketing, 61* (April), 35-51.

Dwyer, R. F., Schurr, P. H., and Oh, S. (1987). Developing Buyer-Seller Relationships. *Journal of Marketing, 51* (2), 11-27.

Ekeh, P. P. (1974). *Social Exchange: The Two Traditions.* Cambridge, MA: Harvard Unversity Press.

Ganesan, S. (1994). Determinants of Long-Term Orientation in Buyer-Seller Relationships. *Journal of Marketing, 58* (2), 1-19.

Geyskens, I., Steenkamp, J. E. M., and Kumar, N. (1998). Generalizations About Trust in Marketing Channel Relationships Using Meta-analysis. *International Journal of Research in Marketing, 15* (3), 223-248.

Giddens, A. (1979). *Central Problems in Social Theory: Action, Structure and Contradiction in Social Analysis.* Berkley, CA: University of California Press.

Giddens, A. (1984). *The Constitution of Society: Outline of the Theory of Structuration.* Cambridge: Polity Press.

Håkansson, H., and Snehota, I. (1995). *Developing Relationships in Business Networks.* London: International Thomson Business Press.

Halinen, A. (1998). Time and Temporality in Research Design: A Review of Buyer-seller Relationship Models. In P. Naudé and P. W. Turnbull (Eds.), *Network Dynamics in International Marketing* (pp. 112-139). Oxford: Elsevier Science.

Hedaa, L., and Törnroos, J.-Å. (2000). *Kairology: An Exposition Toward a Theory of Timing.* Paper presented at the Time and Management, Palermo, Italy.

Hedaa, L., and Törnroos, J.-Å. (2002). Towards a Theory of Timing: Kairology in Business Networks. In R. Whipp, B. Adam and I. Sabelis (Eds.), *Making Time: Time and Management in Modern Organizations*. Oxford: Oxford University Press.

Holm, D. B., Eriksson, K., and Johanson, J. (1996). Business Networks and Cooperation in International Business Relationships. *Journal of International Business, 27* (5), 1033-1053.

Jöreskog, K. G., and Sörbom, D. (1996). *Lisrel VIII*. Chicago: SSI.

Klein, K., and Kozlowski, S. W. (2000). *Multilevel Theory, Research, and Methods in Organizations: Foundations, Extensions, and New Directions*: Jossey Bass.

Kumar, N., Scheer, L. K., and Steenkamp, J. E. M. (1995). The Effects of Supplier Fairness on Vunerable Resellers. *Journal of Marketing Research, 32* (February), 54-65.

Larzelere, R. E., and Huston, T. L. (1980). The Dyadic Trust Scale: Toward Understanding Interpersonal Trust in Close Relationships. *Journal of Marriage and the Family* (August), 595-604.

Lewis, J. D., and Weigert, A. (1985). Trust as Social Reality. *Social Forces*, 967-985.

Lindskold, S. (1978). Trust Development, the GRIT Proposal and the Effects of Conciliatory Acts on Conflict and Cooperation. *Psychological Bulletin, 84* (4), 772-793.

Liu, Y., Tao, L., Li, Y., and El-Ansary, A. I. (2008). The Impact of a Distributor's Trust in a Supplier and Use of Control Mechanisms on Relational Value Creation in Marketing Channels. *Journal of Business and Industrial Marketing, 23* (1), 12 - 22.

Luhmann, N. (1979). *Trust and Power*. New York: John Wiley.

Mattsson, L. G. (2003). Reorganisation of Distribution in Globalisation of Markets: The Dynamic Context of Supply Chain Management. *Supply Chain Management: An International Journal, 8* (5), 416-426.

Malhotra, D. (2004). Trust and Reciprocity Decisions: The Differing Perspectives of Trustors and Trusted Parties. *Organizational Behavior and Human Decision Processes, 94* (2), 61-73.

Medlin, C. J., and Quester, P. G. (2002). *Inter-firm Trust: Two Theoretical Dimensions versus a Global Measure*. Paper presented at the IMP Asia: Culture and Collaboration in Distribution Networks, Perth.

Medlin, C. J. (2003). A Dyadic Research Program: The Interaction Possibility Space Model. *Journal of Business-to-Business Marketing, 10* (3), 63-79.

Medlin, C. J. (2004). Interaction in Business Relationships: A Time Perspective. *Industrial Marketing Management, 33* (3), 185-193.

Medlin, C. J. (2006). Self and Collective Interest in Business Relationships. *Journal of Business Research, 59* (7), 858-865.

Medlin, C. J., Aurifeille, J.-M., and Quester, P. G. (2005). A Collaborative Interest Model of Relational Coordination and Empirical Results. *Journal of Business Research, 58* (2), 214-222.

Moorman, C., Zaltman, G., and Desphande, R. (1992). Relationship between Providers and Users of Market Research. *Journal of Marketing Research, XXIX* (August), 314-328.

Morgan, R. M., and Hunt, S. D. (1994). The Commitment-Trust Theory of Relationship Marketing. *Journal of Marketing, 58*(3), 20-38.

Möller, K., Rajala, A., and Svahn, S. (2005). Strategic Business Nets - Their Type and Management. *Journal of Business Research, 58* (9), 1274-1284.

Parolini, C. (1999). *The Value Net: A Tool for Competitive Advantage*. Chichester: Wiley.

Phillips, L. W. (1981). Assessing Measurement Error in Key Informant Reports: A Methodological Note on Organizational Analysis in Marketing. *Journal of Marketing Research, 18* (November), 395-415.

Pruitt, D. G. (1981). *Negotiation Behaviour*. New York: Academic Press.

Rempel, J. K., Holmes, J. G., and Zanna, M. P. (1985). Trust in Close Relationships. *Journal of Personality and Social Psychology, 49* (1), 95-112.

Rotter, J. B. (1967). A New Scale for the Measurement of Interpersonal Trust. *Journal of Personality, 35* (4), 651-665.

Seppänen, R., Blomqvist, K., and Sundqvist, S. (2007). Measuring Inter-organizational Trust: A Critical Review of the Empirical Research in 1990–2003. *Industrial Marketing Management, 36* (2), 249-265.

Shapiro, S. P. (1987). The Social Control of Impersonal Trust. *American Journal of Sociology, 93* (November), 623-658.

Steiger, J. H. (1989). *EzPATH: Causal Modeling*. Evanston, IL: SYSTAT Inc.

Yoshino, M. Y., and Rangan, U. S. (1995). *Strategic Alliances: An Entrepreneurial Approach to Globalization*. Boston, Massachusetts: Harvard Business School Press.

Zaheer, A., McEvily, B., and Perrone, V. (1998). Does Trust Matter? Exploring the Effects of Interorganizational and Interpersonal Trust on Performance. *Organization Science, 9* (2), 141-159.

Zand, D. E. (1972). Trust and Managerial Problem Solving. *Administrative Science Quarterly, 17* (2), 229-239.

In: Trust, Globalisation and Market Expansion
Editors: J-M. Aurifeille, C. Medlin and C. Tisdell

ISBN 978-1-60741-812-2
© 2009 Nova Science Publishers, Inc.

Chapter 3

TRUST AND ITS IMPLICATIONS FOR ECONOMIC ACTIVITY, WELFARE AND GLOBALISATION

Clem Tisdell[*]

School of Economics,
The University of Queensland,
Brisbane, 4072 Australia

ABSTRACT

Taking account of economic theories and models, this article discusses the influence of trust on the level of economic activity and welfare, and its importance for the process of economic globalisation. After providing some background on the concepts of trust and trustworthiness, it examines trust as a valuable element in contracting and as a consideration in principal-agent relationships and in the sale of goods.

The theory of games is used to highlight the significance of trust for collective outcomes that involve interdependence between entities. This provides a useful introduction to business cooperation and trust because business cooperation involves varied types of economic interdependence between firms. These are captured or highlighted by the theory of games in a general manner.

The role of trust in advancing the process of economic globalisation is given particular attention. Specific consideration is given to its role in facilitating international contracts, its influence on international principal-agent issues, its implications for the international sale of goods and in addition, its consequences for business cooperation and for alliances, the latter may be adopted as a means to meet the challenges of economic globalisation. While economists have given attention to the economic importance of trust, the results presented in this article indicate that its economic importance has been underestimated, and particularly so in relation to the process of economic globalisation.

[*] Email: c.tisdell@economics.uq.edu.au

1. An Introduction to Trust as an Economic Consideration

Although economists have given some attention to trust as an element influencing the level of economic activity and the welfare gains from such activity, its importance in this regard is given less attention than it deserves and virtually no attention has been given by economists to its role in the process of economic globalisation. Trust as an influence on business activity appears to have been given greater emphasis in the literature dealing with business management. Even advocates of the new institutional economies, of whom Williamson (1975, 1993) is a pioneer and who also sometimes contributes to the business management literature, while recognising the importance of trust, have often underplayed its economic importance. For example, Williamson (1993, p.453) states "trust is redundant at best from an economic view." My article stresses the relevance of trust for economic activity and the process of economic globalisation. Because most economic activity in modern economies involves social interdependence, in my view trust plays a central role in determining the extent of that interdependence and the economic benefits obtained from it. This role has increased in importance with growing globalisation.

According to *The Macquarie Dictionary*, (Delbridge, 1981, p.1,855) the word 'trust' (which is of Scandinavian origin) has more than 20 interpretations in English. Therefore, it is important to specify the way in which the word is being used in any discourses about managerial and economic issues. In what respect and to what extent are economic agents to be trusted in their dealings with others? When economic agents are untrustworthy, this adds to economic transaction costs, reduces the level of economic activity and the achievable level of economic welfare as well as potential gains from growing globalisation.

Trust is important in relation to most contracts and the sale of goods. As pointed out by Williamson (1975), contracts are usually incomplete and rely for their full execution on some degree of trust or unspecified expectations. These 'reasonable' expectations may vary from country to country and this creates a challenge for global transactions. Furthermore, problems involving trust are important in relation to principal-agent contracts which are invariably incomplete. Global operations of businesses can provide extra scope for agents to engage in deviant behaviour. Sale of goods can also involve distrust. Scope for fraud and misrepresentation of goods can increase when there is considerable distance between the traders as is often the case in global exchanges. This limits the incentive for trade and can result in market failure and a loss of economic welfare. It reduces the potential extent of economic globalisation and the benefits from it. Measures that can be or have been adopted to reduce these problems are outlined.

In a society in which individuals can be trusted, economic activity will be a greater and economic welfare higher than in a society in which trustworthiness is lacking (Argyle, 1991; Axelrod, 1984). Furthermore, trustworthiness encourages economic exchange even when buyers and sellers are located at considerable distances from one another. The presence of trust is, therefore, favourable to the process of economic globalisation. *Trustworthiness* is used here to mean that one can rely on the integrity of a person (or legal entity) to honour commitments, including customary expectations which accompany such commitments. Similar expectations apply in relation to the sale of goods, for example, one trusts that a good is as represented by the seller and is able to fulfil the purpose for which it is normally intended. Furthermore, when individuals are placed in different social roles in society, it is important that they can be trusted to carry out the functions that are normally assigned to these roles. In the case of business managers of public companies, for instance, it is important that they pursue the basic objectives of their shareholders which in many cases is to maximize the market value of their shares.

Williamson (1985) warns that individuals are liable to behave with guile in business transactions if they have the opportunity to do so. Guileful behaviour can either involve deception or treachery. Taking this into account and other considerations, I suggest that individuals or businesses may be distrusted as parties in economic transactions because

(1) they are knowingly deceptive or treacherous in their economic dealings (even though they may be capable),
(2) they are capable but not conscientious, and
(3) they are conscientious but not capable without being aware of their lack of ability.

In case (1) individuals are morally untrustworthy and in case (2) individuals are virtually morally untrustworthy because they do not exercise care in relation to their economic transactions. In case (3), individuals are untrustworthy but are not morally so. All of these situations lead to mistrust and can add to transaction costs. This indicates that both unethical behaviour and incompetence can result in lack of trust by parties to economic transactions. I am assuming here that if there is no mistrust, then trust exists. These sources of mistrust (according to my comments above) are summarised in Table 1. In this article, attention is concentrated on the possibility of treachery and deception but the occurrence of the other factors listed in Table 1 can also have similar negative impacts on the level of economic transactions and on economic wealth. For example, the market for a particular product may collapse because vendors knowingly sell shoddy goods which they represent as superior, or because they are careless and do not exercise adequate quality control so on the whole their products are shoddy, or because they believe their goods to be superior when they are objectively inferior.

Table 1. A summary and classification of factors that may result in mistrust in business transactions according to my analysis

TYPE OF BEHAVIOUR	EXPLANATION
Morally Untrustworthy	
1. Deceptive	Parties knowingly make false claims about goods for sale or about what they offer as part of an economic exchange.
2. Treacherous	Parties are able to fulfil an agreement but intend not to do so.
Virtually Morally Untrustworthy	
3. Potentially capable but careless	Parties are not conscientious but are potentially competent.
Untrustworthy due to incompetence	
4. Conscientious but incompetent	Parties are not morally untrustworthy but their lack of ability means that they cannot be trusted to complete economic transactions in accordance with agreements or reasonable expectations.

From Table 1, it can also be inferred that trust will be promoted in relation to economic transactions when parties to these transactions are not deceptive, are faithful in their undertakings, are conscientious (careful) and are competent. Note that the classification in Table 1 allows for contractual trust and performance trust but does not extend to a coverage of benevolence trust (see Aurifeille and Medlin, Ch.2) which can be regarded as a non-transactional (non-exchange) element of trust, even though it may promote social bonding and result in long-term reciprocation.

Note that accountants frequently include a monetary allowance in the balance sheet of firms to include goodwill as an asset. Any purchasers acquiring the firm are usually required to pay for this intangible asset. This asset appears to be a reflection of the degree to which the public and those having business dealings with the firm trust the firm. It is further evidence of the economic value of trustworthiness in business.

Business co-operation and alliances can be important for gaining access to international markets, particularly for small and medium-sized firms. Middle traders can play a pivotal role through their cooperation with smaller producers in enabling their products to be exported. However, suppliers at the bottom of the exchange chain tend to become locked into such cooperative arrangements. This can result in their economic exploitation and growing mistrust of such arrangements. Furthermore, once exploitation by a few middlemen occurs, competitors may be forced to follow their practice. Hence, the bad middlemen may drive out the good and cooperative institutional arrangements can be expected to collapse with adverse impacts on economic activity, welfare and exports. Trust is a significant influence on whether business alliances form and whether they last. Trust is also important in relation to the fulfilment of business contracts and for the sale of goods. These aspects are explored in this article and their implications for economic globalisation are examined.

2. CONTRACTS, PRINCIPAL-AGENT ISSUES AND TRUST

Williamson (1975) points out that most contracts or agreements are incomplete. Those entering into contracts trust that the partners will carry out their formal obligations as specified in the contract or agreement as well as their expectations about loosely specified conditions or customary performance associated with such contracts. Therefore, a major element of trust is involved. Although a party to a contract is likely to have legal recourse for its non-fulfilment, this is in most cases inadequate consolation for the non-fulfilment of a contract. The extent of damages to be paid for non-fulfilment when legal action is taken is uncertain, especially as far as 'implied' conditions of the contract are concerned. Consequently, legal action is often only taken as a last resort.

Where there is a widespread expectation that prospective partners to a contract are unlikely to perform the agreement faithfully in accordance either with the conditions specified or its spirit, this can be expected to reduce the extent of economic exchange or add to the costs of monitoring potential parties to contracts and the execution of contracts. Consequently, lack of trust then adds to the cost of economic activity and adds to the transaction costs involved in such activity. As a result, potential economic well-being is less than it would otherwise be.

The problem of incomplete contracts is particularly acute in relation to agents and in relation to employees. This is because it is often difficult to monitor their behaviour, that is, for the principal to monitor and control the behaviour of his/her agent and for an employer to regulate the behaviour of an employee. The monitoring costs are high. Therefore, the principal or employer has to be able to trust the agent or employer to carry out his/her duties faithfully. Considerable time may, therefore, be spent in selecting an agent or an employee, trying not only to assess their competence but how trustworthy they are likely to be in carrying out their duties. Once again, lack of trustworthiness can be expected to reduce reliance on agents and to decrease employment prospects. It can also result in increased monitoring by the principal or employee, all of which adds to transaction costs. A reduction in the amount of economic transactions and an increase in transaction costs reduces the attainable level of economic welfare in society.

3. SALE OF GOODS AND TRUST

Economists have given considerable attention to mistrust as a source of market failure in the sale of goods (Akerlof, 1970; Varian, 1987, Ch. 35; Tisdell and Hartley, 2008, Ch.5). The problem arises because there is often asymmetry of information between buyers and sellers involved in the exchange of goods. In particular, consumers (especially in the sale of complex commodities or the provision of services relying on specialized knowledge, such as the servicing of motor vehicles) are likely to be less knowledgeable about the qualities of the good or service being sold than the seller. This provides scope for cheating by sellers. If such cheating becomes widespread, this can lead to the collapse of the market for commodities of superior quality even though they are in demand. This is because buyers come to believe that there is a high probability that goods which are represented as being of superior quality are in fact defective or of inferior quality. Consequently, the whole market for the product concerned may collapse or only inferior products will be traded and priced accordingly. In essence, the bad products drive out the good ones in such circumstances. Both suppliers of superior products and consumers who wish to purchase superior products suffer an economic loss because a sufficiently large number of sellers cannot be trusted.

Another possibility in this situation is that consumers incur search and monitoring costs to distinguish between superior and inferior products. For example, in the case of a used car sale, they may have the vehicle checked by an independent expert. This all adds to transaction costs and reduces economic welfare. Increased transaction costs reduce the size of the market and in normal circumstances, reduce the economic benefits available to consumers (that is consumers' surplus) and also lowers the economic gains of producers, that is producers' surplus.

This is illustrated in Figure 1. In this case, it is assumed that consumers cannot trust sellers and as a result their market transaction costs are higher than they otherwise should be. For example, suppose that if sellers are completely trustworthy, the market demand for product X is as indicated by line AD. Market equilibrium would then correspond to E_1 if the line GS is the industry's supply curve. But if buyers find that they cannot trust sellers, they may incur market transaction costs equal to AB on each unit of the product purchased.

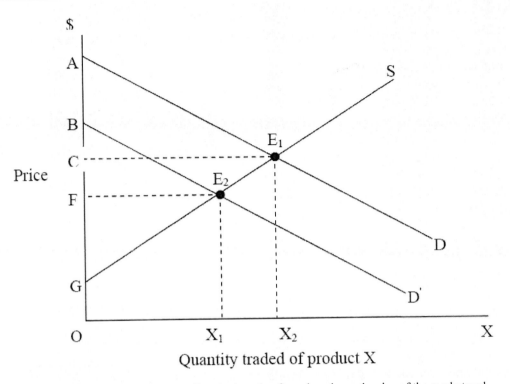

Figure 1. Mistrust of either buyers or sellers in the sale of goods reduces the size of the market and usually damages both buyers and sellers. This diagram illustrates the economic consequences of buyers mistrusting sellers. A similar situation also occurs when buyers cannot be trusted.

When this is taken into account, the market demand curve for product X will fall from AD to BD' and a new market equilibrium will be established at E_2. As a result, the quantity traded of X falls from X_2 to X_1 and its equilibrium price falls from OC to OF. There is a decrease in both consumers' surplus and producers' surplus. Consumers' surplus falls from an amount equivalent to the area of triangle ACE_1 to an amount equal to the area of triangle BFE_2. Producers' surplus declines from an amount equal to the area of triangle CGE_1 to an amount equivalent to the area of triangle FGE_2. It can be shown that the combined loss in economic welfare of buyers and sellers due to sellers being untrustworthy is equivalent to the area of the trapezium ABE_2E_1. If in addition, the seller cannot trust buyers (for example to pay their bills or do so promptly if the good is sold on credit), this will add to the market transaction cost of sellers. This would result in the supply curve of the industry being higher than GS. This will further reduce the economic benefits obtained by both buyers and sellers of X and will reduce the quantity traded of the product. The economic impact of supply-side market transaction costs are illustrated in Tisdell 1966 (Ch. 16).

Thus, it is clear that the market system operates most economically or efficiently when traders can all be trusted. A deterioration in trust amongst traders reduces economic benefits from economic activity and exchange. In the normal situation, both buyers and sellers have reduced economic benefits from trading when trading parties are not to be trusted. In the long run, all lose if traders become unreliable in making their transactions.

4. RELEVANT OBSERVATIONS FROM THE THEORY OF GAMES

The above considerations raise the question of what contributes to the development of trust and the maintenance of it. The knowledge which any potential parties to situations involving trust have of one another is important in judging the extent to which the parties are trustworthy. Experience obtained from previous business dealings with individuals or business entities appears to be widely used as a basis for developing sustained business cooperation (Adam, 2007; Adam and Tisdell, 2008). In some cases, shared values with ethnic or religious groups may also play a role and often, family connections can be very important.

However, penalties for breach of trust, and threat power which can be applied if there is a breach of trust can play an important role in ensuring that agreements are fulfilled. The lower is the legal cost of obtaining damages for a non-fulfilment of an agreement, the higher the claim upheld by the court for damages and the more certain is the legal redress; the more likely are contracting parties to fulfil their agreements. Thus, low legal cost and certainty of the law are factors that reinforce trust in the fulfilment of contracts or formal legal agreements. This reinforcement of trust, because of the ease of applying legal sanctions (compare Shapiro, 1987), implies greater confidence in the fulfilment of the contract but, perhaps paradoxically, there is less call for trusting parties to perform their part of the contract, that is less call to have faith in the integrity of other parties to carry out the contract.

This can be illustrated by the prisoners' dilemma type of problem shown in Table 2. This is assumed to represent either a one-shot game or the normal form of an extensive game. Two parties, 1 and 2 enter into an agreement to respectively adopt strategy s_{11} and s_{21}, or undertake actions corresponding to these. Each has an alternative strategy, s_{12} and s_{22} respectively which would involve breaking that agreement. The payoffs are shown in the body of the matrix in Table 2. If each party keeps to their agreement, each will gain 10 units of payoff. However, if one double-crosses and the other does not, the untrustworthy party gains 12 units of payoff and the trusting party is left with 4 units of payoff. The aggregate benefit of the parties is reduced as a result of this behaviour (from 20 units to 16) but the untrustworthy party benefits. However, the worst outcome occurs when both parties fail to keep to the agreement, that is the strategic combination (s_{12}, s_{22}) is adopted. Each party then only gains 5 units and their potential aggregate benefit is reduced from 20 units to 10 units.

Table 2. A case in which parties to an agreement have an incentive to break it unless adequate external sanctions can be applied for non-compliance

	Strategies of 2 →	
Strategies of 1	s_{21}	s_{22}
s_{11}	(10,10)	(4,12)
s_{12}	(12,4)	(5,5)

If in the case illustrated by Table 2, an injured party to the contract is able to obtain damages from a party that fails to fulfil the agreement of 6 units with certainty plus legal costs, no party will have an incentive to break the agreement. There will be greater trust in the fulfilment of the treatment. However, the lower the probability of obtaining damages of 6 units and the greater the uncertainty about recovery of the amount of legal costs, the lower would be the level of trust in fulfilment of the agreement. The law, therefore, can help to reinforce trust in an agreement being fulfilled.

Nevertheless, there are some types of agreements for which there is no legal redress. Their fulfilment depends entirely on parties acting in complete good faith (Tisdell, 1996, Ch.8). Prisoners' dilemma type situations in which no third (external) party (such as the state) can be called upon to penalize parties who fail to carry out agreements, rely completely on trust to ensure completion of the actions desired by parties involved in these situations (Tisdell, 1966). That is true, for example, in the case illustrated in Table 2 if it is interpreted as a one-shot game.

Improvements in the law internationally can help to contribute to the growth of economic globalization. Such improvements can include the harmonization of the laws of different nations, the simplification of laws and of legal procedures as well as increased precision in the application of laws. Furthermore, institutional developments that allow contracts to be specified in a more precise form can also assist in clarifying and enforcing contracts internationally. The International Standards Organization (ISO) has made (and continues to make) important contributions in this regard. Its classifications help to reduce uncertainty in international trading.

Note that while game theory is useful in illustrating some of the issues that arise in situations involving trust and cooperation, it is doubtful if it can capture all the complexities and nuances involved, some of which have been explored by Axelrod (1984, 1997). For example, it has been suggested that if a cooperative situation has the structure indicated in Table 2 and if it represents a single round in a *replicated* game, 'tit-for-tat' behaviour will eventually result in all parties adopting jointly optimal strategies. However, there are some problems. First, if the number of interactions of the players (that is the number of rounds of the game) is finite, each player has an incentive to renege on a cooperative agreement in the last round. But if each player realizes this, each will have an incentive to renege on the penultimate round. Consequently, by backward deduction, there is an incentive to dishonour the agreement on every round of the game. Secondly, the repetitive (replicated) version of the prisoners' dilemma game assumes that the strategies and payoffs to players remain unchanged as they repeat their rounds of the game. In most cases, this is unrealistic. For example, in the prisoners' dilemma situation, if one prisoner implicates the other (who does not confess) the latter may be hanged or jailed for life, depending on the offence. There is no chance or little chance for the implicated prisoner to retaliate in this case. Similarly, when a business finds that the trust it has placed in a partner is misplaced, it may be so damaged that it is unable to survive or it may be so weakened financially that it cannot take effective retaliatory action. The consequences for a trusting business depend on how vulnerable it is financially to being double-crossed.

The more vulnerable business partners are financially to being double-crossed, the more important is trust for their cooperation. The demand for third parties to act to potentially police any agreement also increases in such cases. It is predicted that when the cost to partners of being double-crossed is low relative to their potential benefits from cooperation, business cooperation will be facilitated but will be less likely to occur if the opposite situation prevails.

5. BUSINESS COOPERATION AND TRUST

There is often scope for businesses to make mutual economic gains by cooperating or forming alliances (Tisdell, 1996, Ch. 13; Tisdell, 2007). For instance, it is not uncommon for a larger business to enter into cooperative supply arrangements with smaller enterprises. If the large enterprise is a manufacturer, the small and medium-sized firms co-operating with it may supply the larger enterprise with components. In return for maintaining a particular quality and regular supply of components, the larger firm may assure its cooperating smaller firms of their market and provide them with technological knowledge. Or the smaller firms may supply a larger cooperating firm with finished products which it retails as, for example, has been the practice of Marks and Spencer (Tse, 1985; Tisdell, 1996, Ch.13) or the larger firm may act as a middleman in the sale of products produced and supplied by the small firms they cooperate with.

The vertical product chain in the latter case is one in which the large firm in the chain cooperates with several small and medium-sized firms to supply it with products which it then retails to end-purchasers. This is illustrated in Figure 2. However, there can be many more steps in this chain. For example, the large firm (or firms) in the chain may sell to intermediate buyers or middlemen who in turn sell to retailers. Here the flow of goods is assumed to be one-way. Hence, the arrows are unidirectional. Other patterns of flows of goods can occur and Adam (2007) outlines a variety of different types of product chains which occur in the Indonesian garment industry.

What is the likely economic advantage of the type of relationship illustrated in Figure 2? One advantage from the point of view of final purchasers is that the large firm in the chain is able to reduce their market transaction costs by ensuring that the products supplied reach acceptable quality standards. This may be reinforced by a promise to buyers from the retailer to refund their purchase price if they are not fully satisfied with the goods purchased. In most cases, it is likely to be valuable to the retailer to maintain its reputation and goodwill.

The larger firm in the chain is likely to find it more economical to check the quality of the products supplied than final purchasers and is able to impose a higher penalty on suppliers who do not meet agreed standards in their supplies, such as by no longer purchasing from them. As part of its cooperative agreement, the larger firm in the chain may provide smaller suppliers with credit, technical knowledge and market information. Normally, the main advantage to the smaller firm of cooperating is an assurance of the market for its products.

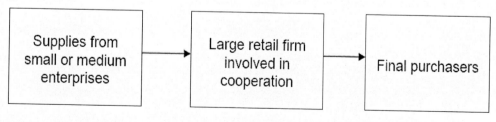

Figure 2. A simple cooperative vertical supply chain involving several small or medium-sized enterprises and a large retailing firm. In this example, the flow of goods is from small and medium enterprises to large retail firms which sell to final purchasers.

Nevertheless, while such cooperative arrangements can be mutually advantageous to business firms, whether or not such alliances are formed and last depends on trust. To some extent, businesses become locked into their cooperative arrangements. However, it is the small and medium-sized enterprises in the chain which are at most risk from 'lock-in'. As a result of the cooperative arrangement, Small and Medium Enterprises (SMEs) may fail to develop alternative markets or only do so to a limited extent. They are, therefore, vulnerable to exploitation by the larger firm in the chain. Furthermore, if the larger firm has *specific* requirements for the products supplied to it, small firms may have to adjust their machinery or production methods to satisfy these requirements. This adds to their lock-in because if the cooperation fails, they incur sunk costs due to the specificity of these items. Therefore, it is important for a small firm to be sure that a large firm with which it cooperates can be trusted to act according to the spirit of their agreement.

Often a larger firm in the type of chain illustrated by Figure 2 has the choice of several small and medium-sized firms from which it can source supplies. This provides scope for unscrupulous middle traders to exploit primary suppliers by enticing some of the primary suppliers into cooperative arrangements and subsequently reducing their profit margins. Once these cooperative arrangements break down, other 'gullible' primary suppliers may be sought and the process may continue. The problem is that this behaviour by unscrupulous traders puts economic pressure on trustworthy secondary traders who have entered into cooperative arrangements with primary suppliers. The unscrupulous traders are able to undercut the prices of the scrupulous in their trading. Consequently, in such cases, those firms that are normally trustworthy may also be forced to act in an unscrupulous way in order to survive (see Varian, 1987, Ch.12). Once these practices become widespread, small and medium-sized firms will shy away from cooperative trading agreements. Consequently, unscrupulous traders are likely to drive out the scrupulous and so interfirm trading cooperation or alliances will no longer occur. As a result of this institutional collapse, there is an economic loss; traders are unable to make mutually advantageous trading arrangements involving cooperation and consumers may have less quality assurance. This case has parallels the type of situation analysed by Akerlof (1970).

In cases where cooperative trading arrangements improve the access of a national industry to international markets, the formation and survival of co-operative business trading arrangements are important if businesses are to take advantage of greater trading opportunities made possible by growing economic globalisation. Furthermore, business cooperation can be important in enabling firms to withstand growing incursions into their home or national market as economic globalisation gathers momentum (Tisdell, 2007).

There are, of course, many other ways in which business enterprises can cooperate. They may for example, enter into joint ventures and into franchise agreements. Whether or not such alliances will eventuate and how durable they prove to be will depend on the trustworthiness displayed by the business partners. In such cooperative arrangements, it may, as pointed out by Tisdell (1966, Ch.12), pay for dominant partners or those with the greatest threat power to be generous to the weaker partners (those with less threat power) since this may provide an incentive for superior performance by the weaker partners. This is because the total benefits from cooperation are unlikely to be a fixed pie. The size of the pie is likely to depend on how those benefits are shared between partners. The solution of von Neumann and Morgenstern (1944) to cooperative games, and that of Nash (1950) to such games (based on the relative threat power of the players) assumes the division of a fixed cooperative pie of gains. This is a limitation of their proposed solution (Tisdell, 1996, Ch. 12). Tisdell (1996, Ch.12) demonstrates that the incentive of individuals to contribute to the size of the pie depends on their relative share of it and hence, the size of it is influenced by its distribution.

While it is recognized in the relevant literature (Andaleeb, 1995, Bromily and Cummings, Joshi, 1999) that trust is a major factor influencing the make-or-buy discussion of enterprises, (because increased business trust reduces market transaction costs and increases the likelihood of a firm buying more of its inputs rather than making them itself thereby increasing economic specialisation by businesses), there is usually no in depth discussion of what leads to the development and maintenance of business trust. There appears also to be no quantitative estimates of the amount by which increasing trust between cooperating firms can reduce market transaction costs. This is probably because trust is an intangible and subjective variable. However, an empirical study by Latif Adam (2007) of producers in the garment industry in Indonesia identified factors that were important in the development and maintenance of business trust between enterprises and provided rankings of the types of economic benefits that cooperating firms said they obtained from their interfirm cooperation. The main findings from this study are summarised in Chapter 7 of this book.

Note that one of the ways in which increasing trust extends the operation of markets is by making firms more willing to buy inputs rather than produce them themselves. This increases the degree of economic specialization in production in an economy and provides greater opportunities for the division of labour and economies of scale in production. As pointed out by Adam Smith (1776; see also Peaucelle, 2007) and as further elucidated on by David Ricardo (1817), these are powerful forces for adding to the economic wealth of nations.

6. TRUST AS AN ELEMENT IN THE FACILITATION OF ECONOMIC GLOBALISATION

Reductions in man-made barriers to international trade and exchange (such as reduced levels of tariffs on imported goods, the abolition of trade quotas, fewer restrictions on foreign investment and fewer qualitative restrictions on imported commodities for example, an easing of phytosanitory restrictions, as well as favourable technological change which for example, lowers transport and communication costs) are important factors that have stimulated the rapid rate of growth of economic globalisation in recent decades (Tisdell and Sen, 2004; Tisdell, 2005). However, the extent to which the business community (and the wider economic community) is able to take advantage of the extra trading opportunities opened up by growing globalisation and withstand the new economic challenges it poses depends on their trust in making economic deals both internationally and locally.

International trade and exchange do not occur in a social vacuum. They can hardly take place in the absence of trust between the parties involved. Trust has an important direct influence on the level of international economic activities and can be important indirectly in making local or national producers who form alliances or cooperative arrangements to be more competitive internationally. This may occur either because business cooperation lowers their costs of supply, improves the quality of their products or more effectively signals the quality of their products to buyers than otherwise. For example, a large secondary supplier acting as a middleman for smaller primary supplier may be able to signal effectively the quality of their products and reduce the market transaction costs which the smaller traders would otherwise have if trading internationally. Indeed, the problem of gaining access to international markets encountered by small producers may be so acute that they may fail to trade internationally in the absence of cooperative business arrangements.

Cole (1988) and Sandee and van Diermen (2004) provide specific examples of how small Indonesian manufacturers have as a result of cooperation with buyers cum consultants from developed countries been able to access markets in developed countries. They respectively provide a detailed account of this for the export of garments from Bali and for Indonesia's exports of furniture. They emphasize that this business cooperation has been successful because it has been profitable for all the parties involved (Adam and Tisdell, 2008).

Trust proves to be important in influencing the extent of international trade, exchange and investment through its influences on the occurrence of business cooperation and the formation of alliances, sale of goods, contracts, and principal-agent issues. The ways in which these factors are relevant for the process of globalisation are summarised in Table 3.

Table 3. Business Relationships Involving Trust and Their Relevance to Globalisation

1	Contracts involving international partners	Similar observations apply as in the sale of goods case
2	Principal-agent issues	In the case of multinational companies, managers of overseas subsidiaries may be difficult to monitor by central management in a company's headquarters and this provides scope for 'deviant' behaviour by the former. Consequently, whether or not an overseas subsidiary is established or is sustained can depend on the trustworthiness of available managers for it. Improvement in communications and transport, however, make monitoring of overseas managers easier than in the past.
3	Sale of goods	Trust lowers the transaction costs of exchanges and expands the size of international markets. The more trustworthy business partners are, the lower is likely to be the cost of insuring against default and the lower is the cost of completing sales.
4	Business cooperation and alliances	Trust is important in fostering these relationships and this can result in cooperating enterprises being more competitive in the international markets or able to withstand increased competition in domestic markets from imports.
5	International direct investment	Where this investment involves joint ventures, trust is important in influencing whether such joint ventures are undertaken and the amount of resources which partners commit to such undertakings. The greater the level of trust between investment partners; the more likely joint ventures are to form and the greater the amount of resources likely to be committed.

CONCLUSION

While artificial restrictions on trade and exchange limit the size of markets, the level of economic activity and welfare, the removal of such restrictions may only reduce these consequences to a limited extent if trust is lacking in relation to economic exchange and business agreements. If wealth maximization is an important goal for society, as for example Posner (1981,1985) claims it to be, it is important for society to foster a culture in which reliability and trustworthiness are valued, and to back this up wherever possible with a supportive and economical legal system. It will also be in the interest of a nation or society to encourage other nations and societies with which it has economic links to do likewise. The spread of such an ethos can increase the magnitude of economic globalisation and add to global wealth.

Strong social reprobation for untrustworthy behaviour can be a powerful force for promoting trust and trustworthy behaviour. Such social sanctions may be exogenous to the codified law. However, they often operate in conjunction with the codified law. Adverse legal outcomes are frequently a basis for social reprobation of guilty parties. In such cases, the actual penalty for breach of trust experienced by guilty people far exceeds the financial penalties imposed by the courts. An adverse court decision may result in social stigma for the guilty party and the transgressions involved may be widely publicized by the press. Apart from this, a further economic penalty can be lost business opportunities as a result of being branded as untrustworthy. The significance of these factors should not be under rated.

Due to growing economic globalisation and the extension of market systems, the efficacy of social reprobation in controlling socially unacceptable behaviour may be weakening and societies may be forced to rely more and more on the codified law to promote social responsible behaviour, including trustworthy behaviour. Reasons for this include the fact that the operation of many companies and business have a geographically wide spread and the prime decision-makers of these businesses often do not live in local communities where they carry out many of their business operations. Their remote location means that they are able to largely escape the wrath of the local community for any anti-social behaviour. Divided responsibility for business decisions (for example, decisions made by a management team or committee) and the respective of ownership and control of businesses as in the case of public companies may further weaken forces for socially responsible business actions. These aspects are discussed in more detail in Tisdell (1990, Ch.2 and in Tisdell, 2009). These considerations indicate that as the institutional structure of societies alter, the social influences and sanctions affecting trust and socially responsible behaviour also change. In short, social mechanisms to promote trustworthy behaviour evolve. In many societies, individuals who are trustworthy and conscientious are highly regarded. This is a cultural influence. In this article, it has also been observed that if these qualities are widespread in a society, they are of substantial economic value because they foster the maximization of a society's economic wealth.

This article has demonstrated the importance of trust (a complex multidimensional concept) as an influence on economic activity, economic transactions and economic relationships between entities. With the extension of market systems and economic interdependence (due, for example, to growing economic globalisation) the significance of trust as a contributor to economic activity and to the level of benefits obtained from it has been shown in this article to be increasing. It is to be hoped that economists will pay more attention in the future to its relevance to the level and nature of economic activity and that they will draw on the business management literature in doing so.

ACKNOWLEDGMENTS

I wish to thank Dr. Christopher J. Medlin and an anonymous reviewer for their detailed comments on an earlier version of this article. These have been helpful in improving its presentation. The usual caveat applies.

REFERENCES

Andaleeb, S. S. (1995). Dependence relations and the moderating role of trust: Implications for behavioural intentions in marketing channels. *International Journal of Research in Marketing, 12,*157-172.

Argygle, M. (1991). *Cooperation: The Basis of Socialability.* London and New York, Routledge.

Adam, L. (2007). *The Economic Role of Formal and Informal Interfirm Networks in the Development of Small and Medium Industrial Enterprises: A Study of Symbiosis in the Indonesian Garment Industry.* PhD thesis, The University of Queensland, submitted September 2007 and accepted for the award October, 2007.

Adam, L. and Tisdell, C. (2008). Interfirm networks in the Indonesian garment industry: trust and other factors in their formation and duration and their marketing consequences. A paper prepared for the 3rd Franco-Australian Workshop of FACIREM held at the University of Adelaide, 25 and 26 March, 2008.

Akerlof (1970). The market for lemons: quality uncertainty and the market mechanism. *Quarterly Journal of Economics, 84,* 488-500.

Axelrod, R. (1984). *The Evolution of Cooperation.* New York, Basic Books.

Axelrod, R. (1997). *The Complexity of Cooperation and Collaboration.* Princeton, NJ, Princeton University Press.

Bromily, P. and Cummings (1992). *Transaction Costs in Organizations with Trust.* Minneapolis, University of Minnesota, Strategic Management Research Center.

Cole, W. (1998). Bali's garment export industry. In H.Hill and K.W. Thee (eds.), *Indonesia's Technological Challenge* (Pp. 255-278). Canberra, Research School of Pacific and Asian Studies, Australian National University, and Singapore, Institute of Southeast Asian Studies.

Delbridge, A. (1981). *The Macquarie Dictionary.* St. Leonards, NSW, Macquarie Library Pty Ltd.

Joshi, A. W and R L Stump (1999). The contingent effect of specific asset investments on joint action in manufacturer-supplier relationships: An empirical test of the moderating role of reciprocal asset investments, uncertainty and trust. *Journal of the Academy of Marketing Science, 27* (3), 291-305.

Nash, J.F. (1950). The bargaining problem. *Econometrica, 18,* 128-140.

Peaucelle, J-L. (2007). *Adam Smith et la division du travail, la naissance d'une idée fausse.* Paris, L'Harmattan.

Posner, R.A. (1981). *The Economics of Justice.* Cambridge, MA and London, UK, Harvard University Press.

Posner, R.A. (1985). Wealth maximization revisited. *Notre Dame Journal of Law, Ethics and Public Policy, 2*, 85-105. Reprinted in R,A. Posner and F. Parisi (2000), *The Economic Structure of Law.* Cheltenham, UK and Northampton, MA, USA, Edward Elgar.

Ricardo, D. (1817). *The Principles of Political Economy and Taxation.* Reprint 1955. London, Dent.

Sandee, H. and van Diermen, P. (2004). Exports by small and medium-sized enterprises in Indonesia. In M. Chatib Basri and P. van der Eng (eds.), *Business in Indonesia: New Challenges, Old Problems.* (Pp. 108-123). Singapore, Institute of Southeast Asian Studies.

Shapiro, S.P. (1987). The social control of impersonal trust. *American Journal of Sociology, 93*, 623-658

Smith, A. (1776). *The Wealth of Nations.* Everyman's edn. 1910. London, Dent.

Tisdell, C. (1990). *Natural Resources, Growth and Development.* New York, Praeger.

Tisdell, C. (1996). *Bounded Rationality and Economic Evolution: A Contribution to Decision Marketing, Economics and Management.* Cheltenham, UK and Brookfield, VT, USA, Edward Elgar.

Tisdell, C. (2005). An overview of globalisation and economic policy responses. In C. Tisdell, (ed) *Globalisation and World Economic Policies.* (Pp. 3-16). New Delhi, Serials Publications.

Tisdell, C. (2007). Business partnerships in a globalising world: economic considerations. In J.-M. Aurifeille, S. Svizzero and C.A. Tisdell (eds.) *Globalization and Partnerships: Features of Business Alliances and International Cooperation.* (Pp. 11-24). New York, Nova Science Publishers.

Tisdell, C. (2009). Economics corporate sustainability and social responsibility. In M. Quaddus and M.A.B. Siddique (eds.). *The Handbook of Corporate Sustainability: Framework, Strategies and Tools.* Cheltenham, UK and Northampton, MA, USA, Edward Elgar. (Forthcoming).

Tisdell, C. and Hartley, K. (2008). *Microeconomic Policy – A New Perspective.* Cheltenham, UK and Northampton, MA, USA, Edward Elgar.

Tisdell, C. A. and Sen, R.K. (2004). An overview of economic globalisation: its momentum and its consequences examined. In C. Tisdell and R.J. Sen (eds) *Economic Globalisation: Social Conflicts, Labour and Environmental Issues.* (Pp. 3-23). Cheltenham, UK and Northampton, MA, USA, Edward Elgar.

Tse, K.K. (1985). *Marks and Spencer: Anatomy of Britain's Most Efficiently Managed Company.* Oxford, Pergamon Press.

Varian, H. (1987). *Intermediate Microeconomics: A Modern Approach.* 4th Edn. New York, London, Norton and Company.

Von Neumann, J. and Morgenstern, O. (1944). *Theory of Games and Economic Behaviour* 1st Edn. Princeton, NJ, Princeton University Press. Also 3rd Edn. by the same publisher in 1953.

Williamson, O.E. (1975). *Markets and Hierarchies: Analysis and Antitrust Implications.* New York, The Free Press.

Williamson, O.E. (1993). Calculativeness, trust and economic organization. *Journal of Law and Economics, 36*, 453-486.

In: Trust, Globalisation and Market Expansion
Editors: J-M. Aurifeille, C. Medlin and C. Tisdell

ISBN 978-1-60741-812-2
© 2009 Nova Science Publishers, Inc.

Chapter 4

TRUST AS AN ELEMENT IN BUSINESS AND ECONOMIC CRISES

Clem Tisdell[*] *and Jacques-Marie Aurifeille*[**]
[*]School of Economics, The University of Queensland,
Brisbane, 4072, AUSTRALIA
[**]University of French Polynesia, FRANCE

ABSTRACT

After summarising the social economic importance of trust and the relationship between crises and trust, globalisation as a potential contributor to business and economic crises is briefly discussed and possible general sources of crises are identified. More detailed analysis then follows of the relationship between business and economic crises and trust. Particular attention is given to loss of trust in financial markets and the mechanisms by which this generates lack of faith in the whole market system and can cause economic depressions, such as the Great Depression of the 1930s, and the economic depression (beginning in 2008 and expected to deepen in 2009) that was triggered by the US financial crisis in 2008. Increased economic globalisation in recent decades has resulted in the rapid global economic contagion of the recent financial and business crisis in the US at its spread to the real economy. The next matter which is given attention is the appropriate management of trust which has been shaken (or is in the process of being shaken) by a crisis. Several concrete suggestions for addressing the matter are made.

A further question given in-depth consideration is whether globalisation adds to the frequency and the depth of occurrence of economic crises and does it make the management of trust in financial systems more difficult?

It is argued that it does pose increased risks for financial and economic stability. The containment of economic and financial crises in major economies now calls for greater international cooperation by governments than in the past because of the increased economic interdependence of economies due to growing globalisation.

1. INTRODUCTION

Trust is important for the efficient operations of economic systems, particularly market systems and to a large extent determines the economic fortunes of businesses. Trust impacts on the level of economic welfare and the volume of economic activity (see Chapter 3) and as well it determines the sustainability of business relationships and can be a critical factor in the survival of businesses. For example, without adequate trust in a firm's product or services, a firm is likely to find that its market will collapse and that it will be forced out of business. Or again, if businesses fail to cooperate due to lack of trust when there are synergetic business benefits from cooperation, they may become uncompetitive, particularly in a world in which globalisation is gathering pace and adding to competitive pressures (Tisdell and Sen, 2004; Tisdell, 2006). In addition to this, misplaced trust in business partners may damage the economic prospects of a business firm, for instance if partners prove to be treacherous or incompetent in carrying out their part in cooperative business agreements.

Bohnet (2007, p.89) summarises the social and economic importance of trust succinctly as follows:

> "Trust pervades our lives and contributes to economic, political, and organizational success. Generalized trust in others has been associated with economic growth (Knack and Keefer, 1997; Zak and Knack, 2001), stable democracy (Inglehart, 1999), better functioning governments (LaPorta et al., 1997), social capital (Putnam, Leonardi, and Nanetti, 1993; Putnam, 2000), a decrease in crime (Rosenfeld, Messner and Baumer, 2001), and cooperation within and between organizations (Kramer and Tyler, 1996; Ostrom and Walker, 2003)."

Business and economic crises often strain arrangements involving trust or beliefs involving trust, for instance the degree of confidence in the operation of economic systems. A crisis places psychological strain and stress on individuals who are affected by it.

"Crisis" comes from the Greek "krisis", meaning a turning point in a disease, from the verb "kinein": to separate, decide, judge. It was progressively transferred into non-medical expressions like "mid-life crisis" or " Torschlusspanik" (shut-door-panic: fear of being on the wrong side of a closing gate) (Aurifeille, 2007). The words "critical" and "critic" derive from the same etymology, with the idea of a decisive moment of separation and judgment. The modern use of "crisis" in Economics and Management Science retains the same sense of a specific moment involving a decisive issue. Because of this temporality and the seriousness of the issue, a critical situation differs from a conflict. Beyond mere conflict(s) between agents, a crisis is a moment when agents have to cooperate to reduce the danger they are all faced with.

Because a crisis exit often requires global cooperation, the question can be raised of how the increasing globalisation of the economy and of the firms should influence the frequency, seriousness and length of the crises. There are several reasons suggesting that a globalising economy or firm could run a greater risk of a crisis. First, the dynamic of globalisation implies constant changes that cannot be perfectly reflected in existing information and control systems. The resulting gap increases with the size of the global investments and the complexity of the globalised activities. Beyond the variety of the partners, consumers and capital providers, these factors reflect also the greater competition among the globalising firms which are striving to maximise their long-term share of the global market before it reaches maturity. An example of the widening information gap met by the globalising firms is given by the so-called "subprime" crisis in the United States. Because of the new financial instruments invented to maximise the liquidity of the markets, banks are now faced with a huge amount of bad debts that nobody seems able to estimate. All over the world, managers, stock brokers, customers and business partners are unsure of the actual situation of their bank. Bank themselves are reluctant to lend to each other, thus illustrating how much information is missing.

Generally a crisis is provoked by a major change in the unfolding of the pattern of events (a change which may or may not be fully foreseen) and it is perceived as resulting in a threat to the future of those affected by it. Those involved in a crisis often find it difficult to cope with the situation that emerges.

They may find that their faith in others or the beliefs about business behaviour and economic systems are completely shaken. In many cases, this can result in emotional and irrational behaviour. 'Flips' or major and sudden shifts in behaviour may occur along the lines modelled in the mathematics of catastrophe (Anon a, 2008, Poston and Stewart, 1998). If the crisis is widespread in the community, emotional and irrational responses to the crisis are likely to become contagious.

Individuals (or businesses) may experience crises due to their own behaviour, due to the behaviour of other individuals in a group to which they belong, or due to widespread societal changes which are completely, or for all intent and purposes, exogenous to them. In all cases, such crises are likely to challenge pre-existing beliefs and may result in those entities caught up in the crisis altering their perceptions from ones of trust to distrust. An over reaction is possible. The consequence of crises is to stultify economic and business progress until trust can be re-established in others or in the economic system. Re-establishment of trust may require reform of business relationships or the economic system. Usually, crises are catalysts for reform.

Let us consider business and economic crisis and their relationship to trust, and then discuss mechanisms for managing business and economic crises before engaging in a broader discussion, which takes account of growing globalisation and competition. These aspects will be examined bearing in mind that when a crisis occurs there is a major change of situation and usually future expectations are dramatically changed. Trust is tested by crises and the consequences or anticipated consequences of a crisis are usually to be so severe as to call for urgent action.

2. BUSINESS AND ECONOMIC CRISES AND THEIR RELATIONSHIP TO TRUST

Business and economic crises can occur at different levels in society. They may occur for individuals, individual firms, groups of entities, in relation to institutions and the general working of socio-economic systems. Consider some of the types of crises that can or have occurred and their implications for trust.

Individuals and individual businesses often experience economic crisis in their activities. For example, individuals may unexpectedly become unemployed or a farmer may experience a crop failure. A business may face a financial crisis because for instance, the demand for its product falls due to no fault of its own, or because an employee defrauds it. A fall in the demand for a company's product could be a result of general economic change or because some person or persons deliberately contaminates its products. In the latter case, buyers come to mistrust the quality of the product. The way in which economic entities deal with such situations is likely to influence the perceptions of others about the trust to be placed in them. If they cope well with a crisis, this may strengthen trust in these economic entities. If they do not, there is likely to be a loss of long-term trust in the entities involved. Thus, if a company tries to 'cover up' the contamination of its produce or defects that have occurred in it and if it does not take visible and convincing actions to prevent further repetition of the problem, buyers are likely to distrust the company's product permanently. For example, an alleged cover up by Mitsubishi of defects in its trucks in the 1990s damaged the reputation of the company globally for a considerable period of time.

In Australia, malicious attempts by extortionists and others to contaminate edible products have resulted in recall of products and the development of 'tamper-proof' packaging. This was, for example, done by Arnotts biscuits in response to an extortion attempt involving contaminated biscuits in supermarkets. The prompt and decisive action of the company quickly restored confidence in its products. A more recent case involved Westons, a wholesale manufacturer of cakes. Razor blades were found in some of the company's products. Its products were withdrawn from the shelves of retail stores and it was found that a disgruntled employee had added the foreign objects during manufacture. In response, the company increased its surveillance equipment at its manufacturing plant and installed equipment to scan its products for metal additions. Confidence was quickly restored in the products of the company.

Sometimes, however, the outcomes are less fortunate. An Australian manufacturer of smallgoods did not take sufficient care to ensure that they were safe to eat. Several cases of food poisoning resulted with one death due to botulism. This company was forced to close down. For a while, however, consumers began to avoid the products of all smallgoods producers. For a period of time, all manufacturers of smallgoods faced a minor-crisis until confidence was restored in the safety of eating smallgoods.

This raises the possibility that if a sufficient number of suppliers in an industry act in a socially unacceptable way, this will result in lack of trust in the products supplied by the whole industry and provoke an economic crisis for it. If sufficient numbers of firms in an industry act in a deceptive manner in relation to prospective buyers, and pass off defective or low quality products as superior ones, buyers may lose confidence in the whole industry. Buyers are likely to reduce their demands for the products supplied by the industry and this may result in an economic crisis for the industry, particularly those in the industries who are involved in the sale of superior products. This situation has been analysed by Akerlof (1970) and is discussed by Tisdell and Hartley (2008, Ch. 5). It is also examined by Tisdell in Chapter 3 of this book.

In Chapter 5 of this book, Marilyn Healy outlines the genesis of a crisis of trust in the diamond jewellery industry. This was precipitated by the marketing of so called blood diamonds. These diamonds were produced in some politically unstable African countries by rebel armies often using forced child labour. Their sale became a threat to the whole diamond jewellery industry and resulted in measures being taken by diamond producers not involved in the supply of blood diamonds to stem this trade; a move supported by the United Nations. For the details of this crisis, see Chapter 5 by Healy in this book.

On a wider scale, individuals may lose confidence in institutions and in socio-economic systems. For example, the subprime mortgage crisis in the United States which was evident in 2007 and 2008, reduced confidence in many major financial institutions which posted losses or became illiquid as a result of their financing of sub-prime mortgages. For instance, the large US investment broker, Bear Stearns collapsed financially as did Lehman Brothers. Several large US financial institutions (for example Citibank) have had to be propped up by the American Government. Even the Northern Rock Bank in the United Kingdom experienced a run on it due to its exposure to the US mortgage loans which meant that depositors in the bank lost confidence in its capacity to repay their deposits. Confidence was only restored by the intervention of the British Government which provided financial backing to the bank.

Note that financial markets have become increasingly globalised. Consequently, a financial crisis in a major economic centre of the world, such as the United States tends to have global domino impacts on economic confidence. This is particularly evident in relation to stock markets. Mistrust of financial operations spreads globally and even financially sound businesses come under suspicion.

The aggregate level of economic activity in market economies usually fluctuates. The reasons for such fluctuations can be quite varied. Economic booms generally generate economic optimism and the economic troughs or depressions that follow result in economic pessimism and gloom. During economic recessions or depressions, there may be a loss of confidence in the ability of market systems to ensure economic security and well-being.

The Great Depression of the 1930s resulted in massive levels of unemployment, depressed levels of economic activity and much human suffering. As a result of their experiences, many individuals lost their faith in the ability of market systems to ensure them of a satisfying and secure economic future. Indirectly this became a threat to democracies based on market systems. The loss of trust in such systems possibly contributed to the rise of Nazi totalitarianism and the spread of communism.

The events of the Great Depression resulted in John Maynard Keynes losing faith in the ability of a completely free market system to maintain full employment and a satisfactory level of activity (Keynes, 1936). He developed the view that governments would have to manage the level of aggregate demand in their economies in order to stabilize the level of economic activity. It was also realized that if faith was to be restored in the Western economic system, the global economic system would also need stabilization.

The Bretton Woods conference held in July 1944, therefore, was convened to establish international institutions designed to stabilize the global economic system and restore global confidence in the economic system (Anon b, 2008). The International Monetary Fund was established to assist with the macroeconomic stabilization of economies. The International Bank for Reconstruction and Development (the World Bank) was also set up and was intended to assist with European economic recovery following World War II, and later increased its emphasis on supporting the economic development of less developed countries. There was also an attempt to set up a body to foster international free trade and override the adoption of 'beggar-my-neighbour' policies by individual nations. This only met with limited success initially because of the resistance of the US Senate to the idea, but eventually resulted in GATT (the General Agreement on Tariffs and Trade). This fell short of what the European powers had hoped for. It was not until the formation of the WTO (World Trade Organization) that a wider institutional conception to foster economic globalization in trade and investment took shape. Nevertheless, even with such institutions in place, macroeconomic crises still occur.

Keynes (1936, Ch.12) stressed the psychological basis of macroeconomic fluctuations, possibly because of his personal experience obtained by investing in the stock market. In his view, variations in confidence and trust of investors in economic returns is the main reason for macroeconomic fluctuations. Interestingly, Keynes (1936, pp.153-158) argued persuasively that market economies have become more precarious or subject to crises of confidence because of institutional change. He states for example, that

> "as a result of the gradual increase in the proportion of the equity in the community's aggregate capital investment which is owned by persons who do not manage and have no special knowledge of the circumstances, either actual or prospective, of the business in question, the element of real knowledge in the valuation of investments by those who own them or contemplate purchasing them has seriously declined." (Keynes, 1936, p.153).

He goes on to point out the disproportionate impact of short-term phenomena on the economic valuation of shares, the significance of mass psychology resulting in "waves of optimistic and pessimistic sentiment", and argues that these waves are not moderated by professional investment advisers because they are "forced to concern themselves with the anticipation of impending changes in the news or the atmosphere of the kind by which experience shows mass psychology of the market is most influenced" (Keynes, 1936, p.155). All these factors add to the inherent volatility of financial markets, place excessive weight on the importance of short-term returns on investments, and waves of sentiments themselves cause actual returns from investments to fluctuate almost synchronistically. Herd-like behaviour or contagion results in the waves of psychological economic expectations becoming self-generating and predictions become self-fulfilling. Keynes felt that these forces could be so strong that monetary policy could become an ineffective force for restoring business confidence and stimulating private investment if these should falter.

This led Keynes to emphasise the so called liquidity trap. This depicts a situation in which lack of confidence in the economic feature results in individuals holding cash or very liquid assets rather than investing their funds in 'real' economic projects or activities. When such economic gloom occurs, a fall in the rate of interest is unlikely to stimulate private investment. Therefore, fiscal rather than monetary policy has to be relied on to bring about macroeconomic recover.

The observation by Keynes mentioned above that professional investment advisers do not help to stabilize financial markets is particularly relevant in the light of the research findings by Manin and Trommsdorf reported in Chapter 14. They find from their empirical study that professional stock investment advisers do not outperform in their stock price predictions those who are less professional and that the predictions of professionals appear to display greater lags. There is furthermore, no clear evidence that professional investment adviser help to stabilize financial markets and prevent crises of confidence.

In recent decades, the view has gained ground that monetary policy maybe a more effective means for the management of the level of aggregate economic activity than portrayed by Keynes. Nevertheless, the importance of psychological factors and future expectations in influencing the level of macroeconomic activity has become widely accepted. Despite this, the significance factor is less widely accepted by some contemporary macroeconomists than seems to be desirable, as is apparent from the critical work of Frydman and Goldberg (2007). Furthermore, a complication has arisen: because of psychological factors, government policies designed to maintain economic activity may have the unfortunate result of reducing business confidence and depressing economic activity. For example, the US Federal Reserve Bank made a series of interest cuts in 2007 and 2008 to shore up the economy and stave off recession. These cuts may have signalled to investors that economic recession was imminent thereby eroding their confidence to undertake new investments and to embark on new economic activities. Thus, in a perverse manner, US government policies designed to avert an economic recession may have contributed to its onset.

3. CRISES AND THE MANAGEMENT OF TRUST

Crises usually prove to be a testing time for trust – they can undermine trust in others and trust in pre-existing beliefs. Trust is likely to become volatile in a crisis and super sensitive to change in external factors. The management of trust in a crisis will depend on the societal unit to which it refers (e.g. individual, firm, institution or a whole socio-economic system) and the object of the trust for example, whether it is trust in a particular belief or theory, or trust in the behaviour of another individual or economic entity or a group of these.

At the individual level, crises may result in individuals radically re-evaluating their beliefs, as for example, is illustrated by Patrick Valéau in Chapter 11 in relation to overseas aid workers. Such personal crises cannot always be avoided but may be less traumatic if prospective aid workers are given a realistic situation briefing on what to expect prior to being sent on their mission.

One should be prepared in advance for the possibility of crises. For example, in relation to economic agreements or contracts, the possibility that disputes could occur and abort the benefits from the agreement should not be overlooked. Therefore, some agreements include clauses that specify arbitration or conciliation in the event of a dispute about the fulfilment agreement.

As pointed out by Aurifeille and Medlin in Chapter 2, trust involves a temporal aspect – it relates to the future. Crises also as a rule involves a dynamic aspect. Normally, crises do not arise out of thin air but have a genesis. By timely action, it is sometimes possible to avoid a crisis and the loss of trust that it may entail. This usually requires action to be taken before the actual crisis emerges. The longer the delay before action is taken the more difficult it usually is to avoid or control a crisis.

Putting it differently, a crisis can be sometimes avoided by 'nipping-in-the-bud' developments which if unchecked will culminate in a crisis. Furthermore, if the possibility of a crisis is foreseen, this should enable individuals to be prepared for the contingency. This accords with the adage that 'to be forewarned is to be forearmed'. In such cases, one does not rely entirely on trust in order to obtain future outcomes.

Crises in interpersonal trust create particular problems. Such crises can occur because one of the parties to an agreement does not act in good faith or turns out to be incompetent. Failure to act in good faith may be curbed by the legal system (see Tisdell, Chapter 3) or by strong social sanctions against those who fail to honour agreements (Batt, Chapter 15). In essence, this means that third parties help to enforce agreements. As a result of such policing, parties may have greater trust in the fulfilment of an agreement and a greater chance of avoiding crises.

If the problem of lack of fulfilment of an agreement arises due to incompetence, then in some cases, a party to a cooperative arrangement may find it worthwhile to provide information and training to the less competent party to improve its performance. Christine Jaeger (Chapter 10) notes this in relation to employees in some telephone call centres in Mauritius. Adam and Tisdell (Chapter 7) find evidence for this in some business-to-business cooperative arrangements in the Indonesian garment industry.

Sometimes however, external events may change to such an extent that a party to an agreement may not be in a position to discharge its obligation under the agreement, or neither party may be able to do so. The wisest course then may be to renegotiate the agreement or cancel it. In any case, the parties need to discuss the problem because avoiding disclosure will merely delay an impending crisis and will probably exacerbate it.

Often governments are faced with the problem of managing financial crises as well as other crises, such as those involving food safety and law and order. The government has a vital role to play in this regard. In such cases, it is not only important for the government to restore confidence or trust in the systems involved but to take action which will sustain that trust.

In the case of financial crisis, it is important for governments at an early stage to curb overly pessimistic expectations. For example, if depositors become worried about the ability of banks to guarantee deposits, this lack of confidence can result in a run on the banks. This lack of trust then results in banks not being able to repay deposits unless the deposits are guaranteed by the central bank; that is indirectly by the government. However, in a free market system, governments would be unwise to guarantee the liquidity of all financial institutions. This would not allow the operation of free market forces and would provide support for speculative financiers. Therefore, government guarantees should normally be limited to supporting the liquidity of the main institutions.

While crises deprive some individuals of opportunities, they also often provide fresh opportunities for other individuals. Some individuals may, for example, take advantage of those experiencing financial crises. This accords with the adage that 'it is an ill wind that brings no good'. Crises can, therefore, be a catalyst for changing ownership of resources which in some cases can be economically advantageous. Also crises often provide a trigger for reforms which may be beneficial in the long run. From this point of view, crises frequently provide an opportunity for personal and social development, as pointed out by some sociologists.

Crisis exit strategies often make a priority of reducing the gap between information and action: the emphasis is put on more detailed, frequent and open communication, in particular concerning the financial results of the firms. Simultaneously, new control systems are implemented. This response is aimed at understanding better the situation and restoring trust among the agents by providing an apparently objective view on the situation. There is also a relatively quick response in times when it is urgent to stop the decay of trust, with "objectivity" likely to dampen the criticisms that head managers are often faced with when a crisis bursts. Indeed, as with any strategy, a crisis exit requires careful planning of the operations. However, they are particularly hard to manage for they deal with asymmetric and discontinuous phenomena (Aurifeille, 2007). Although trust restoration is a priority step towards a broad cooperation among the agents, trust drops faster than it is built and is not a sufficient goal in itself. On the contrary, the restoration of trust may imply preliminary actions that counteract the following steps. The cause of the crisis influences the degree of heterogeneity between the first step of the crisis exit strategy and the following steps. Typically, a crisis may indicate that an ongoing strategy has reached an optimum. From this optimum, there is no continuous way to achieve a better performance. Then, a fundamental revision of the strategy must be undertaken, with the firm projecting itself in a different part of the strategic space and exploring radically different paths to optimality. In such cases, attempts at filling the information gap by focusing on the details of the former strategy would only consolidate the existing control and information processes. A "regression" may then occur, whose focus on security and whose cost of implementation and operation may prolong the crisis instead of taking advantage of the exceptional readiness of agents to reconsider their shares in work and power.

A two-stage process may then be needed to exit the crisis. First, transitory signals are required to restore trust among the agents. Next, this trust permits agents to cooperate for a more fundamental revision where control and information no longer play the dominant role. The first phase is delicate, because the way trust is restored, in particular the time it takes, will decide whether the crisis was an opportunity or a catastrophe. The second phase is also important because, in some way, it has to relax the constraints imposed for restoring trust. This duality is clearly apparent linguistically: while "trust" (ger. "*Vertrauen*") refers to trueness, the corresponding word in the Latin languages (*confiance, confianza*) refers to confidence. Thus, beyond actual/true facts, some faith (lat. *fidere*) is required for an economic entity to go on. In the crisis exit strategies, the transition from phase one (restoration of trust) to phase two (cooperation and fundamental role revision) depends on a variety of actors. Basically, three groups of actors are involved: the employees, the shareholders and the lenders. The objectives of the three groups are often conflicting; giving to the exit crisis the form of a game whose convergence towards a global cooperation requires careful monitoring from the managers in charge of it. Classically, a business crisis materializes with a lack of liquidity. Then, as the lenders are not eager to give more credit, the usual remedy consists in issuing new shares. This was the re-course of banks caught in the "subprime" crisis. However, although a capital increase should reassure the lenders, it creates the risk of another firm's take over, coming with important job cuts. In this context, the reaction of the employees, including some of the top management, may hamper the capital increase and affect the durability of the cooperation of the agents. A solution could be to reserve the new shares to the former shareholders, thus limiting the capital dilution. However, the take over could only be delayed and eased if the shareholders forced to subscribe to the capital feel they are being held hostages.

The critical importance of doing the right thing at the right moment is remarkably illustrated by the contrasted evidence of two majors bank's capital increase. As a reaction to the subprime crisis, France's Societe Generale and England's HBOS both chose to make a capital increase, but did it following different strategies. Societe General reacted 5 months before HBOS, with a capital increase restricted to its shareholders. The operation was a complete success, with all the shares taken up in a few hours. On the contrary, HBOS did not restrict the entry of new shareholders and its reaction was delayed by a cumbersome and slow rights-issue system. It resulted in a failure, with only 8.29% of the new HBOS shares taken up, a failure so unique in the banking system that "The deal will probably enter the City lexicon as the phrase 'doing an HBOS', to mean how not to raise money" (Robert Peston, BBC Business editor). Beyond the different approaches of the two banks, the example draws attention on the fact that regulations often advocated to restore trust may slow the cure rather than mitigate the crises.

4. GLOBALISATION, CRISES AND THE MANAGEMENT OF TRUST

Does globalisation add to the frequency and depth of occurrence of economic crises and make the management of trust in financial systems more difficult? This question cannot be answered categorically at present because one can identify some influences which indicate an affirmative answer and others point to the opposite conclusion and their impacts have not yet been quantified. As pointed out in the introductory section to this chapter, globalisation may alter the dynamics of economic and financial systems in ways that increase the frequency of crises. It may also result in a widening of information gaps. As a result, this can add to the extent of the loss of trust when a crisis occurs and can increase its severity. On the other hand, globalisation has been associated in recent times with the geographical diversification or spread of economic activity. Economic growth in East Asia (particularly China), and to a lesser extent India, has helped to diversify sources of demand for commodities. This has the potential to alleviate international economic crises.

The level of macroeconomic activity of nations has become more interdependent as a result of growing globalisation because world exports constitute a growing proportion of global GDP and the level of global foreign investment has risen in relation to world GDP (see Tisdell and Sen, 2004; Tisdell, 2006). As a result of these developments, the governments of industrial nations have become less able to influence the level of economic activity, including employment, in their economies. However, it does not follow that national economies are more unstable and investors and consumers at greater risk of a loss of economic confidence as a result of growing globalisation. One reason for this in that growing economic globalisation has increased the number of large economies and this process is continuing. Whereas as previously the United States and Europe dominated global economic activity, and to a lesser extent Japan, China has now developed a large and expanding economy as a result of its opening up to the outside world (Tisdell, 1993) and the Indian economy is in the process of expanding its global impact. While there is greater global interdependence, a slow down in the economy of the United States economy may have a smaller economic impact globally than in the past. Australia for example, became more diversified in the geographical direction of its exports and less dependent economically on Europe and the United States compared to earlier times (Tisdell, 2007).

Nevertheless, Australia is not immune to negative impacts from financial crises in the United States and Europe because financial markets in more developed countries have become extremely interdependent. For example, as in Europe, many financial and investing institutions in Australia experienced a financial crisis as a result of the sub-prime mortgage crises in the United States. Some had investments in these mortgage properties, either directly or indirectly, and others relied on a supply of funds from the US which became scarce after the crisis. Australian companies that were borrowing funds short-term from the United States and investing for the long-term experienced a particular difficulty. Furthermore, funds at call were called in by many American financial institutions as they tried to cope with their own liquidity problems. Falling stock prices also meant that many share investors trading on margin were unable to make a profit and the value of their collateral fell with the result that lenders required them to reduce the size of their loans. Thus a contagious concertina effect was started. This had global financial repercussion with the extent of the financial repercussion for individual nations depending upon their level of exposure to financial markets in the United States.

Apart from the type of direct financial impact just mentioned, global financial *sentiments* were undermined by the financial crisis in the United States. Global communications and international financial investment result in financial difficulties in one part of the globe became quickly known elsewhere. This can trigger a lack of trust or confidence in the future performance of financial markets in other parts of the world, particularly if the economy experiencing financial difficulty is seen as playing a pivotal role in the health of the world economy. This may lead to excessive financial panic and contagion of the crisis internationally thereby, making the situation much worse than it need be. Governments in countries subject to such contagion may be able to stem it by appropriate reassurance and timely action to maintain trust in the financial system. For example, the British Government acted in this way in relation to the Northern Rock Bank which suffered financial difficulties due to the sub-prime crisis in the United States and a subsequent run on the bank.

Financial markets can be extremely volatile and speculative. There is a tendency of those operating in such markets to become highly geared (to have a high level of borrowing relative to assets) during boom times and a tendency for this gearing to increase as investors become more optimistic about their economic gains. The end of a boom or bull period is always difficult to predict, but for those who are highly geared it is likely to result in financial crisis. This type of financial crisis can then spread to the 'real' economy resulting in reduced economic activity and less employment because of a general loss of confidence in the economic future. Globally, an economic crisis can spread by two routes: (1) direct international financial contagion which affects economies outside the original source of the crisis and (2) through reduced international trade due to the impacts of the financial crisis on 'real' economies.

The massive increase in global financial trading in recent times, much of which is of a speculative nature and which has far outstripped the growth of international trade and real transactions, has added to the volatility of the world economy and its capacity to generate global economic crises. When there is poor economic management of a major economy (such as appears to have been the case under the presidency of George Bush Jr. in the United States) there is a high chance of the generation of such crises. It is desirable from a global perspective that such economies be more prudently managed. Otherwise, all nations are likely to suffer and trust in the global economic system is likely to be impaired.

The containment of, and avoidance of, economic and financial crisis in major economies now calls for greater international cooperation by governments than in the past because of the increased interdependence of economies due to growing globalisation. Greater prudential supervision of major financial institutions by governments seems to be necessary to avoid the type of 'subprime' financial crisis that began in the United States where there was a lack of prudential supervision of financial institutions because of the belief that the major financial institutions could be trusted to manage their own finances in a prudent manner. It was assumed that they would do so because it was in their self-interest to remain financially solvent. However, this self-regulation failed with considerable economic costs to innocent victims in the United States and globally. The risk has grown that widespread mistrust of the market system will develop.

CONCLUSION

Trust is a complex phenomenon and the word 'trust' has a multitude of meanings. In general, not much progress can be made in analysing trust and its implications unless the object of trust is specified. For example, in analysing trust and its consequences one should consider whether trust relates

(1)   to the degree of confidence in the individual's own beliefs or abilities;
(2)   whether it relates to the reliability of others; or
(3)   whether it applies to the ability of particular systems to deliver specified results.

As indicated above, the occurrence of crises can undermine trust in relation to all these aspects. In discussing trust and its consequences, both the social level at which trust operates and the object of trust should be specified.

Economic globalisation has proceeded at a rapid pace in recent decades. Does this mean that we should now have more confidence in the ability of the economic system to avoid economic recession or depression? While changes in the geographical dispersion of economic activity globally give some grounds for optimism, the evolution of speculative global financial markets makes for greater pessimism. Greater government regulation and international cooperation may be required to ensure that at least, the major financial players in finance markets act in a prudent manner. With greater support for market liberalism, there appears to have been a relaxation of the prudential regulation of major financial institutions. This could undermine trust in the economic system if such institutions begin to act in a bullish manner either because of sentiment or in order to compete more fiercely with other lenders. This might subsequently undermine trust in the whole market system. This would be an unpalatable outcome for those committed philosophically to a liberal market system. Furthermore, trust in the global economic system is likely to be undermined when major powers, such as the United States, fail to adopt prudent economic policies.

Managing trust can, nevertheless, be complicated. Sometimes crises are unavoidable and can have positive effects. For example, as the world evolves beliefs that may have been relevant at an earlier time may become irrelevant but it may take a crisis leading to lack of trust in previous beliefs to develop new ones that can be trusted, at least for a time. Crises may also result in social reforms and adjustment of personal relationships as a means of re-establishing trust in socio-economic systems or in personal relationships. Thus, trust, crises and adjustments are closely interlinked. It also emerges from this discussion that important relationships exist between trust, information gaps and the occurrence and severity of business and economic crises. To the extent that globalisation increases asymmetry of information between agents (that is, information gaps); it raises the risk of behaviours that culminate in business and economic crises and adds to their severity. This creates major challenges for managing trust. It is also interesting to note that, as pointed out in this chapter, Keynes (1936, p.153) identified information deficiencies of economic agents as a major source of economic crises.

ACKNOWLEDGMENTS

This paper has been based in part on the discussion generated by the Open Forum on "Trust and Management of Crises" organized by Professor Jacques-Marie Aurifeille as part of the Franco-Australian Workshop, held at the University of Adelaide, South Australia, March, 2008. Its preparation has benefited from this discussion and we would like to thank participants for their contributions.

REFERENCES

Akerlof, G. (1970). The market for lemons: quality uncertainty and the market mechanism. *Quarterly Journal of Economics, 84*, 488-500.

Anon a (2008). Catastrophe theory. *Wikipedia* http://en.wikipedia.org/wiki/Catastrophe_theory - Accessed 8/5/2008.

Anon b (2008). United Nations Monetary and Financial Crisis. http://en.wikipedia.org/wiki/Bretton_Woods_Conference - Accessed 8/5/2008.

Aurifeille, J.M. (2007). Coordination. In R. Bailey and S.R. Clegg (eds.) *International Encyclopaedia of International Studies* (Pp. 280-283). Thousand Oaks, California. Sage.

Bohnet, I. (2007). Why men and women trust others. In B.S. Frey and A. Stutzer (eds.) *Economics and Psychology: A Promising New Cross-Disciplinary Field* (Pp. 89-110). Cambridge, MA and London, UK. The MIT Press.

Frydman. R. and Goldberg, M.D. (2007). *Imperfect Knowledge Economics: Exchange Rates and Risk*. Princeton, NJ, USA and Oxford, UK. Princeton University Press.

Inglehart, R. (1999). Trust, well-being and democracy. In M. E. Warren (ed.) *Democracy and Trust* (Pp. 88-120). Cambridge, UK. Cambridge University Press.

Keynes, J.M. (1936). *The General Theory of Employment, Interest and Money*. London, UK and St. Martin's Pass, New York. Macmillan.

Knack, S. and Keefer, P. (1997). Does social capital have an economic payoff? A cross-country investigation. *Quarterly Journal of Economics 112*, 1251-1288.

Kramer, R. and Tyler T.R. (eds.) (1996) *Trust in Organizations*. Thousand Oaks, CA, USA. Sage.

LaPorta, R., Lopez-de-Silanes, F., Shleifer, A. and Vishny, R.W. (1997). Trust in large organizations, *American Economic Review 87*, 333-338.

Ostram, E. and Walker, J. (eds.) (2003). *Trust and Reciprocity*. New York, USA. Russel Sage.

Putnam, R.D. (2000). *Bowling Alone: The Collapse and Revival of American Community*. New York, USA. Simon and Schuster.

Putnam, R.D., Leonardi, R. and Nanetti, R.Y. (1993). *Making Democracy Work: Civic Traditions in Modern Italy*. Princeton, New Jersey, USA. Princeton University Press.

Rosenfeld, R., Messner, S.F. and Baumer, E.P. (2001). Social capital and homicide. *Social Forces 80*(1), 283-309.

Tisdell, C. (2003). *Economic Development in the Context of China.* London and St. Martin's Press, New York. Macmillan.

Tisdell, C. (2006). An overview of globalisation and economic policy responses. In C. Tisdell, (ed.) *Globalisation and World Economic Policies* (Pp. 3-16). New Delhi, India. Serials Publications.

Tisdell, C. (2007). Economic and business relations between China and Australia: insights into China's global economic footprint. In P. Basu, G. O'Neill and A. Traglione, *Engagement and Change: Exploring Management, Economic and Finance Implications of a Globalising Environment* (Pp. 11-24). Brisbane, Australia. Australian Academic Press.

Tisdell, C. and Sen, R.K. (2004). An overview of economic globalisation: Its momentum and its consequences examined. In C. Tisdell and R.K. Sen (eds.) *Economic Globalisation: Social Conflicts, Labour and Environmental Issues* (Pp.5-23). Cheltenham, UK and Northampton, MA, USA. Edward Elgar.

Tisdell, C. and Hartley, K. (2008). *Microeconomic Policy – A New Perspective*. Cheltenham, UK and Northampton, MA, USA. Edward Elgar.

Zak, P. and Knack, S. (2001). Trust and growth, *Economic Journal, 111*, 295-321.

In: Trust, Globalisation and Market Expansion
Editors: J-M. Aurifeille, C. Medlin and C. Tisdell

ISBN 978-1-60741-812-2
© 2009 Nova Science Publishers, Inc.

Chapter 5

TRUST IN A GLOBAL VALUE CHAIN: A CASE STUDY OF THE KIMBERLEY PROCESS

Marilyn Healy[*]
Queensland University of Technology,
Australia

ABSTRACT

The thesis of this paper is that the diamond industry is restoring consumer trust through the certification of its global value chain, a concept known as the Kimberley Process Certification Scheme. This process controls the movements of diamonds within the global value chain, from the rough to the finished product at the consumer level. The aim of the Kimberley Process Certification Scheme is to ensure that conflict, or illicit unofficial rough diamonds are excluded from the legitimate value chain. Conflict diamonds have become a major issue in international trade. Diamonds are a symbol of love and devotion, but diamonds are big business. Some may argue that diamonds are a commodity and therefore one cannot trust a commodity nor the process of its value chain. However, the Kimberley Process Certification Scheme is restoring consumer trust in the industry by ensuring the integrity of its global value chain.

Keywords: trust, adaptation, diamonds, Kimberley Process, value chain.

1. INTRODUCTION

A crisis can be described as a situation which requires action to be taken to avoid serious consequences. From that perspective, the diamond industry was facing a crisis. Diamonds represent love and affection. For many years DeBeers and the diamond and jewellery industries globally have built a very strong association between diamonds and romance.

---

[*] Email: m.healy@qut.edu.au

Diamonds have also been romanticised in popular culture, for example, the Marilyn Monroe song, 'Diamonds are a girl's best friend.'

Diamonds may be a girl's best friend, but diamonds are also easy to conceal, transport and store. A small parcel of stones worth many many dollars in value can be placed in the pocket of a jacket and easily moved between borders. While the legitimate diamond trade is, in the main, a closed but well-organised industry, an illegitimate trade was doing serious harm to the industry.

There was a prominent rise in the trade of rough diamonds used by rebel and or terrorist movements to finance their military activities, such as attempts to undermine or overthrow legitimate governments. Diamonds exchanged to finance rebel activities are known by various names such as dirty diamonds (Taylor and Mokhawa, 2003), blood diamonds (United Nations, 2003), terror diamonds (Sulaiman, 2003), or the name most commonly recognised amongst consumers, conflict diamonds (Josipovic, 2003). The official definition of these diamonds is; diamonds that originate from areas controlled by forces or factions opposed to legitimate and internationally recognised governments, and are used to fund military action in opposition to those governments, or in contravention of the decisions of the UN Security Council Forces.

The primary problem was that there was a crisis in the global diamond industry brought about because of the rise in conflict diamonds, which in turn was doing damage to the image and reputation of the industry. Diamonds are positioned in the consumer's mind as a representation of the emotions of love, happiness, romance and self-fulfilment. Knowledge that the mining and distribution of the diamonds they consumed was at the cost of life and limb, damaged the positive image associated with diamonds and sales of diamonds to the consumer market began to decline. Further, the industry needed to alter the image of it being 'secretive, collusive and brutal' to one that was 'progressive, developmental and transparent' (Hughes 2006, p. 1)

The aim of this paper is to explore how an ambitious global plan by the diamond industry addressed the issue of a lack of consumer trust in the industry. Therefore the research question to be answered is: can a process of governance create trust in a globalised industry? To answer this question, a case study approach is taken in which the Kimberley Process Certification Scheme is analysed, a scheme introduced by the global diamond industry to curb the problem of conflict diamonds and to restore confidence in the diamond industry.

For the purpose of this paper, trust is defined as 'having some faith in the workings of systems or processes of which one possesses only limited knowledge (Giddens, 1990). Also, for the purpose of this paper, the *etic* view of trust is adopted, that is, that the concept means the same thing and is measurable the same way across different cultures (Zaheer and Zaheer, 2006). The definition of a value chain is 'the full range of activities from conception of a product/service till its disposal, (Venu and Padmanabhan, 2002, p. 1). In the case of the diamond industry, the value chain starts from the mining of the rough, through to the sale of polished diamonds to the end consumer.

To this end, the paper has three main sections. It begins with an overview of the historical background and effects of conflict diamonds. This section incorporates a discussion of the consequences, problem and process implemented to solve the problem.

The second main section of the paper is a theoretical discussion.

2. HISTORICAL BACKGROUND

The diamond value chain has several manifestations. A simple explanation is that diamonds are mined, sold to buyers who on-sell them to diamond cutters and polishers and then the diamonds are sold to wholesalers or diamond merchants. From there the diamonds are sold to either jewellery manufacturers whose finished products incorporating diamonds are sold to retailers, or direct to retailers, for the final sales to the consumer. Diamonds are mined commercially in a number of different countries or continents, for example, Africa, Canada, Australia and Russia. Conflict free diamonds are defined as those diamonds which have been purchased from legitimate sources not involved in funding conflict and in compliance with the United Nations Resolutions (Anon 2004).

The United Nations has identified conflict diamonds as originating primarily from four countries: Liberia, Sierra Leone, the Democratic Republic of the Congo and Angola. Guinea and Côte d'Ivoire have also been mentioned (Létourneau 2006). There are suggestions that not only are conflict diamonds being sold to finance some ongoing rebel operations within Africa, but also they are being traded to finance terrorist activities around the world. Links have been suggested with Osama Bin Laden, Hezbollah and Al Qaeda (Taylor and Mokhawa, 2003, p. 288). Italian authorities arrested Sanjivan Ruprah, described as a millionaire diamond smuggler, who allegedly sold weapons to Al Qaeda (Bates, 2002). Claims have also been made that senior Al Qaeda members established diamond and gold mining businesses in Tanzania as early as 1993. The expertise gained from these enterprises enabled other operatives to set up diamond trading and laundering operations in Liberia and Sierra Leone in 2000 and 2001 (Sulaiman, 2003).

The dollar value of this trade is large. The rough diamond production was estimated to be valued at US$14.3 billion in 2008 (Ryan, 2008). Estimates of the extent of the conflict diamond trade range from 3% of the total production (Sparshott, 2003) to as high as 20% (Fatal Transaction, a Netherlands organisation for International Development Co-operation in Taylor and Mokhawa 2003).

The Consequences

There are three main consequences from this trade. First, the loss of life, torture, rape and injury to the people, and the destruction of infrastructure in the countries affected by rebel activities financed by the trade in conflict diamonds, as well as the links to wider terrorist organisations. This first issue was recognised by the United Nations General Assembly who began passing a series of resolutions in 1998 calling for the certification of diamonds.

The second consequence was the loss of revenue to the affected producing countries causing fiscal hardships, a situation exacerbated by the destruction caused by the associated conflict. Famine was one consequence of this fiscal hardship, which attracted the interest of global organisations like Amnesty International who actively supported a campaign against conflict diamonds called "did someone else die for that diamond?' This campaign encouraged consumers to write to De Beers to protest about the trade in conflict diamonds. As well, consumers were encouraged to ask retailers what was the origin of the diamond. Furthermore, Amnesty International published a list of jewellers in the United States who supported their campaign against conflict diamonds. In addition, World Vision launched a campaign called 'dying for a diamond' (Taylor and Mokhawa, 2003).

Thus, the third consequence and the one which was the greatest motivator for the diamond industry to find a way in which to identify and to prevent the international transaction of conflict diamonds, was the effect that the negative publicity had on the perceptions that end-consumers of diamonds had of diamonds. This negative publicity was reinforced first, when conflict diamonds were mentioned in a James Bond film and more pointedly in the film Blood Diamonds, starring Leonard De Caprio. These films created awareness of the problem to a far greater audience than possible through other means.

The consumption experience of consumers involves fantasies, feeling and fun and these three F's are of crucial importance when explaining the purchase decision (Holbrook and Hirschman, 1982). Diamonds are positioned in the consumer's mind as representing the emotions of love, happiness, romance and self-fulfilment, all of which are encapsulated in the three Fs. The diamond is the ultimate gemstone which not only is the standard gem for engagement rings throughout much of the world, but also is a symbol of success and status. Research in the United States revealed that in 2003, 26% of consumers were aware of conflict diamonds, an increase from the 7% in 2000 (Anon, 2003). Thus jewellers became concerned that the increased awareness of conflict diamonds was having an impact on the consumer's perception of diamonds and thus would affect demand. This decrease in demand would flow back up the channel from the retailers to the producers. As jewellery represents the greatest market for diamonds by value, this potential reduction in demand became a major concern.

The Problem

From this preamble, the problem then was how to recognise conflict diamonds and how to prevent or limit their sale on the open market, thus protecting the positive positioning of diamonds in the consumer's mind and restoring trust in the industry and the product.

THE SOLUTION

The solution was the introduction of what is known as the Kimberley Process. This process, named after the original diamond producing area in South Africa, requires that each shipment of rough diamonds being exported and crossing an international border not only be transported in a tamper-resistant container but also be accompanied by a government validated Kimberley Process Certificate. Each certificate must contain data describing the shipment's content, be uniquely numbered and be resistant to forgery.

The process was adopted on 5th November, 2002 by the World Diamond Council (WDC) and endorsed by the UN Resolution 1459 on January 29, 2003. Countries agreed that they would only allow for the import and export of rough diamonds if those diamonds come from or are being exported to another Kimberley Process participant, commencing 1st January 2003 (Brown 2004). By November 2006, 71 countries were included in the process (WDC 2006). Note however, that before countries are given access by the WDC to participate in the process they must illustrate that internal mechanisms are in place to monitor the process. Audits are done by the WDC to ensure the integrity of the process.

Once parcels are traded they can be mixed with other Kimberley certified diamonds. If being re-exported, a Kimberley Process Certificate will be issued by the exporting country.

Thus, all buyers and sellers of rough and polished diamonds must make the following statement on all invoices:

The diamonds herein invoiced have been purchased from legitimate sources not involved in funding conflict and in compliance with United Nations Resolutions. The seller hereby guarantees that these diamonds are conflict free, based on personal knowledge and/or written guarantees provided by the supplier of these diamonds (World Diamond Council 2002).

The Result

Today, conflict diamonds represent less than one percent of world diamond production (Létourneau 2006). The process has not only limited the flow of conflict diamonds, but also has unearthed the trade in *illicit* diamonds, that is, diamonds that are not sold through legitimate channels. The number of illicit diamonds was estimated to be in excess of 25% of the total diamond production. For example, one hundred percent of the diamond production from Venezuela was smuggled out of the country in one year (Hughes, 2006; Létourneau, 2006; Partnership Africa Canada, 2006). Similarly, the diamond exports from the Democratic Republic of Congo rose from $331m in 1995 to $895 m in 2005 and the exports from Sierra Leone, which were officially almost zero in 1995, were $142 m in 2005.

3. THEORETICAL DISCUSSION

Given this background the question is then posed – can a process such as the Kimberley Process create or indeed restore consumer trust in the value chain of a global industry and thus in the industry itself? The most opportune time to examine trust is when stress and conflict have created a situation (crises) where confidence is an issue (Rempel, Holmes and Zanna 1985). Research into the retail jewellery market in the United States, one of the largest markets for diamonds, indicated trust in the industry was an issue, as indicated by the research cited above and by anecdotal evidence from within the industry.

Trust is a complex topic. There are many definitions and conceptualisation about what is trust (Raimondo, 2000) and the term trust is often used 'freely and earnestly' (Barber, 1983). For the purpose of this paper, two definitions were adopted. First, trust is having confident positive expectations regarding another's conduct (Lewicki, McAllister and Bies, 1998). In this case, the 'another' is the diamond industry. More specifically, trust is having some faith in the workings of systems or processes of which one possesses only limited knowledge (Giddens, 1990). Consumers generally, have a very limited knowledge of the diamond industry or the diamond value chain.

Based on Barber's (1983) research, it is commonly asserted that trust is based on an expectation that people have for others or themselves (Weber and Carter, 1998). Barber (1983) posited three expectations as being most applicable for the development of trust: first, the expectation for social order; second, the expectation for competent role performance; and finally, the expectation that people will place others' interests before their own.

McAllister (1995) refers to two types of trust; trust based on reasoning (cognitive trust), and trust based on underlying feelings (affective trust). Cognition based trust is based on reasoning and is therefore rational in that 'we choose whom we will trust, in which respects and under that circumstances, and we base the choice of what we take to be 'good reasons', constituting evidence of trustworthiness' (Lewis and Weigert, 1985, p. 970). Affective based trust consists of emotional bonds that develop (McAllister, 1995). Although most authors argue that these emotional bonds are between *individuals* (for example, Molm et al, 2000), it has been shown that consumers develop affective trust with high involvement brands or products (Lau and Lee, 1999).

Diamonds are a high involvement product, where involvement refers to the 'degree of personal relevance of an object, product or services to a customer' (Sheth, Mittal and Newman 1999, p. 361). When a purchase involves a source of self-identification for the buyer, more risk is involved and thus the consumer is more highly involved in the decision to buy (Beaty, Kahle and Homer, 1998). Elliott and Yannopoulou (2007) found that the concept of trust is particularly relevant to symbolic brands with high involvement, due to the high perceptions of purchase risk. Thus, trust is the belief which a consumer relies on in a purchase situation characterised by uncertainty, vulnerability, lack of control and the independent-mindedness of the transaction partner, and is the belief an industry will deliver (Sichtmann, 2007). Furthermore, trust has a strong direct impact on the current purchase intention (Sichtmann, 2007).

Moreover, having an emotional affinity with a brand as one has when one can self-identify with the brand, means that the risk associated with the purchase increases and thus the involvement level increases. The Kimberley Process is therefore a brand based on two points. First, it differentiates non-conflict diamonds from conflict diamonds and second, it increases the benefits to the customers thus reducing the risk in this high involvement purchase.

At the more macro level, trust is one of the most pervasive aspects of life and without the general trust that people have in each other, society itself would disintegrate (Hosking, 2006). Donaldson (2003), in his argument that trust is fundamental to society, suggested the concept of an ethical wealth of nations, a related concept to the thesis of this paper. Societal trust is necessary for consumers to feel good about their purchases, a feeling which in turn creates value. Mauss (1955 cited in Choi, Eldomiaty and Kim, 2007) identified two concepts of value; economic and ideal. Economic value is one in which social interaction is negligible and applies most strongly in the trade of commodities. That is, the market exchange of commodities sees assets being exchanged which are focalised, quantified, and valued at a particular price. One could argue that because diamonds could be viewed as a commodity and therefore are a form of economic value with little social interaction, that trust is not an issue. However, as argued throughout this paper, at the end consumer level, diamonds are a high involvement product and cannot be viewed as a commodity.

Other research found that environmental attributes can increase preferences among certain consumers (Berger and Kanetkar, 1995). Given the global environment of terrorism, actions by the diamond industry to minimise the availability of diamonds to restrict the funds for terrorist organisations will increase the preference for diamonds for some consumers.

The study of trust has generally moved from a level of analysis of individuals to organisations (Medlin and Quester 2002; Seppanen, Blomqvist and Sundqvist, 2007). Nevertheless, it has been argued that in the knowledge and ethics based society in which we now live, there needs to be an emphasis on the collective nature of markets and exchange (Choi, et al, 2007). Thus, this paper takes the debate to a higher level, that is, to that of a global value chain or global industry level.

Trust takes a long time to build, but can be easily destroyed and is hard to regain (Robbins, 1999). A betrayal of trust can lead to the customer's dissatisfaction, that is, a feeling of distrust and defection (Ndubisi, 2004). Distrust is the confidence about a relationship partner's undesirable behaviour, stemming from the knowledge of the individual's capabilities and intentions (Deutsch, 1960).

A key point in the thesis of this paper is that the diamond industry has undertaken what could be referred to as 'adaptation.' Adaption is normally referred to as the adjustments to a company's own operations as well as to the exchange activities with a partner organisation (Canning and Hanmer-Lloyd, 2007). Indeed, adaptation has also been referred to as manifest commitments of a resource to a relationship (Hakansson, 1982), as a transaction specific investment (Williamson, 1985), as a pledge (Anderson and Weitz, 1992) and as a commitment input (Grundlach, Achrol and Mentzer, 1995).

Canning (1999, p. 35 cited in Canning and Hamner-Lloyd, 2007) defines adaptation as '...modifications at the individual, group or corporate level which are carried out by one or both parties in an exchange relationship in order to suit new needs or conditions and which are designed initially for that specific relationship.' In the context of this paper, adaptation is referred to as changes undertaken in the operations of the industry in order to address new conditions in the industry, which in turn affect the affective trust of the end consumer.

CONCLUSION

One part of trust is the articulation and embodiment of a moral code that cares about people (Charlton, 2000). Although this finding was from research done from the organisational perspective, the basic tenet could well be applied to the diamond industry.

Men and women around the world must be reassured that their diamond purchase is just as pure, magical and special as their eternal love, symbolized so well in the unique beauty of a diamond (World Diamond Council, 2006). The diamond industry has moved from a unique selling proposition to a unique industry proposition (Maklan and Knox 1997) by enhancing its reputation and in turn, restoring consumer trust.

Bagozzi (1975) views trust as the degree of perceived validity in the statements or actions of one's partner in a relationship. The perceived validity of the KPCS and the relevant actions of the diamond industry generates trust on the part of the consumer in the industry. The retail diamond industry is reinforcing the message to the consumer to increase the trust that the consumer has in diamonds. For example, Tiffany and Co. have a lengthy statement on their website relating the KPCS which says in part; 'Tiffany and Co. purchases diamonds only in those countries that are full participants in the KPCS. The KPCS has enabled the diamond industry to create a global structure for trust.

The majority of diamond producing and importing countries are adhering to the principles of the Kimberley Process, one exception however, is Venezuela. Although it is claimed that the process may still be open to abuse (Amnesty International 2006) it is concluded that the Kimberley Process and publicity surrounding conflict diamonds is slowly working towards restoring trust in the diamond global value chain and thus in the diamond industry.

Some may argue that when referring to institutions or products or brands that we are in fact referring to confidence rather than trust (Seligman (1997). Given the high involvement of the product however, the crisis facing the diamond industry, the preceding discussion about trust and adaptation, the term 'trust' is justified in this context. The implication of this case analysis is that other industries facing similar crises can learn from the actions of the diamond industry.

REFERENCES

Anderson, E. and Weitz, B. (1992). The use of pledges to build and sustain commitment in distribution channels, *Journal of Marketing Research, 29* (1), 18-34.

Anon. (2003). Awareness of conflict diamonds grow, *Canadian Jeweller,* Oct/Nov 12, 4, 8,10.

Anon. (2004), The Kimberley Process. What is it? *Australian Gemmologist*, April-June, Insert.

Bagozzi, R. (1975). Marketing as exchange, *Journal of Marketing, 39* (4), 32-39.

Barber, B. (1983). *The Logic and Limits of Trust*, New Brunswick NJ: Rutgers University Press.

Bates, S. (2002). Conflict diamonds issues will go on – even without conflicts, *JCK,* Oct, 52.

Beaty, S. E., Kahle, L. R and Homer, P. (1998). The involvement commitment model: theory and implications, *Journal of Business,* 16 March 149-167.

Berger, I. E. and Kanetkar, V. (1995). Increasing environmental sensitivity via workplace experiences, *Journal of Public Policy and Marketing, 14* (Fall), 205-215.

Brown, G. (2004). The Kimberley Process. *Australian Gemmologist, April-June.*

Canning, L. E. (1999). *The Introduction of Environmental (Green) Adaptations in Supplier-Customer Relationships. An Investigation of Inter-Firm Processes in Britain and Germany,* unpublished PhD thesis, University of West of England, Bristol.

Canning, L. and Hanmer-Lloyd, S. (2007). Trust in buyer-seller relationships: the challenge of environmental (green) adaptation, *European Journal of Marketing, 41* (9/10), 1073-1095.

Charlton, G. (2000). *Human Habits of Highly Effective Organisations,* Pretoria:Van Schaik.

Choi, C. J., Eldomiaty, T. I. and Kim, S. W. (2007). Consumer trust, social marketing and ethics of welfare exchange, *Journal of Business Ethics, 74,* 17-23.

Deutsch, M. (1960). The effect of motivational orientation upon trust and suspicion, *Human Relations, 13,* 123-139.

Donaldson, T. (2003). Editor's comments: taking ethics seriously – a mission now more possible, *Academy of Management Review, 28,* 363-366/

Elliott, R. and Yannopoulou, N. (2007). The nature of trust in brands: a psychosocial model, *European Journal of Marketing, 41* (9/10).

Giddens, A. (1990). *The Consequences of Modernity,* Cambridge: Polity Press.

Grundlach, G. T., Achrol, R. S. and Mentzer, J. T. (1995). The structure of commitment in exchange, *Journal of Marketing, 59* (1), 78-92.

Hakansson, H. (1982). *International Marketing and Purchasing of Industrial Goods: An Interactive Approach,* (ed), New York, NY: Cambridge University Press.

Holbrook, M.B. and Hirschman, E.C. (1982). The experiential aspects of consumer behavior: consumer fantasies, feelings and fun, *Journal of Consumer Research, 9* Sept, 132-40.

Hosking, G. (2006). Trust and distrust: a suitable theme for historians? *Transactions of the RHS, 16,* 95-115.

Hughes, T. (2006). Are blood diamonds forever? *BusinessDay,* 8 Nov, http://www.businessday.co.za/articles/topstories.aspx?ID=BD4A312823 accessed 20 March, 2008.

Josipovic, I. (2003). Conflict diamonds: not so clear-cut, *Harvard International Review, 25* (2), 10-12.

Lau, G. T. and Lee, S. H. (1999). Consumers' trust in a brand the link to brand loyalty, *Journal of Market Focused Management, 4,* 341-370.

Létourneau, J. (2006), Killing Kimberley? Conflict diamonds and paper tigers, *Occasional Paper 15, the Diamonds and Human Security Project,* Partnership Africa Canada, Nov. p. 2.

Lewicki, R. J., McAllister, D. J. and Bies, R. J. (1998). Trust and distrust: new relationships and realities, *Academy of Management Review, 23* (3), 438-458.

Lewis, D. J. and Weigert, A. (1985). Trust as a social reality. *Social Forces, 63* (4) (June), 967-985.

McAllister, D. J. (1995). Affect- and cognition-based rust as foundations for interpersonal cooperation in organizations, *Academy of Management Journal, 38* (1), 24-59.

Maklan, S. and Knox, S. (1997). Reinventing the brand: bridging the gap between the customer and brand value. *Journal of Product and Brand Management, 6* (2), 1061-0421.

Mauss, M. (1955). *The Gift,* London: Routledge.

Medlin, C. J. and Quester, P. (2002). Inter-firm trust: two theoretical dimensions versus a global measure, *Proceedings from 18th IMP Conference,* Perth Australia.

Molm, L. D., Takahashi, N. and Peterson, G. (2000). Risk and trust in social exchange: an experimental test of a classical concept, *American Journal of Sociology, 105* (5), 1396-1427.

Ndubisi, N. O. (2004). Understanding the salience of cultural dimensions on relationships and aftermath, *Cross Cultural Management, 11* (3), 70-89.

Raimondo, M. R. (2000). The measurement of trust in marketing studies: a review of models and methodologies, IMP Conference.

Rempel, J., Holmes, J. and Zanna, M. (1985). Trust in close relationships, *Journal of Personality and Social Psychology, 49* (1), 95-112.

Robbins, S. P. (1996). *Essentials of Organizational Behavior. Concepts, Controversies, Applications,* 7th ed., Englewood Cliffs, NJ:Prentice-Hall.

Ryan, 2008, « Rough diamond supply to drop this year, miningm[x], 24th July, accessed http://www.miningmx.com/diamonds/686521.htm, date accessed Sept 30, 2008.

Seligman, A. (1997). *The Problem of Trust,* Princeton NJ: Princeton University Press.

Seppanen, R., Blomqvist, K. and Sundqvist, S. (2007). Measuring inter-organizational trust – a critical review of the empirical research in 1990-2003, *Industrial Marketing Management, 36* (2), 249-265.

Sichtmann, C. (2007). An analysis of antecedents and consequences of trust in a corporate brand, *European Journal of Marketing, 41* (9/10), 999-1015.

Sparshott, J. (2003). United States: other countries step up monitoring of shady diamond trading, *Knight Ridder Tribune Business News*, 3 Jan, Washington, 1.

Sulaiman, T. (2003). Clean diamond act to help U.S. buyers stay clear of 'conflict diamonds', *Knight Ridder Tribune Business News*, 7 May, Washington, 1.

Taylor, I. and Mokhawa, G. (2003). Not forever: Botswana, conflict diamonds and the bushmen, *African Affairs, 102,* 261-83.

'Tiffany and Co. purchases diamonds only in those countries that are full participants in the Kimberley Process Certification Scheme (KPCS).'

http://www.tiffany.com/sustainability/mining_diamonds.aspx accessed 1 Dec 2008.

United Nations (2003). General assembly text strongly supports 'Kimberley Process' Certification Scheme, *MS Presswire,* 14 April, Coventry, 1.

Venu, S. and Padmanabhan, K. (2002). Globalising by value chain, *Businessline,* 17 Dec., 1. Chennai.

Weber, L. R. and Carter, A. (1998). On constructing trust: temporality, self-disclosure and perspective-taking, *International Journal of Sociology and Social Policy, 18* (1), 7-26.

Williamson, O. E. (1985). *The Economic Institutions of Capitalism: Firms, Markets, Relational Contracting,* New York, NY: The Free Press.

World Diamond Council. (2006), Diamond industry hails success of conflict conference, *Press Release,* Nov. 9, http://72.32.101.83/pdfs/media/news/2006_11_9_WDC.pdf, accessed 20 March, 2008.Zaheer, S. and Zaheer, A. (2006). Trust across borders, *Journal of International Business Studies, 37,* 21-29.

Part III. The Role of Trust within Institutional and Network Elements of Globalising Business

In: Trust, Globalisation and Market Expansion
Editors: J-M. Aurifeille, C. Medlin and C. Tisdell

Chapter 6

DO WE NEED TRUST TO GET ALONG? THE INFLUENCE OF TRUST ON HARMONY IN NETWORKS

Giselle Rampersad
University of Adelaide, Australia

ABSTRACT

Globalization has led to an increased prominence of RandD networks amongst members of universities, businesses and government. However, empirical studies examining the performance of these networks are sparse. To fill this gap, this study applies confirmatory factor analysis using structural equation modelling to ascertain the influence of trust on harmony within these networks. It is based on 235 responses of network participants from a range of technology-driven industries in Australia. It adopts a network perspective by analysing and comparing the views of network members from universities, businesses and government. It reveals that trust has a significant impact on harmony from the perspectives of varied network participants.

1. INTRODUCTION

Globalization has significantly increased the prevalence of inter-organizational RandD networks amongst members of government, universities and businesses. A number of factors have contributed to this phenomenon. First, there have been many attempts to spread growing RandD costs and risks across multiple stakeholders. Second, there have been shifts in public RandD funding and incentives towards encouraging multi-institutional research in various countries including the United Kingdom, the United States and Australia (Provan and Milward, 1995). Third, the permeation of enabling technologies such as information and communications technology (ICT) has blurred traditional organizational boundaries.

Management approaches within these networks have also shifted. For instance, inter-organizational coordination is characterized by 'soft assembled strategies' which are less controlling and more moderate compared to traditional intra-organizational management that are more hierarchical (Clark, 1997; Ojasalo, 2004; Williamson, 1975). Cooperationist or harmonious approaches have become prevalent (Kozan et al., 2006; Kumar, 1996). Additionally, relational factors such as trust are playing increasingly important roles in governance structures (Healy and Jonhson, 2007; Izquierdo and Cillan, 2004).

Despite the increased importance and the managerial shifts of these RandD networks, empirical research particularly at network level of analysis remains limited. To date, the relationship marketing (RM) and industrial networks literatures have placed more attention on private sector organizations than on relationships involving government and academic partners (Plewa and Quester, 2006). Furthermore, although the extant literature upholds constructs associated with ideal relationship management styles, it is biased towards an organizational rather than a network level of analysis.

To address these shortcomings, this study adopts a network level of analysis to investigate the impact of trust on harmony within networks. It is based on a network level of analysis as the responses are compared from members of government, businesses and universities. This paper is organized as follows. First, we review the extant literature and present our hypotheses. We then discuss the methodology, including our survey-based data collection process and our data analysis, using confirmatory factor analysis (CFA), and more specifically structural equation modelling (SEM). Finally, we offer managerial implications for organizations involved in innovation networks and also highlight future research directions.

2. THEORETICAL BACKGROUND

The advent of globalization has intensified the prominence of networks which aim at strengthening the innovation capacity, and in turn, the international competitiveness of countries (Furman et al., 2002; Ruttan, 2001; Tushman, 2004). These innovation networks can be defined as groups of loosely interconnected organizations including universities, businesses and government agencies that share scientific discovery and application goals (Moller and Rajala, 2007). They are instrumental in assisting countries in nurturing their innovation capabilities towards obtaining revenues for their own innovations rather than solely paying for foreign innovations (Gans and Hayes, 2004).

In order to derive the anticipated benefits from innovation networks, it is extremely important to enhance our understanding of the key factors leading to their success. While networks may provide numerous advantages such as access to new markets, knowledge and resources, they can also be problematic (Barringer and Harrison, 2000; Ford and Johnsen, 2000; Hakansson, 1987; Wilkinson et al., 2004). They may, in fact, drain resources as relationships can be demanding, sensitive information may be lost, and intellectual property may create contention amongst network members (Ford and Johnsen, 2000 ; Hedaa, 1999). Therefore, identifying the drivers that improve network performance is useful in the innovation process.

Extant literature has largely ignored the network perspective and has focused primarily on the organizational perspective. While the RM and network literatures use constructs associated with relationship management styles, those pertaining to joint outcomes remain mainly untested and their focus is on the firm rather than on the relationship or on network levels of analysis (Aurifeille and Medlin, 2007; Provan and Milward, 1995). Additionally, innovation and technology management literatures are either biased towards organizational perspectives or have considered mainly the views of one type of participant in the network and together they have ignored the combined perspectives of university, business and government participants (Bozeman, 2007; Jensen, 2007). Consequently, principles and constructs proven for the organizational perspective require further validation to determine and improve their applicability to wider network contexts.

In particular, trust, one of the most prevalent constructs in the RM literature, should be examined from a network perspective. It may be defined as 'confidence in an exchange partner's reliability and integrity' (Morgan and Hunut, 1994, p. 23). Although studies on inter-organizational relationships have consistently established the importance of trust for relationship performance since the early 1990s (Seppanen et al., 2007), its examination at the network level remains limited. The study of trust has generally moved from a level of analysis of individuals to organizations (Medlin and Quester, 2002; Seppanen et al., 2007). In business research and particularly in the field of marketing, trust features in numerous studies on business-to-business/RM, sales management and channel management (Doney and Cannon, 1997; Ganesan, 1994; Morgan and Hunt, 1994). However, trust remains under-explored empirically at the network level of analysis with extant studies focusing predominantly on organizational or even individual levels of analysis with one type of informant such as CEOs (Aulakh et al., 1996; Coote et al., 2003; Norman, 2002), salespersons (Ganesan, 1994; Nooteboom et al., 1997; Smith and Barclay, 1997), buyers (Mollering, 2002; Plank et al., 1999) and purchasers (Chow and Holden, 1997; Doney and Cannon, 1997; Zaheer et al., 1998) or, at best, dyadic relationships e.g. universities and businesses (Plewa, 2005). Understanding trust from a wider variety of actors will be of interest to the multiplicity of participants of innovation networks.

Harmony is a construct that also requires further empirical investigation at the network level. The literature contains numerous studies on conflict and cooperation. Harmony is a term used in the new product development (NPD) literature that can be applied to innovation networks. It encompasses both the notions of conflict and cooperation while retaining a more positive connotation for management than mere conflict. While harmony is related to the concept of functional conflict it is different in two main respects. The term functional or constructive conflict is defined as an 'evaluative appraisal of the results of recent efforts to manage disagreements' (Rawwas et al., 1997, p. 52). It varies from harmony as it is reactive or evaluative or based on past disagreements (Anderson and Narus, 1990; Robicheaux and El-Ansary, 1976; Rosenberg and Stern, 1971; Skarmeas, 2006) compared to the proactive approach of harmony in incorporating key players early in the process and encouraging debates. Additionally, harmony also focuses on efforts to facilitate cooperation, rather than simply addressing disagreements (Song and Thieme, 2006). Harmony is more closely related to the concept of cooperation, which implies that 'the partners are willing to pursue mutually compatible interests rather than act opportunistically' (Das and Teng, 1998 in Luo and Park, 2004, p. 142).

Harmony is desirable as globalization has led to a blurring of the boundaries between conflict and cooperation and has resulted in a shift towards a more positive cooperationist style (Rojot, 2007). Harmony is reflected in whether actors are 'involved from the early phases of innovation, if they attempt to understand each other's point of view, if conflicts between them are resolved at the lowest possible level ... and if they discuss issues rather than simply accept them' (Gupta et al., 1986, p.12). It, therefore, does not involve simply suppressing concerns and being obliged to agree, but also encompasses open and healthy debates addressing fundamental issues (Song and Thieme, 2006). A degree of conflict may be required for innovation while at the same time cooperation may be needed for efficiency (Laine, 2002; Vaaland, 2001). The NPD literature on harmony predominantly adopts an intra-organizational focus, mainly on the relationship between internal RandD and marketing functions, rather than one on inter-organizational collaborations. Hence, exploring harmony in an inter-organizational network context should contribute to a better definition of this construct. Furthermore, understanding harmony from a network perspective is important given that globalization has resulted in both the prevalence of networks and shifts towards harmonious management approaches (Kozan et al., 2006; Kumar, 1996).

3. HYPOTHESES

Despite limited empirical studies of trust at the network level of analysis, network theorists have emphasized its influence on harmony, albeit conjecturally (Cravens et al., 1994). Consequently, we hypothesize that trust is positively related to harmony within networks. Trust may impact on harmony as it facilitates conflict management: Trusting network actors may forego short-sighted goals, voice their views openly and focus on developing shared initiatives (Achrol and Kotler, 1999; Powell, 1990; Rowley et al., 2000; Seppanen et al., 2007; Uzzi, 1996). Rojot (2007) argues that functional flexibility (i.e. harmony) is influenced by mutual trust between parties. In addition to influencing the flexibility that firms show to each other, it also affects their level of solidarity (Sezen and Yilmaz, 2007). Therefore, adopting a network perspective by incorporating the variety of views of network participants, we hypothesize the following:

Hypothesis 1:   Based on the perspective of a university network participant, trust is positively related to harmony.

Hypothesis 2:   Based on the perspective of a government network participant, trust is positively related to harmony.

Hypothesis 3:   Based on the perspective of a business network participant, trust is positively related to harmony.

4. METHODOLOGY

The study is based on a mixed-method approach of qualitative followed by quantitative research. Qualitative research was deemed essential for ensuring the applicability of constructs at the network level of analysis and for developing scales where necessary. Quantitative research via CFA and SEM was crucial due to the sparse empirical research available on the constructs of trust and harmony and the subsequent relationship between them at the network level.

The quantitative survey-based data collection was carried out across a range of industries and sectors. Industries were selected on the basis of Australia's research strengths and priorities and which were also of international importance. These included responses from technology driven industries and their related counterparts, such as, defence/ICT, biotechnology/advanced materials, and wine. Responses were also drawn from a range of sectors such as universities (112), businesses (62) and government agencies (61). It should be noted that although three categories are chosen, it does not reflect a triadic relationship but a network focus as responses are drawn from 38 organisations, not only three. The study categorizes responses in these three main sectors in order to compare their views and determine the degree to which they are aligned in order to recognize patterns and generalise results to these sectors. Multiple informants (different from those in the qualitative stage) from each organization were surveyed to improve the reliability of responses of each organization (Marsden, 1990).

Respondents were identified using snowballing, and through the analysis of secondary data. From interviewees during our qualitative research, a group of initial possible respondents were suggested. These findings were also triangulated with information on collaborations from annual reports, public documents, respondents' co-authors from collaborating organizations found in publication lists, and collaboration reports from various organizations in the network. At the end of the survey, respondents were asked to refer us to up to 5 contacts within the network. As an incentive for each referral, they were placed in a draw to receive one year subscription for a topical magazine on innovation management. Given the connected nature of networks, snowballing and triangulation with secondary data were deemed suitable methods in order to more specifically define the boundaries of the population (Brito, 1999; Iacobucci, 1996; Sarantakos, 1998). A total of 808 potential respondents were sent emails with a request to participate in an online survey during the period February to December 2007. Second reminder emails were sent after two weeks of the first one. A total of 235 responses were obtained in total, representing a response rate of 31%.

The scale for trust used in this study was adapted from the existing Relationship Marketing literature while more extensive scale development was necessary for harmony. Existing scales for trust were previously applied in the contexts of university – industry relationships in Plewa (2006). Therefore, they only required slight adjustments via in-depth interviews and a pre-test to improve relevance to the wider variety of network participants including businesses, government and universities. Items for trust were sourced from Doney and Canon (1997) and also Morgan and Hunt (1994). However, scales for harmony found in the literature were predominantly used either in an intra-organizational or dyadic context of SCM, rather than at the network level of analysis. Consequently, scale development was carried during the qualitative part of this research via interviews which contributed to the item pool from the literature for harmony (Gupta et al., 1986; Song and Thieme, 2006). Following Churchill (1979), after the sourcing of items, a pilot study was conducted to purify the scales using exploratory factor analysis and reliability testing. Appendix I contains a list of the scales used in the study. All items were placed on 7-point Likert scales ranging from 1 – strongly disagree to 7 – strongly agree.

5. RESULTS

Prior to testing our hypotheses using CFA with SEM, several steps were taken. An assessment of validity and reliability was carried out for all measures. Additionally, one factor congeneric models for each construct were tested for fit. The structural model was then developed and an assessment of fit was done. Once fit was established, hypothesis testing followed.

Validity of Scales

Information on construct reliability and validity for our scales is summarised in Appendix I.

Reliability

Reliability was assessed using coefficient alpha and construct reliability. Coefficient alpha was calculated using SPSS 15.0. Although there is little consensus on acceptable levels, values above 0.7 are deemed acceptable with those above 0.5 being desirable in early stages of research (Hair et al., 2006; Kline, 2005). Coefficient alpha for all constructs exceeded this value, thereby demonstrating acceptable reliabilities. Construct reliabilities were calculated using AMOS 6.0. Congeneric models for each separate construct were developed and these provide information on standardized item loadings and error measurement (ε_j) that was essential in the calculation of construct reliability (Byrne, 2001; Kline, 2005). Convention suggests that construct reliability scores should exceed 0.5 (Hair et al., 2006) with those above 0.5 being desirable in early stages of research (Fornell and Larcker, 1981). All constructs achieved acceptable construct reliability.

Convergent Validity

Convergent validity assesses the extent to which measures of the same construct correlate (Churchill, 1979). Using one factor congeneric models, item loadings were acceptable as they all exceed the threshold of 0.5 except one item in each construct (Steenkamp and van Trijp, 1991). However, these deviant loadings only pertained to the small samples for government and business network members. Therefore, it was deemed too premature to delete these items or be too exacting as these may load well with larger samples as indicated by the acceptable loadings for the larger university sample. However, it should be noted that the low loading for the government sample for the first item of the harmony construct may be an indication that further work is needed to develop this item. The item focuses on the involvement of university and industry participants from early stages of innovation. While the previous qualitative research revealed that early input from these two players is important for overall network outcomes, government respondents may not be in a position to comment on this relationship and therefore, the item may be in need of adjustment to incorporate a wider set of roles including those pertaining to government.

As an alternative test, convergent validity was calculated by examining the proportion of variance extracted. This is a measure of the amount of variance reflected in the construct relative to the variance lost to measurement error (Fornell and Larcker, 1981). It is recommended that variance extracted exceed 0.5 (Hair et al., 2006). If it is less than 0.5, this means that the construct captures less than 50% of the variance and more than 50% of it is due to measurement error (Fornell and Larcker, 1981). Evidence of convergent validity was provided for all constructs as variance extracted either equates or exceeds the lower limit of 0.5.

Discriminant Validity

In contrast to convergent validity, discriminant validity measures the distinctness and novelty of each individual measure (Churchill, 1979; Page and Meyer, 2000). We assessed discriminant validity using a widely used test from Fornell and Larcker (1981) which compares variance extracted of each construct with the square of the highest correlation that each factor shares with other factors (Ramani and Kumar, 2008; Rokkan et al., 2003; Straub et al., 2004). All factors exhibited discriminant validity as their variances extracted all over 0.500, exceed the square of the highest shared variance between factors which was 0.319.

Congeneric Models for Each Construct

In addition to assisting in the assessment of reliability and validity, we ran one factor congeneric models prior to analyzing the full structural model in order to evaluate model fit for each construct. Checking for model fit at the construct level prior to combining them structurally is important for diagnosing and reducing an amalgamation of problems at that later stage. The model fit for all constructs was acceptable as shown in Appendix I.

The Structural Model

Once our one factor congeneric models were assessed, a structural model was developed. Table 1 shows that the fit achieved for the causal model for each sector was acceptable.

Table 1. Fit indices used to evaluate fit of structural model

Type of Index	Name of Index	Acceptable Level	University Level	Government Level	Business Level
Model Fit	Chi-square		7.873	18.613	16.521
	degrees of freedom (df)		19	19	2
	P Value	> 0.05	0.988	0.482	0.583
Absolute Fit	Normed Chi-square (Chi-square/df)	< 2	.414	.979	.870
	Goodness-of-Fit (GFI)	> 0.90/0.95	0.983	0.927	0.941
	Adjusted Goodness of Fit (AGFI)	GFI -AGFI < 0.6	0.967	0.862	0.889
	Root Mean-Square Error or Approximation (RMSEA)	< .05	0.000	0.000	0.000
Incremental Fit	Comparative Fit Index (CFI)	> 0.95	1.000	1.000	1.000
	Tucker-Lewis Index (TLI)	> 0.95	1.026	1.003	1.019

Hypotheses Support

Given that the model exhibits good fit, tests of hypotheses emerging from the literature review were deemed suitable. As demonstrated in Table 2, all hypotheses were supported.

Table 2. Hypotheses tests

Hypothesis	Perspective	Independent Variable	Dependent Variable	P Value	Support
1	university	trust	harmony	.000***	YES
2	government	trust	harmony	.019***	YES
3	business	trust	harmony	.077*	YES

Note: *** Represents a 99% confidence level where as * represents a 90% confidence level.

CONCLUSION

Given the increasing prominence of networks, this study provides empirical evidence for the substantial impact of trust on network harmony from the perspective of universities, businesses and government agencies. Unlike previous studies, the level of analysis has shifted from predominantly organizational focus towards a genuine network focus which encompasses the variety of perspectives of the network actors. Consequently, a number of important constructs were validated in a network context.

Based on the evidence provided, the study offers useful managerial implications to a broad spectrum of organizations involved in innovation networks including universities, businesses and government agencies. These players should not underestimate the importance of fostering trust in achieving harmony when participating in networks. Government agencies may incorporate these findings in RandD grant policies and in designing technology transfer and innovation initiatives across sectors. Similarly, university technology transfer units responsible for university clusters and incubator centres may find these results of interest. Businesses operating in innovation networks could also use our findings in extending their understanding of key managerial factors in effective collaboration.

Of course, it should be noted that these results are preliminary and, therefore, should be interpreted in light of a number of limitations. For instance, the business and government samples are quite small and thus larger samples may be required to strengthen results. Additionally, given the reach of these networks across international borders, studies involving several countries should also be considered. Nevertheless, this study is a first step towards validation of key constructs from the perspectives of varied network actors.

APPENDIX I: MEASURES

Trust	Standardized Loadings		
	U	G	B
This partner was frank in dealing with us.	.92	.94	.82
This partner could be counted on to do what is right.	.96	.93	.87
The partner was genuinely concerned that our efforts succeeded.	.78	.58	.82
This partner kept promises it made to our organization.	.80	.51	.27
We felt that this partner was on our side.	.88	.57	.72

Chi-square = 2.424(U) 10.325(G) 4.18(B), d.f. = 5(U) 5(G) 5(B), P value = .788 (U) .067 (G) .524(B)
GFI = .991(U), .932(G), .974(B), CFI = 1.000(U), .964(G), 1.000(B)
Coefficient alpha = .936(U) .817(G) .793(B), Construct reliability = .832(U) .824(G) .820(B)
Variance extracted = .500(U) .500(G) .500(B)

Harmony	U	G	B
The research institution and the industry partner were involved in the early phases of discussion in setting the research agenda.	.50	.25	.51
Conflicts between participants were resolved locally among the disagreeing participants rather than via escalation throughout the wider network.	.69	.60	.59
There was compromise among participants in decision-making and each party obtained value from the network.	1.04	.78	.99

Chi-square = 7.873(U) 18.613(G) 16.5(B), d.f. = 19(U) 19(G) 19(B), P value = .988(U) .482(G) .639(B)
GFI = .983(U), .927(G), .941(B), CFI = 1.000(U), 1.000(G), 1.000(B).
Coefficient alpha = .706(U) .720(G) .546(B), Construct reliability = .733(U) .725(G) .510(B).
Variance extracted = .500(U) .506(G) .510(B).

Abbreviations:
U = University;
G = Government;
B = Business

REFERENCES

Achrol, R. S. and Kotler, P. (1999) 'Marketing in the Network Economy'. *Journal of Marketing,* Vol.63 No.4, pp.146-163.

Anderson, J. C. and Narus, J. A. (1990) 'A Model of Distributor Firm and Manufacturer Firm Working Partnerships'. *Journal of Marketing* Vol.54 pp.42-58.

Aulakh, P. S., Kotabe, M. and Sahay, A. (1996) 'Trust and Performance in Cross-Border Marketing Partnerships: A Behavioral Approach'. *International Business Studies,* Vol.27 No.5, pp.1005-1032.

Aurifeille, J. M. and Medlin, C. J. (2007) 'Segmentation for Dyadic Analyses of International Business Relationships'. In Aurifeille, J.-M., Svizzero, S. and Tisdell, C. (Eds.) *Globalization and Partnerships: New Features of Business Alliances and International Co-operation.* London, Nova Science Publishers, Inc.

Barringer, B. R. and Harrison, J. S. (2000) 'Walking a Tightrope: Creating Value through Interorganizational Relationships'. *Journal of Management,* Vol.26 No.3, pp.367-403.

Brito, C. M. (1999) 'Issue-Based Nets: a Methodological Approach to the Sampling Issue in Industrial Networks Research'. *Qualitative Market Research: An International Journal,* Vol.2 No.2, pp.92-102.

Byrne, B. (2001) *Structural Equation Modeling With AMOS: Basic Concepts, Applications, and Programming,* New Jersey, Lawrence Erlbraum Associates, Inc., Publishers.

Chow, S. and Holden, R. (1997) 'Toward an Understanding of Loyalty: The Moderator Role of Trust'. *Journal of Managerial Issues,* Vol.93 No.3, pp.275-298.

Churchill, G. A. (1979) 'A Paradigm for Developing Better Measures of Marketing Constructs'. *Journal of Marketing Research,* Vol.16 No.1, pp.64-73.

Clark, A. (1997) *Being There: Putting Brain, Body and the World Together,* Boston, MA, MIT Press.

Coote, L., Forrest, E. J. and Tam, T. W. (2003) 'An Investigation into Commitment in Non-Western Industrial Marketing Relationships'. *Industrial Marketing Management,* Vol.32 No.7, pp.595-604.

Cravens, D. W., Shipp, S. H. and Cravens, K. S. (1994) 'Reforming the Traditional Organization: The Mandate for Developing Networks'. *Business Horizons,* Vol.37 No.4, pp.19-28.

Das, T. K. and Teng, B. S. (1998) 'Between Trust and Control: Developing Confidence in Partner Cooperation in Alliances'. *Academy of Management Review* Vol.23 No.3, pp.491-512.

Doncy, P. M. and Cannon, J. P. (1997) 'An Examination of the Nature of Trust in Buyer-Seller Relationships'. *Journal of Marketing,* Vol.61 No.2, pp.35-51.

Ford, D. and Johnsen, T. (2000) 'Managing Collaborative Innovation in Complex Networks: Findings from Exploratory Interviews'. *Proceedings from the 16th IMP Conference.* Bath, UK.

Fornell, C. and Larcker, D. F. (1981) 'Evaluating Structural Equation Models with Unobservable Variables and Measurement Error'. *Journal of Marketing Research,* Vol.18 No.1, pp.39-50.

Furman, J. L., Porter, M. E. and Stern, S. (2002) 'The Determinants of National Innovative Capacity'. *Research Policy,* Vol.31 No.6, pp.899-933.

Ganesan, S. (1994) 'Determinants of Long-Term Orientation in Buyer-Seller Relationships'. *Journal of Marketing,* Vol.58 No.2, pp.1-19.

Gans, J. and Hayes, R. (2004) http://www.ausicom.com/01_cms/details.asp?ID=303, Last Accessed May 8, 2006.

Gupta, A. K., Raj, S. P. and Wilemon, D. (1986) 'A Model for Studying RandD-Marketing Interface in the Product Innovation Process'. *Journal of Marketing,* Vol.50 No.2, pp.7-17.

Hair, J. F., Anderson, R. E., Tatham, R. L. and Black, W. C. (2006) *Multivariate Data Analysis,* New Jersey, Prentice Hall.

Hakansson, H. (1987) *Industrial Technological Development: A Network Approach,* London, Routledge.

Healy, M. and Jonhson, G. (2007) 'Trust or Predictablity in International Small Business Relationships?' In Aurifeille, J.-M., Svizzero, S. and Tisdell, C. (Eds.) *Globalization and Partnerships: New Features of Business Alliances and International Co-operation.* London, Nova Science Publishers, Inc.

Hedaa, L. (1999) 'Black Holes in Networks'. *Advances in International Marketing,* Vol.9 pp.131 - 148.

Iacobucci, D. (1996) *Networks in Marketing,* California, London, New Delhi, Sage Publications.

Izquierdo, C. C. and Cillan, J. G. (2004) 'The Interaction of Dependence and Trust in Long-term Industrial Relationships'. *European Journal of Marketing,* Vol.38 No.8, pp.974-994.

Kline, R. B. (2005) *Principles and Practice of Structural Equation Modeling,* New York, London, The Guilford Press.

Kozan, K. M., Wasti, N. S. and Kuman, A. (2006) 'Management of Buyer-Supplier Conflict: The Case of the Turkish Automotive Industry'. *Journal of Business Research,* Vol.59 pp.662-670.

Kumar, R. (1996) *Research Methodology: A Step-by-step Guide for Beginners,* Addison Wesley Longman.

Laine, A. (2002) 'Sources of Conflict in Cooperation between Competitors'. *Proceedings from the 18th IMP conference.* Dijon, France.

Luo, Y. and Park, S. H. (2004) 'Multiparty Cooperation and Performance in International Equity Joint Ventures'. *Journal of International Business Studies* Vol.35 No.4, pp.334-335.

Marsden, P. V. (1990) 'Network Data and Measurement'. *Annual Review of Sociology,* Vol.16 No.1, pp.435-463.

Medlin, C. J. and Quester, P. (2002) 'Inter-firm Trust: Two Theoretical Dimensions Versus a Global Measure'. *Proceedings from the 18th IMP Conference.* Perth, Australia.

Moller, K. K. and Rajala, A. (2007) 'Rise of Strategic Nets - New Modes of Value Creation'. *Industrial Marketing Management,* Vol.36 No.7, pp.895-908.

Mollering, G. (2002) 'Perceived Trustworthiness and Inter-firm Governance: Empirical Evidence from the UK Printing Industry'. *Cambridge Journal of Economics,* Vol.26 No.2, pp.139-160.

Morgan, R. M. and Hunt, S. D. (1994) 'The Commitment-Trust Theory of Relationship Marketing'. *Journal of Marketing,* Vol.58 No.3, pp.20-38.

Nooteboom, B., Berger, H. and Noorderhaven, N. G. (1997) 'Effects of Trust and Governance on Relational Risk'. *Academy of Management Journal,* Vol.40 No.2, pp.308-338.

Norman, P. M. (2002) 'Protecting Knowledge in Strategic Alliances: Resource and Relational Characteristics'. *Journal of High Technology Management Research,* Vol.13 No.2, pp.177-202.

Ojasalo, J. (2004) 'Management of Innovation Networks - Two Different Approaches'. *Proceedings from the 20th IMP Conference.* Copenhagen, Denmark.

Page, C. and Meyer, D. (2000) *Applied Research Design for Business and Management,* Sydney, McGraw-Hill Companies, Inc.

Plank, R. E., Reid, D. A. and Pullins, E. B. (1999) 'Perceived Trust in Business-to-Business Sales: A New Measure'. *Journal of Personal Selling and Sales Management,* Vol.19 No.3, pp.61-71.

Plewa, C. (2005) 'Key Drivers of University-industry Relationships and the Impact of Organizational Culture Difference; A Dyadic Study'. *School of Commerce.* Adelaide, University of Adelaide.

Plewa, C. and Quester, P. (2006) 'Satisfaction with University-Industry Relationships: The Impact of Commitment, Trust and Championship''. *Journal of Technology Transfer and Commercialisation,* Vol.5 No.1/2, pp.79-101.

Powell, W. W. (1990) 'Neither Market nor Hierarchy: Network Forms of Organization'. *Research in Organizational Behavior,* Vol.12 pp.295-336.

Provan, K. G. and Milward, H. B. (1995) 'A Preliminary Theory of Interorganizational Network Effectiveness: A Comparative Study of Four Community Mental Health Systems'. *Administrative Science Quarterly,* Vol.40 No.1, pp.1-33.

Ramani, G. and Kumar, V. (2008) 'Interaction Orientation and Firm Performance'. *Journal of Marketing,* Vol.72 No.1, pp.27-45.

Rawwas, M., Vitell, S. and Barnes, J. H. (1997) 'Management of Conflict Using Individual Power Sources: A Retailers' Perspective'. *Journal of Business Research* Vol.40 No.1, pp.49-64.

Robicheaux, R. and El-Ansary, A. (1976) 'A General Model for Understanding Channel Member Behaviour'. *Journal of Retailing*, Vol.52 pp.13-30.

Rojot, J. (2007) 'Globalization: The End of Industrial Relations?' In Aurifeille, J.-M., Svizzero, S. and Tisdell, C. (Eds.) *Globalization and Partnerships: New Features of Business Alliances and International Co-operation.* London, Nova Science Publishers, Inc.

Rokkan, A. I., Heide, J. B. and Wathne, K. (2003) 'Specific Investments in Marketing Relationships'. *Journal of Marketing Research,* Vol.40 No.2, pp.210-224.

Rosenberg, L. J. and Stern, L. W. (1971) 'Conflict Measurement in the Distribution Channel'. *Journal of Marketing Research* Vol.8 pp.437-442.

Rowley, T., Behrens, D. and Krackhardt, D. (2000) 'Redundant Governance Structures: an Analysis of Structural and Relational Embeddedness in the Steel and Semiconductor Industries'. *Strategic Management Journal,* Vol.21 No.3, pp.369-387.

Ruttan, V. W. (2001) *Technology, Growth and Development: An Induced Innovation Perspective,* New York, Oxford, Oxford University Press.

Sarantakos, S. (1998) *Social Research,* Australia, Macmillan Education.

Seppanen, R., Blomqvist, K. and Sundqvist, S. (2007) 'Measuring Inter-Organizational Trust - A Critical Review of the Empirical Research in 1990-2003'. *Industrial Marketing Management,* Vol.36 No.2, pp.249-265.

Sezen, B. and Yilmaz, C. (2007) 'Relative Effects of Dependence and Trust on Flexibility, Information Exchange, and Solidarity in Marketing Channels'. *Journal of Business and Industrial Marketing,* Vol.22 No.1, pp.41 - 51.

Skarmeas, D. (2006) 'The Role of Functional Conflict in International Buyer–Seller Relationships: Implications for Industrial Exporters'. *Industrial Marketing Management* Vol.35 No.5, pp.567.

Smith, J. B. and Barclay, D. W. (1997) 'The Effects of Organizational Differences and Trust on the Effectiveness of Selling Partner Relationships'. *Journal of Marketing,* Vol.61 No.1, pp.3-21.

Song, M. and Thieme, R. J. (2006) 'A Cross-National Investigation of the RandD-Marketing Interface in the Product Innovation Process'. *Industrial Marketing Management,* Vol.35 No.3, pp.308-322.

Steenkamp, J. B. E. M. and van Trijp, H. C. M. (1991) 'The Use of LISREL in Validating Marketing Constructs'. *International Journal of Research in Marketing,* Vol.8 No.4, pp.283-299.

Straub, D., Rai, A. and Klein, R. (2004) 'Measuring Firm Performance at the Network Level: A Nomology of the Business Impact of Digital Supply Networks'. *Journal of Management Information Systems,* Vol.21 No.1, pp.83-114.

Tushman, M. L. (2004) 'From Engineering Management/RandD Management, to the Management of Innovation, to Exploiting and Exploring Over Value Nets: 50 Years of Research Initiated by the IEEE-TEM'. *IEEE Transactions on Engineering Management,* Vol.51 No.4, pp.409-411.

Uzzi, B. (1996) 'The Sources and Consequences of Embeddedness for the Economic Performance of Organizations: The Network Effect'. *American Sociological Review,* Vol.61 No.4, pp.674-698.

Vaaland, T. I. (2001) 'Conflict in Business Relations. The Core of Conflict in Oil Industrial Development Projects.' *Proceedings from the 17th IMP Conference.* Oslo, Norway.

Wilkinson, I., Ritter, T. and Johnston, W. (2004) 'Ability to Manage in Business Networks: A Review of Concepts'. *Industrial Marketing Management,* Vol.33 No.3, pp.175-183.

Williamson, O. E. (1975) *Markets and Hierarchies,* New York, The Free Press.

Zaheer, A., McEvily, B. and Perrone, V. (1998) 'Does Trust Matter? Exploring the Effects of Interorganizational and Interpersonal Trust on Performance'. *Organization Science,* Vol.9 No.2, pp.141-159.

In: Trust, Globalisation and Market Expansion
Editors: J-M. Aurifeille, C. Medlin and C. Tisdell

ISBN 978-1-60741-812-2
© 2009 Nova Science Publishers, Inc.

Chapter 7

INTERFIRM NETWORKS IN THE INDONESIAN GARMENT INDUSTRY: THEIR DEVELOPMENT, DURATION, DETERMINANTS AND BENEFITS

Latif Adam[*] *and Clem Tisdell*[**]

[*]Centre for Economic Research (P2E),
The Indonesian Institute of Sciences (LIPI), Jakarta, Indonesia
[**]School of Economics, The University of Queensland,
Brisbane, 4072, QLD, Australia

ABSTRACT

After a brief overview of the relevant literature on the theory of business networks, this paper discusses the development of interfirm networks in the Indonesian garment industry, their determinants, duration, and benefits. The discussion indicates that business cooperation is a significant feature of the Indonesian garment industry. Of the 210 enterprises surveyed, 132 enterprises have at one stage developed business cooperation and 88 of them have succeeded in maintaining their cooperation continuously.

Trust and competence play an important role in cementing long-term business cooperation. Moreover, repeated business contact in the market and family connection are found to be the key factors leading to the long-term cooperation. This suggests that repeated business contact and family connection are more accurate than other factors in assessing the trustworthiness and competency of potential partners. Also, this implies that these two factors are more favourable than other factors in facilitating the creation of trust. While several benefits from business cooperation are revealed, the most obvious expected benefit is to expand the market of cooperating businesses and reduce their marketing uncertainty and transaction costs. Evidence is provided that cooperative business networks have played an important role in expanding Indonesia's exports of garments.

[*] Email: latif_adam@yahoo.com.au

1. INTRODUCTION

The focus of this chapter is on the *empirical* analysis of interfirm cooperative networks or alliances in the garment industry in the Bandung region of Indonesia, particularly networks that involve small- or medium- sized firms. While many of the networks studies are confined to regional cooperation, some extend beyond the Bandung region and have an international dimension. For example, it was observed that some of the regional networks were linked to garment distributors in Nigeria. One of the most important benefits reported by participants from networking in the garment industry in the Bandung area was its ability to facilitate the widening of markets available to network participants. While there has been much theoretical work on the role of business networks in facilitating economic competition, much less work of an empirical nature has been completed.

Nohria and Eccles (1992) provided an overview of the theory of the role of networks in business organization as it has developed by the early 1990s. Nohria (1992) claimed that interest in the subject had burgeoned because of evidence that business networking increases the competitiveness of businesses that engage in networking within their own business and with other firms. Networking implies a more fluid form of organization than that typical of the traditional hierarchal insular business firm. In its widest usage, business networking is typified by "lateral and longitudinal linkages within and among firms". (Nohria, 1992, p.2). In this chapter, however, it is only interfirm connections that receive attention.

Linkages between firms can be very heterogeneous and the theory on how to best classify such linkages is still evolving. Perrow (1992) provides some useful insights into the classification of economic organizations (see especially Perrow, 1992, pp. 446-447). Some of the organizational forms that he identifies overlap with those found to be present in this study of the garment industry in Indonesia, for example sub-contracting and small firm networking.

Achrol (1997) claims that business networking is going to become the dominant industrial organizational form in the 21st century and explains why this evolution is taking place. He includes a useful discussion of the role of trust in the formation and sustainability of such networks (Achrol, 1997, pp.65-66) as well as the role of social norms. He concludes: "...it seems inevitable that any company that is going to be a significant player in dynamic global markets is going to be actively networked in one form or another" (Achrol, 1997, p.69). We present evidence from Indonesia that interfirm networking has been a positive factor in the export of Indonesian manufactured products.

It is not possible in this short chapter to consider all aspects of interfirm cooperation. Some additional insights into this cooperation can, for example, be found in Skinner et al. (1992), Khanna et al. (1998) and Payan (2007). The article by Skinner et al. (1992) is particularly interesting because it deals with the relative power of suppliers and dealers (retailers) particularly in the American context and ways to improve cooperation between businesses involved in such relationships. Welch et al. (1996) and Welch and Wilkinson (2004) consider aspects of the role of governments in the development of business networks. The Indonesian government has been active in encouraging such development but our study found that business networks promoted by the Indonesian government were not very sustainable and that this approach in Indonesia has had little economic value.

As stated above, very few in depth quantitative empirical studies have been done on interfirm networks and cooperation involving small- or medium-sized firms as at least one of the partners in a network. This paper reports on and analyses the results from a survey of 210 small or medium-sized garment enterprises in Bandung, Indonesia. This survey involved direct interviews conducted in 2004 by Latif Adam as part of his research for his PhD thesis (Adam, 2007) and this article is based to a considerable extent on a part of his thesis, principally Chapter 8. The procedure adopted to obtain a representative sample of small and medium-sized manufacturers in the Bandung area is outlined in detail in Adam (2007). A list of relevant questions (English translation) asked managers of small and medium-sized garment enterprises in the Bandung area, (the results of which are reported here) is given in the Appendix to this chapter.

The survey was designed to ascertain whether the firms surveyed engaged in cooperative interfirm agreements, the type of cooperative arrangements made, factors (such as trust) influencing business cooperation, reasons for discontinuing interfirm cooperation, factors favouring the success of business cooperation, and the benefits expected by firms from interfirm business cooperation. Each of these matters is considered in this article and then the implications for Indonesia's export of garments of cooperation between garment enterprises are considered as well interfirm networking generally as a means for Indonesian small and medium sized firms to access global markets.

Two previous studies of Indonesia's garment industry came to different conclusions about the importance of business cooperation for the economic performance of Indonesia's garment industry. van Diermen (1997), after studying garment firms in the Jakarta area, concluded that business cooperation played an insignificant role in their economic performance. In contrast, Cole (1998) found that business cooperation had made a significant contribution to the development of Bali's garment industry. Adam (2007) also found that interfirm cooperation contributed significantly to the economic performance of Bandung's garment industry. Whether or not Jakarta is an 'odd case' is unclear. Latif Adam also wanted to conduct a similar survey in Jakarta to that in Bandung but because of the unsettled political situation at the time and lack of cooperation from managers of garment firms in Jakarta, was unable to proceed with that. Nevertheless, the Bandung survey provides useful insights into factors influencing business cooperation generally.

2. TYPES OF BUSINESS COOPERATION ENGAGED IN BY THE SMALL AND MEDIUM-SIZED ENTERPRISES SURVEYED

More than half the garment enterprises surveyed (62.9%) said that they had been involved in business cooperation. Cooperation sometimes included firms outside the Bandung area but located in other cities or regions of Indonesia.

Activities involving business cooperation of the enterprises surveyed are summarised in Table 1. This reveals that Small and Medium Enterprises (SMEs) were most commonly involved in putting out of garment manufacture (51.5%) followed by subcontracting (30.3%) and clustering accounted for the remainder.

The process of putting out involves one firm (a secondary firm) arranging with another (a primary firm) to produce garments for it which it then resells. The primary firm may also produce garments but in some cases it may merely act as a 'middleman'. Subcontracting is the process by which some components for the manufacturers of a garment are made (on contract) for secondary firms by a primary firm. Whether or not clustering should be classified as a form of business cooperation is unclear but it facilitates interfirm cooperation and has been included as a feature of interfirm cooperation in previous studies. By clustering together, small garment makers find it easier to make any useful trades with each other. Such interfirm trading may not be continuous but may vary according to needs of the individual garment maker and cooperative arrangements are usually informal. The main advantage of clustering from the point of view small and medium-sized garment makers is that it reduces their market transaction costs.

**Table 1. Types of Business Cooperation that the SMEs Surveyed
Have Been Involved in, (%), Bandung, 2004**

Types of Business Cooperation	Discontinued	Continued	Total
Putting out	20.5	29.6	26.5
Putting out and clustering	27.3	23.9	25.0
Subcontracting	18.2	18.2	18.2
Clustering	20.5	17.1	18.2
Subcontracting and clustering	13.6	11.4	12.1
TOTAL	100 (N=44)	100 (N=88)	100 (N=132)

Source: Adam 2007.

3. FACTORS ASSOCIATED WITH THE DEVELOPMENT OF BUSINESS COOPERATION IN THE BANDUNG GARMENT INDUSTRY

The Bandung survey revealed that the two most important factors in fostering initial business cooperation between garment manufacturers were principally repeated business contact in the market and family connections. The results are summarised in Table 2.

Table 2. Factors Fostering Initial Business Cooperation, %, Bandung, 2004

Factors	Discontinue	Continue	Total
Repeated business contact in the market	9.1	54.6	39.4
Family connection	25.0	12.5	16.7
Family connection and repeated business contact in the market	4.6	22.7	16.7
Family connection and industry and trade associations	11.4	2.3	5.3
Family connection and government program	11.4	1.1	4.5
Industry and trade association	13.6	3.4	6.8
Government program	15.9	2.3	6.8
Ethnic group connection	9.1	1.1	3.8
Religious connection	0.0	0.0	0.0
TOTAL	100 (N=44)	100 (N=88)	100 (N=132)

Source: Adam 2007.

Both repeated business contacts and family connections provide knowledge to entrepreneurs about potential factors. It assists them in judging the trustworthiness of potential business partners as well as how well they are likely to perform. Not much weight was placed by the respondents on ethnic group connection as a factor making for initial business cooperation. Religious connection was given no weight at all. However, the reason why this could be so is that Bandung's entrepreneurs in the garment industry are relatively homogenous – they are all Sudanese and followers of Islam.

Contacts through industry and trade associations and through Indonesia government schemes to sponsor business cooperation were influences in fostering business cooperation in some instances but paled in importance compared to repeated business contacts and family connection as factors leading to interfirm cooperation.

The low importance of the Indonesian Government's scheme to sponsoring business cooperation and the lack of durability of cooperation (evident from Table 2) needs to be explained. Since 1984, the Government has operated the *Bapak Angkat* (Foster Parent) program to promote the development of vertical business cooperation between small and medium industrial enterprises (SMIEs) and their larger counterparts. To strengthen the implementation of the *Bapak Angkat* program, the Indonesian Government introduced several regulations. For instance, in 1989 the Ministry of Finance through a Decree No. 1232/KMK.013/1989 ordered all state-owned enterprises (BUMN) to provide financial assistance between of 1 and 5% of their profit to SMIEs as part of the *Bapak Angkat* program. In addition, on 14 February 1991, President Soeharto endorsed the *Bapak Angkat* program as a national movement (*gerakan nasional*). To support this national movement, the President asked not only state-owned but also private enterprises to participate in the *Bapak Angkat* program. According to van Diermen (1997), the President's personal support for the *Bapak Angkat* program pressured and forced many large private enterprises to enter the program.

However, this study indicates that there are several weaknesses not only in the implementation process, but also in the concept that resulted in it not facilitating the development of long-term business cooperation. For example, some SMIEs mentioned that vague criteria and requirements about the types of SMIEs that can participate in the program may result in the benefits offered by the program being unavailable to some potential SMIEs. Furthermore, they also pointed out that the *Bapak Angkat* program has largely been enjoyed by SMIEs that have close relationships with government officers (compare Welch and Wilkinson, 2004).

In addition, in discussion with Latif Adam, top managers from two (anonymous) large state-owned enterprises that have involved in the program for years emphasized that engaging in the *Bapak Angkat* program does not bring great economic benefits for their enterprises. The difference in core business between these two stated-owned enterprises and their SMIEs partners is one factor reducing their economic incentives from their engagement in the *Bapak Angkat* program. These two stated-owned enterprises are involved in the program as a result of a sense of obligation to government rather than economic benefit. Accordingly, they are only half-hearted in developing cooperation with SMIEs. Indeed, as some SMIEs interviewed confirmed, after receiving financial assistance, there was no follow-up contact carried out by large enterprises to maintain contact and cooperation. This implies that these large enterprises do not have any intention of establishing continuous business cooperation with SMIEs.

The frequency with which most large enterprises involved in the *Bapak Angkat* program preferred to provide financial assistance to SMIEs rather than other types of assistance is an indication that they entered the program only to comply with the government's order. The difference in terms of core business and technological acquisitions between large enterprises and their SMIEs partners make the provision of financial assistance to SMIEs the easiest way for large enterprises to show to the government that they have participated in the program. For large enterprises, recognition from the government that they participate in the *Bapak Angkat* program is important because it may bring indirect benefits for them. This government recognition of involvement may in turn open the opportunities for large enterprises to enjoy several privileges, such as easy access to state-owned banks.

Based on the explanation so far, it becomes apparent that the emphasis of the *Bapak Angkat* program on social-political considerations results in its failure to promote continuous vertical cooperation between SMIEs and their larger counterparts. The involvement of large enterprises in the program is not motivated by their direct economic gain. Rather, they entered the program due to government pressure. Thus, except for SMIEs receiving financial assistance, there may be no economic gain for either party to be involved in the program (Sato, 2001).

Interestingly, Table 2 also shows that the initial route that the firms chose to establish business cooperation correlates with whether or not their business cooperation can be maintained continuously. On the one hand, most small and medium enterprises (SMEs) that developed business cooperation through repeated business contact and family connection were able to maintain and continue their cooperation. On the other hand, the majority of SMEs that used ethnic group connections, industry and trade associations, and government programs, to facilitate their initial business cooperation tended to discontinue their cooperation.

Theoretically, trustworthy and competent partners are considered to be fundamental determinants for cementing long-term business cooperation. It was found that most SMEs surveyed which succeeded in maintaining their long-term business cooperation pointed to trustworthy and competent partners as the keys to their success (Table 4). The presence of trustworthy and competent partners is an incentive for firms to keep engaging in business cooperation. This is because trustworthy and competent partners enable them to lower monitoring costs and reduce uncertainty due to less fear of opportunism. Accordingly, such partners ensure that the SMEs interviewed obtain optimum benefits from their involvement in business cooperation.

It seems from Table 2 that repeated business contact and family connections are the most reliable sources for assessing how trustworthy and competent potential partners are. Similarly, it becomes apparent that repeated business contacts and family connections are more favourable than the three other sources in developing trust. Thus, SMEs that use repeated business contact and family connection to facilitate initial development of their business cooperation are more likely to succeed in maintaining long-term business cooperation than those that do not.

Cooperation developed through repeated business contact, as Haugland and Gronhaug (1996), Cole (1998), and Huemer (2004) emphasized, is mainly motivated by a long-term profit motivation. In contrast, cooperation formed through ethnic group connections, industry and trade associations, and government program is, according to van Diermen (1997) and Sato (2001), frequently driven by a socio-political motives. Because cooperation developed through the former is more likely to survive over a long period of time than that established through the latter, this suggests that economic gains provide a more secure basis than socio-political factors in building trust- and competent-based long-term cooperation. Indeed, as Tisdell (1996) pointed out, long-term business cooperation may survive over a longer period of time if it is motivated by economic considerations.

However, this study also found that economic consideration is not the only factor that supports the survival of business cooperation. The fact that cooperation formed through family connection can also be often maintained continuously suggests that family imperatives can also play an important role in the development of long-term business cooperation. This may be because family members are usually close to one another (Ouchi, 1980). This close relationship means family connections can function not only as a foundation to build trust, but also as a reliable source for assessing the competency of prospective family partners.

As part of this study, a binomial logit model based on the personal attributes of entrepreneurs was also considered. The three factors considered were length of business experience of the entrepreneur, level of educational achievement and type of work experience. The results are summarized in Table 3.

Table 3. Results of Binomial Logit Model for the Development of Business Cooperation, by Personal Attributes of Entrepreneurs

Variable	The Development of Cooperation (Y_1)	
	Coefficient	Marginal Effect
Constant	-1.039*	-0.237*
	(-1.869)	(-1.830)
Length of business experience	0.013	0.003
	(0.200)	(0.200)
Educational level		
Lower High School	0.546	0.119
	(1.304)	(1.378)
Upper High School	1.316***	0.278***
	(3.033)	(3.369)
University	1.592**	0.287***
	(1.995)	(2.756)
Working experience		
Worked at other similar SMIEs	0.905**	0.190***
	(2.217)	(2.449)
Worked at large enterprises	1.277***	0.248***
	(2.622)	(3.239)
Child of the owner	0.685	0.148
	(1.531)	(1.637)
Log-Likelihood		-122.494
Pseudo R²		0.116
χ^2		32.091
N		210

Note: 1. t-ratio is given in parentheses.
2. * Statistically significance at the 0.10 level;
** at the 0.05 level; *** at the 0.01 level.

It was found that among the independent variables, the estimated coefficient and marginal effect of educational level are the largest, suggesting that this is the dominant variable in influencing the decision of SMEs to develop business cooperation. The higher the educational level of entrepreneurs, the more likely they are to develop business cooperation. This may be because educational level correlates positively with the ability to have contact and communicate with others. It means that the higher the educational levels of entrepreneurs, the more probable they are to have contact and communicate with others. As Weaver's study (1998) found, the more entrepreneurs communicate with each other, the more capable they are of developing business cooperation (strategic alliances).

Surprisingly, the estimated coefficient and marginal effect of length of business experience are not only statistically insignificant, but also are the lowest. This suggests that length of business experience has little bearing on the decision of SMEs to develop and maintain business cooperation.

4. REASONS FOR DISCONTINUING BUSINESS COOPERATION

Of these businesses interviewed, 52 had discontinued cooperating with other firms after commencing it. In the case of those involved in *putting out,* the most common reason given for discontinuing cooperation was that the down payment by buyers was too small and partners were always late with their payment. Also profit margins became too small as partners asked for a lower price than the general market price, and partners were unwilling to make a price adjustment when there was a considerable increase in the price of new materials. The most frequent reason given for discontinuing subcontracting was that partners frequently rejected the products supplied even though these accorded with the design and quality stated in the agreement. Also many respondents complained that they were 'squeezed' by partners so that their profit margins became too small compared to that which they could obtain without the agreement. Fewer, but still some, complained that partners were unwilling to make price adjustments when the price of new materials rose substantially. Similar complaints were also recorded by firms involved in *cooperation in business clusters* but some also said that because the demand for their products declined they were able to meet this demand from their own production and therefore, discontinued cooperation.

5. FACTORS MAKING FOR THE LONG-TERM SUCCESS AND VIABILITY OF BUSINESS COOPERATION

Trustworthiness of partners and their competency were the factors most frequently mentioned by the entrepreneurs interviewed, who had continuing business contracts as important for the success of long-term business cooperation. Similarity in objections of partners was also considered to be important by several entrepreneurs interviewed. The distribution of responses by garment entrepreneurs who continued to be involved in business cooperation at the time of their interview is shown on Table 4.

From Table 4, it is apparent that in an attempt to develop successful business cooperation, a firm needs to find trustworthy partners.

Table 4. Factors for the Success of Long-Term Business Cooperation, %, Bandung, 2004

Factors	Municipality	District	Municipality and District
Partners have required competency and are trustworthy	41.7	40.0	40.9
Partners are trustworthy	20.8	20.0	20.5
Partners have required competency	16.7	12.5	14.8
Similar objectives	8.3	12.5	10.2
Similar objectives and partners are trustworthy	4.2	7.5	5.7
Autonomy of participants	4.2	5	4.6
Similar objectives and partners have competency	4.2	2.5	3.4
TOTAL	100 (N=48)	100 (N=40)	100 (N=88)

Source: Adam 2007.

Choosing untrustworthy partners, as Granovetter (1985; 1992), McAllister (1995), Gulati (1995), Gulati and Gargulio (1999), and Nooteboom (1999; 2003; 2004) mention, will result in attempted business cooperation bring detrimental rather than beneficial to the firm and will not improve its efficiency, competency, and competitive advantage. Similarly, cooperating and interacting with untrustworthy partners will make it likely that business cooperation will not survive over a long period of time. Accordingly, the firm should have sufficient information to decide whether or not its potential partners are trustworthy.

The managers of garment firms involved in business cooperation at the time of the survey were asked what important actions they took to maintain their long-term business cooperation. The distribution of their responses is shown in Table 5. Overall, taking action to show that they are trustworthy was most important. Being competent, however, was also important and in many cases, was interlinked with being trustworthy.

Table 5. Important Actions to Maintain Long-Term Business Cooperation, %, Bandung, 2004

Actions	%
1. Ensuring partners always trust the firm by producing the same products as previously stated in the agreement in terms of design, quality, and punctuality, and improving competency in order to adjust quickly to the change in design, quality, and punctuality ordered by partners	43.2
2. Ensuring partners always trust the firm by producing the same products as previously stated in the agreement in terms of design, quality, and punctuality	29.6
3. Improving competency in order to adjust quickly to the change in design, quality, and punctuality ordered by partners	18.2
4. Appreciating autonomy of partners by refraining from interfering in the internal issues of partners' enterprises	4.6
5. Opening and providing honest information about their enterprises	4.6
TOTAL	100 (N=88)

Source: Adam 2007.

Besides requiring trustworthy and competent partners, the SMEs surveyed agreed that long-term business cooperation can only be maintained successfully if they themselves are also trustworthy and are competent. Hence, as can be seen in Table 5, the majority of SMEs surveyed claimed that their efforts to create an image of being trustworthy and competent are important for maintaining their long-term business cooperation.

It is important to note that although the SMEs surveyed apparently distinguished the development of trust and competency as two different important actions to maintain long-term cooperation (Table 5), interviews with some SMEs indicated that these two important actions are actually inter-related. The SMEs interviewed argued that their (potential) partners usually assess whether or not they are trustworthy from their competency. The firms that are highly competent will ensure their partners that they have an ability to act and perform in predictable manners. In contrast, the firms that are lacking in competency may send bad signals to their partners, namely that they will not be able to meet their partners' expectation. Hence, in an attempt to portray that they are trustworthy, some SMEs interviewed mentioned that they consistently improved their competency. Likewise, other SMEs pointed out that their motivation to improve their competency is to present a good image to their partners that they are sufficiently reliable and competent to be trusted.

A binomial logit model was used to identify factors that are likely to be associated with continuing business cooperation. It was found that business associations formed as a result of any of the following three factors were statistically significant at the one per cent level:

(1) Repeated business contacts;
(2) family connections; and
(3) family connections and repeated business contacts.

These business alliances tended to last whereas those formed through connections with industry and trade associations or sponsored by government did not display statistically significant sustainability. In relation to competency, only improvements in quality of products was statistically significant for the sustainability of cooperation. This was at the 5 per cent level. The economic results are summarized in Table 6.

As specified in Table 6, when business cooperation is established as a result of repeated business contact, its marginal effect on continuing business cooperation is the highest, and the relationship is statistically significant. Thus, repeated business contact is the most significant variable in determining the survival of business cooperation. In other words, it tells that cooperation developed through repeated business contact has the highest probability of surviving over a long period of time.

Besides repeated business contact, family connections alone or jointly with repeated business contact are other variables that have significant impact on developing continuous business cooperation. The firms that developed their cooperation through either family connection or family connection combined with repeated business contact have a high probability of maintaining their long-term cooperation. As noted previously, this may be because family members are close to one another. This close family relationship may deter network members from behaving opportunistically towards one another. One who behaves opportunistically with family members will have a bad reputation because others may think if he/she can be disloyal to his/her family, he/she can be more easily disloyal to non-family members. In addition, such close family relationships enable the firm to have sufficient required information about the trustworthiness and competency of its family-partners. As discussed above, the better the firms know how trustworthy and competent their potential partners are, the higher is the probability that they will succeed in maintaining business cooperation.

Table 6. Results of Binomial Logit Model for Continuing Business Cooperation

Variables	Continuing Cooperation (Y_2)	
	Coefficient	Marginal Effect
Constant	-12.365***	-1.955***
	(-4.388)	(-3.995)
Initial Mechanism		
Repeated business contact	3.764***	0.495***
	(3.066)	(3.799)
Family connection	2.809**	0.258***
	(2.173)	(3.192)
Family connection & Repeated business contact	4.144***	0.321***
	(2.902)	(3.937)
Family connection & Industry and trade association	1.081	0.125
	(0.764)	(1.116)
Family connection & Government program	0.543	0.073
	(0.337)	(0.406)
Industry and trade associations	-0.824	-0.158
	(-0.604)	(-0.521)
Government program	-0.446	-0.079
	(-0.340)	(-0.308)
Competency		
Range of products	0.462	0.073
	(0.851)	(0.826)
Design of products	0.122	0.019
	(0.176)	(0.175)
Quality of products	1.312**	0.207**
	(2.090)	(2.066)
Finishing products	1.158	0.183
	(1.373)	(1.372)
Machinery sophistication	0.821	0.130
	(1.001)	(1.039)
Log-Likehold		-41.348
Pseudo R²		0.508
χ^2		85.344
N		132

Note: 1. t-ratio is given in parentheses.

2.* Statistically significance at the 0.10 level; ** at the 0.05 level; *** at the 0.01 level.

As for the competency variables, the quality of products is the only variable for which the estimated coefficient and its marginal effects are statistically significant. This finding is surprising because previously, based on theoretical argument and initial findings, it was expected that all of the estimated coefficients and marginal effects of the competency variables would have a significant impact on increasing the probability of business cooperation surviving continuously. Two explanations are possible for this result. First, it may arise from collection and measurement errors in data used in this study. Secondly, it may be because the econometric model used in this study omits relevant variables or includes irrelevant variables.

When asked to name important actions to maintain continuing cooperation, most SMEs surveyed mentioned punctuality to be one of the most important actions. Indeed, as Prabatmojo (1999) emphasized, the ability of enterprises to deliver ordered products to their partners on time will strengthen cooperation. This suggests that punctuality is significantly important to be included in the econometric testing. Unfortunately, the punctuality variable was omitted in the econometric model, as it could not be measured and collected adequately.

Apart from the type of business cooperation, the length of an enterprises' involvement in business cooperation influences the extent of the gain to firm from business cooperation and its probability of continuing. At the beginning of cooperation a firm is naturally not completely sure how trustworthy and competent its partners are. Hence, in the beginning the firm usually starts to cooperate with its partners on a small scale and with a low-level of mutual dependence, suggesting that during this period the cooperating firm may not obtain maximum benefits (Nooteboom, 1999: 2004). When the firms continue their involvement in business cooperation for a longer period of time, they may enjoy increased benefits. This is because as firms continue their involvement in business cooperation, there will be simultaneous growth in trust of and commitment to their partners (Shapiro, 1987). This increases the likelihood of the cooperation continuing.

6. MOTIVATIONS FOR DEVELOPING BUSINESS COOPERATION AS RATED BY GARMENT PRODUCERS INVOLVED IN BUSINESS COOPERATION AND THEIR BENEFITS

Table 7 provides a measure of the relative importance of the benefits those respondents involved in continuing business cooperation (88 garment producers) expected to obtain from business cooperation. In most cases, securing and expanding markets was the major benefit sought. This was so for situations involving putting out and subcontracting but not for clustering. Reducing transaction costs and uncertainty was important for all categories of cooperation as was obtaining capital. Improving technological capabilities was also rated as important for all categories of cooperation, except clustering. A similar situation is apparent for the possibility of exporting products. Increased access to new materials was only rated as important to cooperative situations involving clustering.

Ratings of the stated benefits which garment manufacturers said they obtained from business cooperation are given in Table 8. Except in the case of firms relying solely on clustering, (which seems to bring fewer benefits than other forms of business cooperation) the main technological benefits were said to be improved quality control and the provision of technological information; the main financial benefits were advance payments and capital participation; the principal marketing benefits were information about and guidance on the market and assistance in securing and expanding the market; and in some cases, the provision of raw materials was important. In a few categories, the provision of managerial training proved to be important, as is apparent from Table 8.

Table 7. Stated Motivations of SMEs surveyed (that were continuing interfirm cooperation) to Develop Inter-Firm Networks, (Average Score), Bandung, 2004

Motivations	PO	S	C	PO & C	S & C	Total
Securing and expanding markets	3.00	2.94	2.00	3.00	3.00	2.82
Reducing transaction costs and uncertainty	2.62	2.81	2.07	2.71	2.80	2.60
Obtaining capital	2.62	2.69	2.00	2.57	2.70	2.52
Improving technological capabilities	2.00	2.44	1.47	2.00	2.60	2.06
Obtaining raw materials	1.85	1.88	2.00	1.86	2.00	1.90
Exporting products	2.00	2.06	1.00	2.00	2.40	1.89
TOTAL ENTERPRISES	26	16	15	21	10	88

Source: Adam 2007. Note: 1. PO is putting out, S is subcontracting, and C is clustering. 2. Entrepreneurs were asked about the motivation in developing business cooperation. The entrepreneurs' are then scored. The scores are: 1 for not important, 2 for important, and 3 for very important. The average score is calculated from the total score in each motivation divided by total sample in each type of business cooperation.

Table 8. The Various Stated Benefits of Business Cooperation, Cooperating Firms (Average Score), Bandung, 2004

Benefits	PO	S	C	PO & C	S & C	Total
I. Technological Benefits						
Quality control	2.62	2.69	1.27	2.71	2.80	2.44
Technological information	2.08	2.56	2.13	2.29	2.80	2.31
Production technique	1.85	2.25	1.67	1.95	2.60	2.00
Providing machinery	1.38	2.00	1.73	1.62	2.20	1.70
Instruction in machinery use	1.19	2.19	1.00	1.10	2.70	1.49
Worker training	1.12	1.94	1.00	1.00	2.20	1.34
TOTAL ENTERPRISES	26	16	15	21	10	88
II. Financial Benefits						
Advance payment	2.73	2.69	1.13	2.81	2.80	2.48
Capital participation	2.38	2.44	1.07	2.48	2.50	2.20
Machinery leasing	1.38	2.00	1.73	1.62	2.20	1.70
Borrowing & lending capital	0.00	0.00	2.67	2.76	2.70	1.42
Investment loan	1.08	1.13	1.40	1.57	1.50	1.31
TOTAL ENTERPRISES	26	16	15	21	10	88
III. Marketing Benefits						
Informational/guidance on market	2.65	2.63	1.73	2.71	2.50	2.42
Securing & expanding market	2.65	2.69	1.07	2.67	2.60	2.35
Exchange of market information	0.00	0.00	2.53	2.76	2.70	1.40
TOTAL ENTERPRISES	26	16	15	21	10	88
IV. Other Benefits						
Providing raw materials	2.19	2.25	1.00	2.33	2.30	2.05
Managerial training	1.08	2.56	1.00	1.00	2.70	1.50
Sharing in the provision of raw materials	na	na	2.53	2.67	2.70	1.38
TOTAL ENTERPRISES	26	16	15	21	10	88

Source: Adam 2007. Note: 1. PO is putting out, S is subcontracting, and C is cluster. Entrepreneurs were asked about their perception of the importance of business cooperation in providing various benefits. The entrepreneurs' perceptions were then scored. The scores are: 1 for not important, 2 for important and 3 for very important. The average score is calculated from the total score in each motivation divided by total sample in each type of business cooperation; na is not applicable.

Table 9 probably provides a clearer picture of the relative importance of business cooperation in improving the performance attributes of the 88 cooperating firms. According to the perceptions of the 88 entrepreneurs of firms involved in business cooperation, improving marketing capabilities was the most important performance factor. Improved production capabilities and quality control were also of high importance. Performance factors are listed in Table 9 in declining levels of overall importance.

Table 9. Cooperating Entrepreneurs' Perception of the Importance of Business Cooperation in Improving the Performance of their Enterprises, (Average Score), Bandung, 2004

Motivations	PO	S	C	PO & C	S & C	Total
Marketing capabilities	4.54	4.56	3.47	4.62	4.70	4.40
Production capabilities	4.27	4.25	3.47	4.38	4.30	4.16
Quality control	4.35	4.44	3.00	4.38	4.50	4.16
Competitiveness	4.19	4.25	3.33	4.29	4.30	4.09
Financial capabilities	3.92	4.00	3.13	4.33	4.20	3.93
Productivity	3.73	4.13	2.87	3.86	4.40	3.76
Profitability	3.58	3.88	3.27	3.71	4.00	3.66
Efficiency	3.65	3.88	3.07	3.71	4.10	3.66
Technological capabilities	3.31	4.38	2.67	3.76	4.50	3.64
TOTAL ENTERPRISES	26	16	15	21	10	88

Source: Adam 2007

Note: 1. PO is putting out, S is subcontracting, and C is clustering.

Entrepreneurs were asked about the importance of business cooperation in improving the performance of their enterprises. The entrepreneurs' perceptions were then scored. The scores are: 1 for not important, 2 for little important, and 3 for moderate, 4 for important, and 5 for very important. The average score is calculated from the total score in each motivation divided by total sample in each type of business cooperation.

Inspection of Table 9 suggests that several of the motivations mentioned are likely to be positively correlated. For example, an improvement in production capabilities, quality control, competitiveness, efficiency and technological capabilities are likely to be reflected in greater marketing capability. Or to give another example, improved technological capabilities may result in better quality control.

7. THE ROLE OF BUSINESS COOPERATION IN EXPANDING INDONESIA'S INTERNATIONAL TRADE IN GARMENTS

From Table 7, it can be seen that in cases including either putting out of garment production or the subcontracting of parts of it, gaining access to export markets was an important motivation for small and medium Indonesian garment manufacturers to cooperate, even though overall this factor did not have the highest rating. This is, understandable because many of cooperating garment suppliers in Bandung would be satisfied with having a larger market in Indonesia as a result of their cooperation.

In Adam's (2007) study no data was collected directly on the mechanisms used by small and medium-sized manufacturers of garments to gain access to overseas markets. However, Cole (1998) found from his study of Bali's garment export industry that cooperation between buyers cum consultants from developed countries with small manufacturers of garments played a pivotal role in their export to developed countries. In this regard, Cole (1998, pp. 275-276) observes:

"Information transfer and assistance provided by foreign buyers achieved a level of efficiency and accuracy unimaginable through any other mechanism. The specific assistance in the production process that was offered at each stage of a producer firm's development was *precisely* and *only* what was appropriate for improving production quality and quantity at that level. Translated into the language of business support programs: the assistance was provided on a for-profit basis; it was tied specifically to tangible product output results; the provider of the assistance received no compensation unless the assistance was successful; and the firms targeted for assistance were those with the best potential and a demonstrated willingness to absorb assistance inputs. There is surely no other source of assistance that would be more accurate and timely, and certainly no mechanism for delivering it that would involve more performance-based incentives for the provider."

Similarly, Sandee and van Diermen (2004, p.108) bring attention to:

"the importance of foreign buyers and investors in promoting SME exports [from Indonesia]. Small firms that have a relatively large share of exports in total sales tend to have better developed links with foreign counterparts than do other firms. [Sandee and van Diermen] show the importance of strategic alliances between foreign buyers and Indonesian small firms in promoting exports. Buyers are involved in a much wider range of supporting activities than is generally assumed. [They] show that strategic alliances are an essential part of upgrading technological and marketing capabilities of small firms and provide examples based mainly on [their] fieldwork in Indonesia"

Despite the valuable studies by the above mentioned authors, there is not as yet a comprehensive study of the different types of cooperative mechanisms which Indonesian businesses use to gain access to global markets and increase their exports. For instance, the role of internal Indonesian business networks and alliances have been little explored. The emphasis of the research conducted so far has been on direct cooperation between overseas buyers and small and medium-sized enterprises in Indonesia. Extending mutually profitable forms of business cooperation is, however, seen by many researchers to be a promising way of improving the international competitiveness of many of Indonesia's industries, including its textile industry (Cole, 1998; Van der Kamp et al., 1998; Sandee and van Diermen, 2004)

CONCLUSION

The empirical study reported here highlights that the trustworthiness and competence of potential business partners have a major influence on whether interfirm business cooperation occurs and lasts. The findings are based on a survey of 210 garment producers in Bandung, Indonesia, nearly two-thirds of which had been involved in interfirm business cooperation and 42 per cent of which continued to be involved in such cooperation at the time of the survey.

Repeated business dealings in the market and family connections were found to be the major factors leading to the establishment of interfirm cooperation in the garment industry in the region studied. Furthermore, business cooperation established via these routes was more likely to last than that established through trade association contacts or those sponsored by the Indonesian Government.

In most cases where interfirm business cooperation had been discontinued, it seems that either breach of trust or lack of competence on the part of one of the partners was involved. In any case, problems leading to breakdown of cooperation included

(1) the slowness of payment by the partner (causing liquidity problems);
(2) the low price paid by the partner compared to the market price;
(3) the unwillingness of the partner to adjust the price paid to allow adequately for steep rises in the price of raw materials; and for some firms
(4) the failure of suppliers to supply goods of the quality specified on time.

While several benefits from business cooperation were mentioned, the most important expected benefit was that it would expand the market of the cooperating business and reduce their marketing uncertainty and transaction costs. Business continuing to be involved in cooperation claimed that interfirm cooperation had increased their marketing and production capabilities, that is had increased their market access and their business competency. These however, are the views of those who have as a whole, been able to sustain business cooperation. It does not follow that all other firms in the sample would have had similar success as a result of cooperating. Suitable preconditions must be satisfied if business cooperation is to benefit all the parties involved in it and is to provide wider economic benefits. There must be the prospect of economic synergies from the cooperation, the partners should be trustworthy and should display at least a reasonable degree of business competence.

In several circumstances, interfirm cooperation (compared to the lack of such cooperation) can lead to the extension of markets (including enhanced access to global markets), results in greater economic activity and growth, and can add to economic welfare. This Indonesian case study underlines the global importance of such issues.

ACKNOWLEDGMENTS

We wish to thank Dr. Christopher J. Medlin for constructive suggestions that helped to improve an earlier version of this paper and also an anonymous reviewer for critical comments on an earlier draft of this paper. The usual *caveat* applies.

APPENDIX

THE LIST OF RELEVANT QUESTIONS ABOUT BUSINESS CO-OPERATION ASKED TO MANAGERS OF SMALL AND MEDIUM-SIZED GARMENT ENTERPRISES IN THE BANDUNG AREA

Note that the numbering of this set of questions is the same as the ones extracted from the longer questionnaire used for the study by Adam (2007)

34] Since starting the business, what types of business cooperation have you ever been involved in (probably more than 1)
1) Putting out system
2) Subcontracting system
3) Clustering systems
4) Other (specify) _____
5) Never (why) _____
6) No answer

35] What was the factor fostering your initial business cooperation
Repeated business contact in the market
1) Family connection
2) Ethnic group connection
3) Religious connection
4) Industry and trade associations
5) Government program
6) Other (specify) _____
7) No answer

36] Do you still continue to cooperate with those whom you have business cooperation with earlier?
1) Yes
2) No (Why?) _____
3) Other (specify) _____
4) No answer

37] If yes, what factors for the success of your long-term business cooperation
Similar objectives
1) Autonomy of participants
2) Partners have required competencies
3) Partners are trustworthy
4) Others (specify) _____
5) Non answer

38] How important are such cooperation in providing the following benefits to you?

Benefits	Not Important (1)	Important (2)	Very Important (3)
1. Technological Benefits			
Technological information			
Instruction in machinery use			
Providing machinery			
Quality control			
Production technique			
Worker training			
Other (specify)			
2. Financial Benefits			
Capital participation			
Investment loan			
Advance payments			
Machinery leasing			
Other (specify)			
3. Marketing Benefits			
Information/guidance on market			
Securing and expanding market			
Other (specify)			
4. Other Benefits			
Providing raw materials			
Managerial training			
Other (specify)			

41] How important are the following reasons/motivations in establishing business cooperation?

Reasons	Not Important (1)	Important (2)	Very Important (3)
Reducing transaction costs and uncertainty			
Improving technological capabilities			
Obtaining raw materials			
Securing and expanding markets			
Exporting products			
Obtaining capital			
Other (specify)			

43] In your opinion, what are the important actions to maintain permanent business cooperation?

_____

_____

_____

46] How important business cooperation for improving the performance of your enterprise for the following areas

Statements	Not important 1	Little important 2	Moderate 3	Important 4	Very important 5
Production capabilities					
Technological capabilities					
Marketing capabilities					
Financial capabilities					
Profitability					
Productivity					
Efficiency					
Competitiveness					
Quality of product					

REFERENCES

Adam, L. (2007). The Economic Role of Formal and Informal Networks in the Development of Small and Medium Industrial Enterprises: A Study of Symbiosis in Indonesian Garment Industry. PhD thesis of The University of Queensland, Brisbane, submitted September 2007 and approved October 2007.

Achrol, R.S. (1997). Changes in the theory of interorganizational relations in marketing: Toward a network paradigm. *Journal of Academy of Marketing Science*, 25 (1) 56-71.

Cole, W. (1998) Bali's garment export industry. Pp.225-278 in H. Hill and K.W. Thee (eds.) Indonesia's Technological Challenge. Research School of Pacific and Asian Studies, Australian National University, Canberra and Institute of Southeast Asian Studies, Singapore.

Granovetter, M. (1985). Economic actions and social structure: the problem of embedding. *American Journal of Sociology*, 91, 481-510.

Granovetter, M. (1992). Problem of explanation in economic sociology. Pp. 25-56 in N. Nohria and R.G. Eccles (eds.) *Networks and Organizations: Structure, Form and Action.* Harvard Business School Press, Boston, MA.

Gulati, R. (1995). Does familiarity breed trust? The implications of repeated ties for contractional choice. Academy of Management Journal, 38, 85-112.

Gulati, R. (1998). Where do inter-organizational networks come from? *American Journal of Sociology*, 104, 1439-1493.

Haugland, S.A. and Gronhaug, K. (1996). Cooperative relationships in competitive markets. *Journal of Socio-Economics*, 25, 359-371.

Huemer, L. (2004). Balancing between stability and variety: identity and trust trade-offs in networks. *Industrial Marketing Management*. 33, 251-259.

Khanna, T., Gulati, R. and Nohria, N. (1998). The dynamics of learning alliances: Competition, cooperation and relative scope. *Strategic Management Journal*, 19, 193-210.

McAllister, D.J. (1995). Affect and cognition-based trust as foundation for interpersonal cooperation in organizations. *Academy of Management Journal*, 38, 24-59.

Nohria, N. (1992). Is a network perspective a useful way of studying organizations? In N. Nohria and R.G. Eccles (eds.), *Networks and Organizations: Structure, Form and Action* (pp. 2-22). Harvard Business School Press, Cambridge, MA.

Nohria, N. and Eccles, R.G. (1992). *Networks and Organizations: Structure, Form and Action*. Harvard Business School Press, Boston, MA.

Nooteboom, B. (1999). *Inter-Firm Alliances: Analysis and Design*. Routledge, London.

Nooteboom, B. (2003). The trust process. Pp. 16-36 in B. Nooteboom and F. Six (eds.) *The Trust Process in Organizations*. Edward Elgar, Cheltenham, UK.

Nooteboom, B. (2004). *Inter-Firm Collaboration, Learning and Networks: An Integrated Approach*. Routledge, London.

Ouchi, W.G. (1980). Market bureaucracies, clans. *Administrative Science Quarterly*, 25, 129-141.

Payan, J.M. (2007). A review and delineation of cooperation and coordination in marketing channels. *European Business Review*, 19 (3) 216-233.

Perrow, C. (1992). Small-firm networks. In N. Nohria and R. G. Eccles (eds.), *Networks and Organizations: Structure, Form and Action* (pp.445-470). Harvard Business School Press, Boston.

Prabatmojo, H. (1991). Prospects for Flexible Specialisation in Less Developed Countries: *The case of Small-scale Footwear Production in Cibaduyui*, Bandung, Indonesia. PhD Thesis, The University of Queensland, Brisbane.

Sandee, H. and van Diermen, P. (2004). Exports by small and medium sized enterprises in Indonesia. Pp. 108-121 in M.C. Basri and P. van der Eng (eds.) *Business in Indonesia: New Challenges, Old Partners*. Institute of Southeast Asian Studies, Singapore.

Sato, Y. (2001). *Structure, Features of Determinants of Vertical Inter-Firm Linkages*. PhD Thesis, University of Indonesia, Jakarta.

Shapiro, S.P. (1987). The social control of impersonal trust. *American Journal of Sociology*, 93, 623-658.

Skinner, S.J., Gassenheimer, J.B. and Kelley, S.W. (1992). Cooperation in supplier-dealer relations. *Journal of Retailing*, 68 (4) 174-93.

Tisdell, C. (1996). *Bounded Rationality and Economic Evolution: A Contribution to Decision Making, Economics and Management*. Edward Elgar, Cheltenham, UK and Brookfield, VT, USA.

van der Kamp, R., Szirmai, A. and Timmer, M. (1998). Technology and human resources in the Indonesian textile industry. Pp. 279-300 in H.Hill and K.W. Thee (eds.) *Indonesia's*

Techological Challenge. Research School of Pacific and Asian Studies, Australian National University, Canberra and Institute of Southeast Asian Studies, Singapore.

van Diermen, P. (1997). *Small Business in Indonesia.* Ashgate Aldershot, UK.

Weaver, K.M. (1998). *Strategic Alliances and SME Development in Indonesia.* The Asia Foundation and USAID, Jakarta.

Welch, C. and Wilkinson, I. (2004). The political embeddednes of international business networks. *International Marketing Review*, 21 (2) 216-231.

Welch, D.E., Welch, L.S., Young, L.C. and Wilkinson, I. (1996). Network development in international project marketing and the impact of external facilitation. *International Business Review*, 5 (6) 579-602.

In: Trust, Globalisation and Market Expansion
Editors: J-M. Aurifeille, C. Medlin and C. Tisdell

ISBN 978-1-60741-812-2
© 2009 Nova Science Publishers, Inc.

Chapter 8

INFLUENCE, TRUST AND TRADE IN THE KEIRETSU OF TOYOTA: A CENTRALITY ANALYSIS

*Takao Ito[*1], Christopher J. Medlin[2], Katia Passerini[3] and Makoto Sakamoto[4]*

[1]Ube National College of Technology, Japan
[2]Business School, University of Adelaide, Australia
[3]New Jersey Institute of Technology, USA
[4]University of Miyazaki, Japan

ABSTRACT

Many constructs such as influence, trust and trade can be considered as important in network organizations. Here we examine trust by measuring 'influence' as forms of cross-shareholdings and use inter-firm trade as a proxy for interdependence. We introduce the Keiretsu of Toyota, a typical network organization, and focus on a theoretical discussion based an analysis using centrality index graph theory. The centrality indexes of transactions and cross-shareholdings have been measured. We discuss the implications of the centrality measurement results with reference to influence, trust and interdependence, and clarify the associations between transactions and cross-shareholding.

1. INTRODUCTION

The pace of globalization and the ability to react to economic change has caused more firms to develop flexible organizational forms. These flexible forms provide a higher degree of responsiveness to change that cannot be obtained within hierarchical organizational structures (Achrol and Kotler 1999; Bleeke and Ernest 1993; Powell 1987). Among the flexible organizational forms, we have seen the development of networked business

---

[*] (visiting research professor of School of Management, New Jersey Institute of Technology in USA from March 29, 2008 to March 28, 2009) Email: ito@ube-k.ac.jp

organizations, where the ties between firms range from cross-shareholdings, to joint ventures, strategic alliances and contractual arrangements and even to gentleman's agreements (Cravens et al. 1993; Hergert and Morris 1988; Richardson 1972; Yoshino and Rangan 1995). These networked organizations gain flexibility through committing to common goals and a common future based on trust. Nonetheless, conflict regarding goals might still exist as self and collective interests do not always coincide (Medlin 2006).

A network is generally defined as a set of actors interrelated and connected by activities or lines of communication, or channels of resource/product flow. Generally, networks exist through time (Halinen and Törnroos 1995; Hedaa and Törnroos 2002; Medlin 2004) and may not have specific boundaries (Ford and Håkansson 2006). Organizations, and especially complex combinations of organizations, can be seen as networks. Nohria (1992) stated that "the term 'network' has become the vogue in describing contemporary organizations. From large multinationals to small entrepreneurial firms, from manufacturing to service firms, from emerging industries such as biotechnology to traditional industries such as automobiles, from regional districts such as those of Silicon Valley and Italy's Prato district to national economics such as those of Japan and Korea, more and more organizations are being described as networks" (pp.1). To say that a network exists is to make a statement about how one sees the reality of organizational structure. A network approach focuses on connections between firms.

Managing within networked organizations is a process that can not be achieved by fiat or hierarchical power. This follows directly from the concept that each firm has different goals within the network (Halinen 1998). However, there are three main methods of managing within the economic sphere: hierarchical power, relationships/trust and market exchange (Bonoma 1976; Perrow 1981; Richardson 1972). Within networked organizations, the role of hierarchical power is decreased and instead there is a reliance on relationships based on trust and mutual gain through interdependence (Easton and Araujo 1994). Trust in this perspective is psychological-sociological and is future oriented with firm-level economic consequences. Only people can trust (Lewis 1992) and yet the goals that managers seek are in the future interests of firms. Trust allows managers to accept the influence of another firm on the basis that mutual goals will be achieved.

This is not to say that the application of power and hierarchy is removed from networks, rather their role is partly reduced and may better be termed as 'influence'. Here 'influence' is defined as the ability to strongly suggest a specific future deployment of resources and commercial exchanges. Importantly, there is a clear theoretical link between 'influence' and 'trust', as they are both future oriented and refer to expectations on future behaviors. Influence, in the sense defined earlier and in contrast to hierarchical power through subsidiaries, is only possible where a form of mutual trust exists.

In this paper we explore the linkage between trust and mutual interdependence by examining the Keiretsu network of Toyota. In our analysis we examine trust by measuring 'influence' as forms of cross-shareholdings. Interdependence on the other hand is displayed as a covariate of influence, and in this study we use inter-firm trade as a proxy for interdependence. When firms undertake continuing trade, they are fulfilling their attempts to influence through the network. The main contribution of this paper is to introduce the Keiretsu of Toyota, one of the typical network organizations, and focus on a theoretical discussion of measurements of centrality index using graph theory. The centrality indexes of transaction and cross-shareholdings have been measured. We discuss the implications of the centrality measurement results with reference to influence and interdependence by focusing on the relationship between transaction and cross-shareholding.

The Chapter is structured in the following manner. The second section introduces the Keiretsu network organization. The third section focuses on a theoretical discussion of measurements using graph theory, and data collection methods. Next, we analyze the data and discuss the implications of the centrality measurement results with reference to influence and interdependence in section 4. The conclusion discusses limitations and future research.

2. KEIRETSU NETWORK ORGANIZATION

The Keiretsu is a specific network of organizations with integrated and interlocking business relationships and joint shareholdings. As an affiliation of enterprises, the Keiretsu plays an important role in the growth of automotive manufacturing in Japan. For example, Asanuma and Kikutani (1997) conduct an empirical study of supply chain relationships in the auto-parts industry and electric machine manufacturing and found that the longstanding transactional relationships among the Keiretsu are a crucial factor for ensuring economic rationality. According to Lincoln and Gerlach (2004), "the most distinctive form of network organization in Japan – and the most critical to understanding its economy – is the clusters of industrial, commercial, and financial corporations known as the Keiretsu "(pp.15).

Both historical and qualitative analyses of the Keiretsu have been recently undertaken (Moloney 2005; Lincoln and Gerlach 2004). However, a quantitative descriptive approach, using graph theory, is also an accepted technique. For example, Brass and Burkhardt (1992) conduct an empirical study of centrality and power in the organization of a newspaper publishing company. Other recent studies have also focused on the analysis of the relationships among the firms in the Keiretsu of Toyota and other organizations (Ito 2002; Wakabayashi 2003). Ito (2004) examines the correlation coefficients between the centrality index of a network and corporate performance indicators, such as sales and ordinary profit. Furthermore, the importance of individual firms is discussed in the Keiretsu of Toyota using a model called "strengthening, neutral and weakening (SNW) analysis" (Ito and Sakamoto 2005). These studies have focused on the Keiretsu of Toyota and other organizations as the limit of cross-shareholdings provides a theoretical basis for implying a network boundary. The correct identification of network boundaries is a major issue when applying graph theory. The cross-shareholding of a specific corporation provides a reasonable limit to the connections of a network, as they indicate the managers' interest in some form of control.

3. NETWORK MEASURES, DATA COLLECTION AND ANALYSIS

Network research in organizational theory deals with the study of the network organization or organizational networks. Its roots lie in the sociometry of small groups (Moreno 1934), the psychology of sentiments (Heider 1946), and the mathematical approach with graph theory (Harary 1959). Graph theory supports the study of networks. A graph consists of a set of points and a set of lines connecting pairs of points. In graph theory the points, which compose a network, are called 'nodes'; and the line, which connects any two nodes directly, is called an 'edge'. The shortest path linking a given pair of nodes is called 'geodesic'. To understand the structure of network, a family of centrality indexes could be considered.

Measurements

Freeman (1978, 1979) identifies key measures of network interactions based on the centrality of each node within the entire network from three points of view: a) degree, b) betweenness and c) closeness. Ito (2008) explains these concepts in details. Much more information about centrality measurement is given by Ito, et al. (2008).

a) Degree
Degree of a node is defined as the number of nodes that are directly connected. Freeman calculates it based on Nieminen (1974). Mathematically, the central degree of node pk, denoted as CD(pk), is defined as follows.

$$C_D(p_k) = \sum_{i=1}^{n} a(p_i, p_k) \tag{1}$$

where
$a(p_i, p_k) = 1$ if and only if p_i and p_k are connected by a line
$a(p_i, p_k) = 0$ otherwise

The number of nodes adjacent to a given node in a symmetric network is represented by the degree of that node. For asymmetric networks, the in-degree of a node pk is the number of ties received by pk, and the out-degree is the number of ties initiated from pk. The degree of a node, in symmetric and asymmetric networks, means the proportion of other nodes that are adjacent to pk and is viewed as an important index of its potential communication activity.

b) Betweenness
The index of betweenness is calculated as a probability that node pk falls on a randomly selected geodesic linking pi with pj. Freeman (1977) defines the index of betweenness of node pk, denoted as CB(pk), as follows.

$$C_B(p_k) = \sum_{i}^{n} \sum_{j}^{n} b_{ij}(p_k) = \sum_{i}^{n} \sum_{j}^{n} \frac{g_{ij}(p_k)}{g_{ij}} \tag{2}$$

where
$i \neq j \neq k$;
$g_{ij}(p_k)$: the number of geodesics linking p_i and pj that contains p_k
g_{ij}: the number of geodesics linking p_i and p_j

Betweenness is useful as an index of the potential of a node to control communication, and betweenness is also useful as an index of the network structure. Betweenness means that a firm serves as a bridge to reduce the gap between the other two firms in the network of transactions and cross-shareholdings respectively.

c) Closeness

The third index is an index of closeness, that is a distance from pk to all other nodes linking with pk directly or indirectly. It expresses the distance conditions from a node pk to other nodes in a network. The central degree of node pk, denoted as CC(pk), is calculated and ddeveloped by Sabidussi (1966).

$$C_C(p_K)^{-1} = \sum_{i=1}^{n} d(p_i, p_k)$$

(3)

where

$d(p_i, p_k)$: the number of edges in the geodesic linking p_i and p_k

CC (pk)-1 grows with increasing distance between pk and other nodes. It is an inverse of centrality for node pk, CC (pk).

Closeness is useful when measures based upon independence or efficiency need to be identified.

The betweenness index is valid when all geodesics are equal. But sometimes it may not be appropriate, and even the geodesic may not be only one path in realistic communication networks. In other words, paths with distances greater than minimum path length attained by the geodesics have been overlooked. At the same time, the fact that if some nodes on the geodesics have different degrees, then the geodesics containing these expansive nodes are more likely to be used as shortest paths than other geodesics. To answer these concerns, Stephenson and Zelen (1989) develop a new concept of centrality: the information centrality index.

d) Information Centrality

The information centrality of a node p_k is the harmonic mean of all the information measures between p_k and all other nodes in the network. The information centrality of node p_k, denoted as $C_I(p_k)$, is calculated as follows.

$$C_I(p_k) = \frac{1}{c_{kk} + (T - 2R) / N}$$

(4)

where

c_{kk} .... the diagonal entries of the inverse of matrix
T......... the trace or the sum of the diagonal entries of the matrix
R......... the row sums of the matrix
N......... the number of the matrix

This index measures how much information is contained in the paths that originate and end at a specific node.

Another measure is Bonacich's eigenvector centrality. It is calculated based on centrality measure for every node. The eigenvector of the largest positive eigenvector is a measure of centrality.

e) Eigenvector Centrality

This index follows that the centralities will be the elements of the corresponding eigenvector (Bonacich, 1972). Given an adjacency matrix A, the centrality of node pk, denote as Ce (pk), is given by

$$C_e(p_k) = \alpha \sum A_{ki} C_e(p_i) \tag{5}$$

where

α .... a parameter, the inverse of eigenvalue of matrix

Eigenvector centrality weights ties with others according to their centralities while degree weights every contact equally.

Data-Collection

The Keiretsu of Toyota is deemed an appropriate object for three reasons. First, it is a typical successful example of network organization. Second an automobile is a complex product with various components that must work together. A typical motor vehicle has about 30,000 parts. Mutual adjustment and effective coordination are required on the part of suppliers and automakers since each component is part of a large system. Third, and importantly, the network is bounded by the data definitions of cross-shareholdings and automotive parts purchased. While the boundary could be equivocal with regard to automotive parts (as the network extends to second-tier and third-tier suppliers, or beyond), this is not the case for Toyota cross-shareholdings, which creates a definite boundary of control and direct information flow among firms owning other firms' shares.

In this study, we collected the data on transactions and cross-shareholdings in the Keiretsu of Toyota from secondary data sources including publications in the Japan Automotive Parts Industries Association - JAPIA - and the Automotive Trade Journal Co., Inc. - ATJC- (JAPIAandATJC 2005), and interviews with selected organizations. There are two steps in the process of data collection. The first is to collect the data on transactions and cross-shareholdings, and the second is to input the data into a matrix table.

Table 1 illustrates a small part of a larger transaction matrix grouping data on more than 200 firms. In table 1, the firms listed in the rows refer to the observed firms (which correspond to the same firm in the column format), and the value 0 indicates that no transaction occurred between the selected firm in the row and the firm listed in the column.

A value of 1 indicates that transactions have occurred. For example, there are three 1s in the first column. This means that three firms, Asmo Co., Ltd, Inoac Corporation, and Usui Kokusai Sangyo Kaisha, Ltd supplied their automotive-parts to Toyota in 2004.

Table 1. Selected part of the transaction matrix of Toyota in 2004

	1	2	3	4	5	6	7	8	9	10
1: Toyota Motor Corporation	0	0	0	0	0	0	0	0	0	0
2: Aisin Chemical Co., Ltd	0	0	0	0	0	0	0	0	0	0
3: Aichi Hikaku Industry Co., Ltd	0	0	0	0	0	0	0	0	0	0
4: Asahi Glass Co., Ltd	0	0	0	0	0	0	0	0	0	0
5: Asmo Co., Ltd	1	0	0	0	0	0	0	0	0	0
6: Iida Industry Co., Ltd	0	0	0	0	0	0	0	0	0	0
7: Ichikouh Indsutries, Ltd	0	0	0	0	0	0	0	0	0	0
8: Inoac Corporation	1	0	0	0	0	0	0	0	0	0
9: Usui Kokusai Sangyo Kaisha, Ltd	1	0	0	0	0	0	0	0	0	0
10: Eguchi Iwao Co., Ltd	0	0	0	0	0	0	0	0	0	0

For the network of cross-shareholdings or for transactions relationships, each firm in the columns accepts investments or automotive-parts from other firms listed in the rows in the matrix table of cross-shareholdings or the matrix table of transactions. The total number of firms considered in the data sample (whose relationships were further specified in a matrix like table 1) is represented in Table 2.

Table 2. Number of the firms in the Keiretsu of Toyota

	1996	2004
Firms related to transactions	194	208
Firms related to cross-shareholdings	251	255

Relationships among the firms in each category were identified through graph modeling. A graph is a model with an undirected dichotomous relation. In other words, a tie is present or absent between each pair of actors. The data consist of valued directed relations in which the strength or intensity of each tie is recorded. We collected directed 0-1 relationship to compute the centrality of each firm. The graphical representation of the network of transactions and cross-shareholdings in the Keiretsu of Toyota is illustrated in Figure 1.

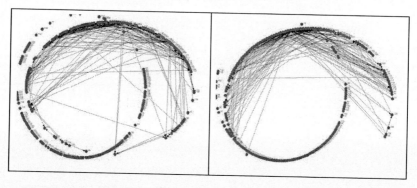

Figure 1. Cross-Shareholdings (left) and Network of Transactions (right) of Toyota in 2004.

Figure 1 shows the complexity of network structure. It is difficult to understand which firms are located at the centre of the network, and whether there are significant differences between transactions and cross-shareholdings from the visual analysis only. However, applying centrality analysis to the Keiretsu of Toyota, the centrality of the firms that are part of the business network of Toyota as well as those connected through cross-shareholdings (reciprocal business ownership) can be calculated.

4. ANALYSIS AND DISCUSSION

We measured the centrality indexes described above using the *Ucinet* software application. Closeness centrality cannot be computed because the Keiretsu of Toyota is not connected, as there are infinite distances. The data matrix is transformed as a symmetric by taking the larger of X_{ij} and X_{ji}, even though it is asymmetric when calculating centrality of information and eigenvector. Further, data is adjusted by adding '0.1' to all nodes' data when it has degree zero for calculation of information. The results are presented in tables 3 and 4.

Table 3. Ranking and Results for Cross-Shareholdings Network of Toyota in 2004[#]

No*	No**	Firm	In-de	Out-d	Betwe	Infor	Eigen
1	1	Sumitomo Mitsui banking Corporation	0	19	0	0.181	0.169
2	2	Japan Trustee Service Bank, Ltd	0	36	0	0.182	0.36
3	3	The Master Trust Bank of Japan, Ltd	0	37	0	0.182	0.364
4	4	NISSAY	0	21	0	0.181	0.224
5	9	Mizuho Corporate Bank, Ltd	0	13	0	0.179	0.096
6	16	Bank of Tokyo-Mitsubishi	0	8	0	0.178	0.078
7	17	The Daiichi Mutual Life Company	0	8	0	0.178	-0.087
8	19	The UFJ Bank, Ltd	0	12	0	0.179	0.101
9	48	Toyota Motor Corporation	0	31	0	0.181	0.253
10	70	Koito Manufacturing Co., Ltd	10	0	0	0.179	0.178
11	80	Sumitomo Electric Industries, Ltd	5	2	12	0.177	0.118
12	102	Tokai Rubber Industries, Ltd.	4	1	12	0.172	0.078
13	103	Tokai Rika Co., Ltd	7	0	0	0.177	0.121
14	108	Toyota Gosei Co., Ltd	10	0	0	0.179	0.148
15	112	Toyota Boshoku Corporation	7	0	0	0.176	0.062
16	129	The Furukawa Electric Co. Ltd	4	1	2	0.174	0.074
17	135	Maruyasu Industries Co., Ltd	1	2	7	0.147	0.007
18	149	Aisin Seiki Co.,Ltd	9	8	54.5	0.18	0.192
19	156	Arai Seisakusho Co. Ltd	7	0	0	0.174	0.036
20	161	Exedy corporation	7	0	0	0.176	0.103

Table 3. (Continued)

No*	No**	Firm	In-de	Out-d	Betwe	Infor	Eigen
21	164	NOK corporation	**8**	*0*	*0*	*0.178*	*0.126*
22	165	NTN Corporation	**9**	*0*	*0*	*0.178*	*0.12*
23	176	Koyo Seiko Co., Ltd	**10**	*0*	*0*	**0.179**	**0.148**
24	190	Taiho Kogyo Co., Ltd	*3*	*1*	**3**	*0.173*	*0.036*
25	200	Denso	*6*	**10**	**38.5**	**0.18**	**0.196**
26	205	Topy Industries Ltd.	**8**	*0*	*0*	*0.177*	*0.09-*
27	206	Toyoda Machine Works Ltd	**9**	*0*	*0*	**0.179**	**0.178**
28	217	NSK Ltd	**7**	*0*	*0*	*0.177*	*0.108*
29	220	NGK Spark Plug Co. Ltd	**7**	*0*	*0*	*0.178*	*0.116*
30	221	NHK Spring Co., Ltd.	*5*	*3*	**13**	*0.177*	*0.094*
31	222	Nippon Piston Ring Co. Ltd	**7**	*0*	*0*	*0.175*	*0.063*
32	228	Bando Chemical Industries, Ltd	**7**	*0*	*0*	*0.176*	*0.04*
33	243	Matsushita Electric Industrial Co., Ltd	*4*	*1*	**1**	*0.175*	*0.106*
34	254	Riken corporation	**9**	*0*	*0*	*0.178*	*0.121*

[#]1) There are 17 firms in In-degree, 11 firms in Out-degree, 9 firms in Betweenness, 13 firms in Information and 11 firms in Eigenvector ranked in the group of top 10th.

2) * is the series number in Table 1.

3) **is the series number in the data matrix of cross-shareholdings.

4) The data in bold and in italic express the firms ranked in the top 10 and below the top 10 respectively.

Table 4. Ranking and Results for Transaction Network of Toyota in 2004[#]

No*	No**	Firm	In-de	Out-d	Betwe	Infor	Eigen
1	1	Toyota Motor Corporation	**79**	*0*	*0*	**0.186**	**0.494**
2	5	Asmo Co.,Ltd	*2*	*5*	*3.25*	*0.181*	**0.122**
3	29	Jeco Co., Ltd	*0*	**8**	*0*	**0.182**	**0.122**
4	33	Sumitomo Electric Industries, Ltd	*2*	*4*	**4.833**	*0.179*	*0.09*
5	41	Pacific Industrial Co., Ltd	*0*	**9**	*0*	**0.182**	**0.121**
6	50	Chuyo Spring Co., Ltd	*0*	**6**	*0*	**0.18**	*0.107*
7	51	Tsuchiya Co., Ltd	*0*	**7**	*0*	*0.181*	*0.108*
8	62	Toyota Auto Body Co., Ltd	**11**	*0*	*0*	**0.182**	*0.082*
9	63	Toyota Tsusho Corporation	**4**	*0*	*0*	*0.177*	*0.033*
10	65	Toyota Boshoku Corporation	*3*	*7*	**18**	**0.182**	**0.121**
11	77	Hamanako Denso Co. Ltd	*0*	**6**	*0*	**0.18**	*0.094*
12	88	Maruyasu Industries Co., Ltd	**4**	*3*	**4**	*0.181*	*0.108*
13	92	Muro Corporation	*0*	**11**	*0*	**0.183**	**0.161**
14	98	Aisan Industry Co., Ltd	*2*	*5*	*3.583*	*0.181*	*0.114*
15	99	Aisin AI Co.,Ltd	**4**	*0*	*0*	*0.176*	*0.029*

Table 4. (Continued)

No*	No**	Firm	In-de	Out-d	Betwe	Infor	Eigen
16	100	Aisin AW Co., Ltd	**12**	*2*	**17**	**0.183**	**0.139**
17	102	Aisin Seiki Co., Ltd	**10**	*3*	**11**	**0.183**	**0.146**
18	103	Aisin Takaoka Ltd	*0*	**7**	*0*	*0.18*	*0.079*
19	107	Asahi Iron Works Co., Ltd	*0*	**8**	*0*	*0.181*	*0.09*
20	119	Ohashi Iron Works Co., Ltd	*0*	**7**	*0*	*0.181*	*0.12*
21	129	Koyo Seiko Co., Ltd	*3*	*3*	**3.5**	*0.18*	*0.105*
22	141	Daihatsu Motor Co., Ltd	**40**	*0*	*0*	**0.185**	**0.297**
23	153	Denso	**18**	*3*	**13.917**	**0.184**	**0.233**
24	159	Toyoda Machine Works Ltd	*3*	*4*	**7.5**	*0.181*	*0.098*
25	160	Toyota Industries Corporation	**14**	*0*	*0*	**0.183**	*0.109*
26	170	NSK Ltd	*0*	**9**	*0*	*0.181*	*0.116*
27	182	Hikari Seiko Co. Ltd	*0*	**6**	*0*	*0.18*	*0.11*
28	184	Hitachi Ltd	**4**	*0*	*0*	*0.176*	*0.023*
29	185	Hino Motors Ltd	**30**	*0*	*0*	**0.185**	**0.241**
30	191	Fujitsu Ten Limited	*1*	*2*	**5**	*0.75*	*0.074*
31	198	Mannoh Industrial Co. Ltd	*0*	**6**	*0*	*0.18*	*0.105*
32	203	Meidoh Co. Ltd	*0*	**6**	*0*	*0.179*	*0.083*
33	204	Yamaha Motor Co. Ltd	**9**	*0*	*0*	**0.182**	*0.059*

[#]1)There are 13 firms in In-degree, 14 firms in Out-degree, 10 firms in betweenness, 13 firms in Information and 11 firm in Eigenvector ranked in top 10th.
2)* is the series number in Table 1.
3)** is the series number in the data matrix of transaction.
4)The data in bold and in italic express the firms ranked in the top 10 and below the top 10th respectively.

Analysis

There are 34 firms in Table 3 (cross-shareholdings), and these are presented in figure 2 on three dimensions (i.e. in-degree, out-degree, and betweenness). Figure 2 shows the firms can be divided into three groups, except for firm number 18 (i.e. Aisin Seiki Co. Ltd). In Group A are located 8 banks (e.g. Firm 2 - Japan Trustee Service Bank Ltd, and Firm 3 - The Master Trust Bank of Japan Ltd.) and Toyota Motor Corporation; indicating that Toyota plays a role similar to a bank.

The cooperative part-makers can be divided into two groups. Group B has high value of in-degree. These firms (e.g. Firm 10 - Koito Manufacturing Co Ltd, and Firm - 15 Toyota Boshoku Corporation) have core technologies and accept stock-investment from other firms or banks. The firms in Group C (e.g. Firm - 25 Denso, and 30 of NHK Spring Co Ltd) have high value of betweenness suggesting they invest in stocks of other firms and also accept investment from other firms or banks. Denso is one of the wholly-owned subsidiaries of Toyota, and its capital and net sales on the consolidated basis reaches US$ 1.8 billion and

US\$ 26.2 billion each[1]. The independent firm, located away from three groups is 18 of Aisin Seiki Co. Ltd., because it has extra high value of both in-degree and betweenness.

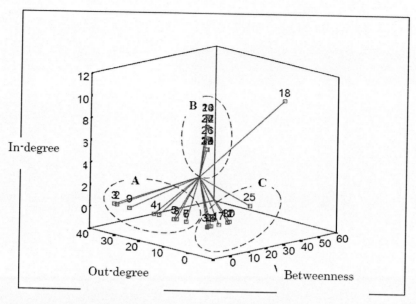

Figure 2. Firms in Cross-Shareholdings Network of Toyota in 2004.

The three ways grouping of the Toyota Keiretsu is similar to that reported by Fukuoka, et al. (2006) for the Nissan group in financial year 2004. However, the structure of the two Keiretsu is quite different. Toyota is composed of core firms, while Nissan is not. There are 15 common firms in the two Keiretsu groups, with four of them being subsidiaries of Toyota (i.e. Firm 14 - Toyota Gosei Co. Ltd., Firm 18 - Aisin Seiki Co. Ltd., Firm 25 – Denso, and Firm 27 - Toyoda Machine Works Ltd).

Figure 3 shows that the firms can be divided into three groups on the basis of transactions. Group A includes 11 firms all with high centrality of in-degree. These firms purchase many auto-parts, and play an important role in the network of the Toyota group. In particular four of them are auto-makers and assemblers (i.e. Firm 1 - Toyota Motor Corporation, Firm 8 - Toyota Auto Body Co Ltd, Firm 22 - Daihatsu Motor Co Ltd, and Firm 29 - Hino Motors Ltd). Firm 9 (Toyota Tsusho Corporation) has the same character as an assembly auto-maker, because it is a trade company engaged in exporting for the Toyota group. Firm 10 (Toyota Boshoku Corporation) and Firm 25 (Toyota Industries Corporation) are directly under the control of Toyota, and they are core firms in the network. Firm 33 (Yamaha Motor Co Ltd) is not an assembly auto-maker or wholly-controlled subsidiary of Toyota; rather this firm manufacturers motorcycles. Firm 28 (Hitachi Ltd) is a huge information and electronic device company with sales and profit reaching US\$ 78.87 billion and US\$ 2.13 billion in fiscal year of 2006[2]. These last two firms appear to represent a change in the Keiretsu of Toyota.

---

[1] http://www.denso.co.jp/en/aboutdenso/company/ (Retrieved April 8th, 2006) The former is 187.4 billion and the later is 2,799.9 billion in Japanese Yen.

[2] http://www.hitachi.co.jp/IR/financial/highlight/pl/index.html (Retrieved January 10th, 2007) The former is 9,464.801 billion and the later is 256.012 billion in Japanese Yen.

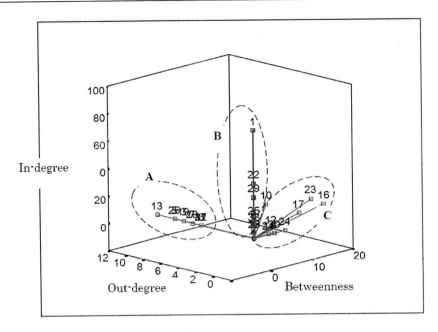

Figure 3. Transactions of the 33 Firms of Table 4.

Group B is composed of 13 firms with a high value of out-degree and all, except Firm 13 (NSK Ltd), solely transact with Toyota. NSK Ltd inaugurated its business in 1916 and produced the first ball bearings made in Japan. It is highly respected in other fields such as automotive products, precision machine parts and mechatronics products. Their capital and annual sales are US$ 0.67 billion and US$ 5.81 billion each[3]. Group C includes 9 firms with high values of betweenness. All of them are Toyota subsidiaries, except Sumitomo Electric Industries Ltd and Aisin AW Co. Ltd. These firms purchase many auto-parts, and sell their products to assembly auto-makers and other firms actively. When we compare the centrality measures for cross-shareholdings and transactions we find 12 core firms in the Keiretsu of Toyota. These firms have high degrees of centrality, betweenness and information (or eigenvector). The 12 core firms are Toyota Industries Corporation, Aichi Steel Corporation, Toyoda Machine Works, Ltd., Toyota Auto Body Co. Ltd., Toyota Tsusho Corporation, Aisin Seiki Co. Ltd., Denso, Toyota Boshoku Corporation, Kanto Auto Works, Ltd., Toyoda Gosei Co. Ltd., and two automakers Hino Motors, and Daihatsu Motor Co. Ltd[4].

As a final step in our analysis we calculate the correlation coefficients between the centrality of cross-shareholdings and transactions (see table 5).

---

[3] http://www.nsk.com/company/about/index.html (Retrieved April 8th, 2006) The former is 67 billion and the later is 581 billion in Japanese Yen.

[4] Besides, There are still two companies, Towa Real Estate Co. Ltd and Toyota Central Research and Development laboratories, Incorporated in the Toyota group.

Table 5. Correlation coefficient of centrality between the cross-shareholdings and transactions[#]

	C-Ind	C-Outd	C-Bet	C-Infor	C-Eig	T-Ind	T-Outd	T-Bet	T-Infor	T-Eig
C-Ind	1	0.037	0.263**	0.808**	0.847**	-0.006	0.403**	0.326**	0.501**	0.337**
	.	0.592	0.000	0.000	0.000	0.932	0.000	0.000	0.000	0.000
	208	208	208	208	208	208	208	208	208	208
C-Outd		1	0.358**	0.223**	0.461**	0.843**	-0.028	0.184**	0.176*	0.630**
		.	0.000	0.001	0.000	0.000	0.683	0.008	0.011	0.000
		208	208	208	208	208	208	208	208	208
C-Bet			1	0.199**	0.387**	0.161*	0.098	0.508**	0.159*	0.259**
			.	0.004	0.000	0.020	0.158	0.000	0.022	0.000
			208	208	208	208	208	208	208	208
C-Infor				1	0.784**	0.219**	0.392**	0.289**	0.618**	0.503**
				.	0.000	0.001	0.000	0.000	0.000	0.000
				208	208	208	208	208	208	208
C-Eig					1	0.364**	0.335**	0.367**	0.517**	0.573**
					.	0.000	0.000	0.000	0.000	0.000
					208	208	208	208	208	208
T-Ind						1	-0.056	0.182**	0.240**	0.751**
						.	0.425	0.009	0.000	0.000
						208	208	208	208	208
T-Outd							1	0.234**	0.687**	0.570**
							.	0.001	0.000	0.000
							208	208	208	208

Table 5. (Continued)

	C-Ind	C-Outd	C-Bet	C-Infor	C-Eig	T-Ind	T-Outd	T-Bet	T-Infor	T-Eig
T-Bet								1	0.252**	0.349**
								.	0.000	0.000
								208	208	208
T-Infor									1	0.701**
									.	4.31E-32
									208	208
T-Eig										1
										.
										208

#C means cross-shareholdings network and T means transaction network. These data means correlation coefficient/ significant probability/ number of sample.

** p< 0.01(two-sided test).

* p< 0.05(two-sided test).

Generally, Table 5 shows strong correlations between cross-shareholdings and transactions. The correlation coefficients of in-degree (T) and out-degree (C), out-degree (T) and in-degree (C), betweenness (T) and in-degree (C) are 0.843, 0.403 and 0.326 respectively, and they are all significant at p<0.01. It is clear that the level of a firm's transactions with another firm is linked to stock investment from the other firm, and vice versa.

This suggests that influence in the form of cross-shareholding and control in the form of transactions are closely linked. From this study we can not suggest which comes first; influence or control, and likely one would find different answers depending on when a study was said to begin. The beginning of influence and the beginning of control, like networks extend back into time.

In order to understand the character of the Toyota group and whether it was stable through time, we compared the indexes by measuring the correlation coefficients between two indices: r1 (based on out-degree (C) and in-degree (T)) and r2 (based on in-degree (C) and out-degree (T)) for data on Toyota from 1996 and 2004. To give a basis for comparison we completed the same analysis for the Nissan group (see table 6).

Table 6. Correlation Coefficient of the Network of Toyota and Nissan

		r_1	r_2
Toyota group	1996	0.340	0.826
	2004	0.843	0.403
Nissan group	1996	0.399	0.985
	2004	0.023	0.053

Table 6 shows that the changes in the Toyota group are small; meaning that higher centrality of cross-shareholdings is linked more with the centrality of transactions. This suggests that a mutual relationship will be maintained, if the core firms retain their influence. In other words, the goal of the core firms is what shapes the interactions and organization of the firms in the network.

CONCLUSION

A strong capital relationship may be one of the key conditions to maintain longstanding relationship. Whether trust and influence through cross-shareholdings leads to further transactions remains a moot point, however, the analysis presented in this chapter shows that they are strongly correlated. The limitation of this paper is that data of transactions and cross-shareholdings are restricted to two fiscal years. Data from more years would be required in order to more completely study the trend of these identified indexes through time series analysis. To better understand the rationality of longstanding relationships among the Keiretsu, more quantitative analysis such as density and capacity analysis of transactions and cross-shareholdings and further detailed analysis of multiple points and years is required.

In addition, corporate performance is affected by many factors including business conditions and corporate strategy. Our future research will try to identify and control the multiple factors that explain why, for example, the corporate performance measured by sales and profits of companies such as Nissan is decreasing, while that of Toyota is on the rise. While the difference in the companies' network structure may play a role as discussed in the paper, we will continue to investigate other environmental and strategic factors that may provide holistic views of corporate performance differences.

ACKNOWLEDGMENTS

This research was partially supported by the Ministry of Education, Science, Sports and Culture, Granted-in-Aid for Exploratory Research, 19651071, 2007.

We would like to thank P. Benjamin Chou, and the anonymous reviewers for their constructive comments and useful advice.

REFERENCES

Achrol, R. S. and Kotler, P. (1999) *Marketing in the Network Economy,* Journal of Marketing, 63 (4), 146-164.

Asanuma, B. and Kikutani, T. (1997) *Mechanism of the Adaptation to Organizational Innovation in Japanese Firm*, 143-196, Touyou Keizai Shinpo (Japanese Edition).

Bleeke, J. and Ernest, D. (1993) *Collaborating to Compete*, New York: John Wiley and Sons.

Bonacich, P. (1972) *Factoring and weighting approaches to status scores and clique identification*, Journal of Mathematical Sociology 2, 113-120.

Bonoma, T. (1976) *Conflict, Cooperation and Trust in Three Power Systems,* Behavioral Science, 21 (November 1976), 499-514.

Brass, D. J. and Burkhardt, M. E. (1992) *Centrality and power in organizations* in Nitin Nohria and Robert G. Eccles (Eds.) *Networks and Organizations*, 191-215, Harvard Business School Press.

Cravens, D. W., Shipp S. H. and Cravens K. S. (1993) *Analysis of Cooperative Interorganizational Relationships, Strategic Alliance Formation, and Strategic Alliance Effectiveness,* Journal of Strategic Marketing.

Easton, G. and Araujo, L. (1994) *Market Exchange, Social Structures and Time,* European Journal of Marketing, 28 (3), 72-84.

Ford, D. and Håkansson, H. (2006) *The Idea of Business Interaction*, The IMP Journal, 1 (1), 4-27.

Freeman, L.C. (1977) *A Set of Measure of Centrality Based on Betweenness*, Sociometry, Vol. 40, No.1, 35-41.

Freeman, L.C. (1978/79) *Centrality in Social Networks Conceptual Clarification*, Social Networks 1, 215-239.

Fukuoka, S., Ito, T., Passerini, K., and Sakamoto, M. (2006) *An Analysis between Transaction and Cross Shareholdings in the Keiretsu of Nissan*, Proceedings of the 6th International Business Information Management Association, International Conference, Managing Information in Digital Economy, pp. 163-169, June19-21, 2006, Bonn, Germany.

Halinen, A. (1998) *Time and Temporality in Research Design: A Review of Buyer-seller Relationship Models* in Network Dynamics in International Marketing, P. Naudé and P. W. Turnbull Oxford: Elsevier Science, 112-139.

Halinen, A. and Törnroos, J.-Å. (1995) *The Meaning of Time in the Study of Industrial Buyer-Seller Relationships* in Business Marketing: An Interaction and Network Perspective, K. Möller and D. Wilson Boston, Dordrecht and London: Kluwer Academic Publishers, 493-530.

Harary, F. (1959) *Graph Theoretic Methods in the Management Sciences*, Management Science 5, p.387-403.

Hedaa, L. and Törnroos, J.-Å. (2002) *Towards a Theory of Timing: Kairology in Business Networks* in Making Time: Time and Management in Modern Organizations, R. Whipp, B. Adam and I. Sabelis Oxford: Oxford University Press.

Heider, F. (1946) *Attitudes and cognitive Organization*, Journal of Psychology 21, p.107-112.

Hergert, M. and Morris D. (1988) *Trends in International Collaborative Agreements* in Cooperative Strategies in International Business, F. J. a. L. Contractor, Peter Lexington, Mass: Lexington Books.

Ito, T. (2002) *Network Organization and Information*, Hakuto Shobo (Japanese Edition).

Ito, T. (2004) *Quantitative Analysis of a Firm's Relationship in the Keiretsu of Toyota Group*, Proceedings of the 2004 Information Resources Management Association, International Conference, Innovations Through Information Technology, 1078-1079, May 23-26, 2004, New Orleans, USA.

Ito, T. and Sakamoto, M. (2005) *Importance Analysis of firm in the Keiretsu of Toyota*, Proceedings of the 2005 Information Resources Management Association, International Conference, Managing Modern Organizations with Information Technology, pp. 930-933, May 15-18, 2005, San Diego, USA.

Ito, T., Passerini K., and Sakamoto M., (2008) *Structure Analysis of Keiretsu of Toyota*, in Putnik G. D. and Cunha M. M. (Eds.), *Encyclopedia of Networked and Virtual Organizations*, Idea Group Publishing, pp.1542-1548.

JAPIAandATJC, (2005) *Japanese Automotive Parts Industry* '05, Automotive Parts Publishing Company (Japanese Edition).

Lewis, J. D. (1992) *The New Power of Strategic Alliances,* Planning Review, Spec.I (Sept./Oct. 1992), 45-62.

Lincoln, J. R. and Gerlach, M. L. (2004) *Japan's Network Economy*, Cambridge University Press.

Medlin, C. J. (2004) *Interaction in Business Relationships: A Time Perspective,* Industrial Marketing Management, 33 (3), 185-193.

Medlin, C. J. (2006) *Self and Collective Interest in Business Relationships,* Journal of Business Research, 59 (7), 858-865.

Moloney, J. (2005) *Keiretsu in Japan*, Last Access: October 10th, 2006 from http://encyclopedia. thefreedictionary.com/keiretsu.

Moreno, J.L. (1934) *Who Shall Survive?* Washington DC: Nervous and Mental Disease Publishing Co.

Nieminen, J. (1974) *On centrality in a graph,* Scandinavian Journal of Psychology 15, 322-336.

Nohria, N. (1992) *Is a Network Perspective a Useful Way of Studying Organizations?* In Nitin Nohria, and Robert, G. Eccles (Eds.) *Networks and Organizations*, Harvard Business School Press.

Perrow, C. (1981) *Markets, Hierarchies and Hegemony* in Perspectives on Organization Design and Behaviour, A. Van de Ven and W. F. Joyce NY: Wiley-Interscience, 371-381.

Powell, W. W. (1987) *Hybrid Organizational Arrangements: New Form or Transitional Development?,* California Management Review, 30 (1987), 67-87.

Richardson, G. B. (1972*) The Organisation of Industry,* Economic Journal, 82 (September), 883-896.

Sabidussi, G. (1966) *The Centrality Index of a Graph,* Psychometrika 31, 581-603.

Stephenson, K. and Zelen, M. (1989) *Rethinking Centrality*, Methods and applications, Social Networks 11, 1-37.

Wakabayashi, N. (2003) *Social network and the trust of continuous cooperation within firms*, Shakaigaku Nenpo Vol. 32, 71-92, (Japanese Edition).

Yoshino, M. Y. and Rangan, U. S. (1995) *Strategic Alliances: An Entrepreneurial Approach to Globalization,* Boston, Massachusetts: Harvard Business School Press.

In: Trust, Globalisation and Market Expansion
Editors: J-M. Aurifeille, C. Medlin and C. Tisdell

ISBN 978-1-60741-812-2
© 2009 Nova Science Publishers, Inc.

Chapter 9

A STUDY OF TRUST, COMMITMENT AND SATISFACTION ACROSS RESEARCH-INDUSTRY RELATIONSHIPS

Christopher J. Medlin and Carolin Plewa
Business School, University of Adelaide, Australia

ABSTRACT

The role of trust, commitment and satisfaction in a buyer-supplier relationship are examined within an interaction framework, so that effects between firms from each side of a buyer-supplier relationship are modelled. An empirical study is undertaken in the context of firms commercialising products (buyers) with university research entities (suppliers). By examining both sides of the relationship an understanding is developed of how interaction and perceptions of trust and commitment influence the other party's level of commitment and satisfaction in the relationship. An ordering effect is found where the actions of the suppliers influence the perceptions of the buyers. This ordering reflects the direction of intellectual property flow. Further research is required to determine the causes of this ordering effect.

Keywords: Trust, Commitment, Interaction.

INTRODUCTION

The nature of on-going interaction between a buyer and a supplier shapes the development of a business relationship (Grönroos 1990; Håkansson 1982). In the case of a commercial relationship between a research supplier and a commercialising firm the quality of the relationship is a critical factor in global commercialisation. Research outcomes are highly intangible and intellectual property can be shaped to become a multiplicity of commercial products and services. Research institutions ultimately rely on successful global commercialisation for a major part of their revenue stream, while commercialising firms must manage various risks, e.g. the risk that a technology can not be taken through to a final product with value in global markets.

The time between research outcomes and commercialisation adds another dimension to the nature of the relationship between researching entity and commercialising firm. The time dimension means that some degree of trust and commitment to the relationship is required. The role of trust and commitment is well recognised in normal commercial situations where there is continuing interaction between the parties (Andaleeb 1995; Anderson and Weitz 1992; Morgan and Hunt 1994). Finally, the researching entity and commercialising firm must feel a continuing satisfaction with their relationship, if they are to continue to pursue an outcome requiring joint effort.

In a globalising world, the speed with which products are commercialised is increasing, but the essential human dynamics between buying and supplying firm remain as a continuing source of difficulty. Managing is at least two-sided in business relationships (Halinen 1998). This paper takes an interaction perspective and examines the two sides of the relationship between supplying and buying firms, which are respectively university researching entities and commercialising firms. The research aim is to examine how trust, commitment and satisfaction in a partner influence the degree of trust, commitment and satisfaction to the relationship by the other partner.

The remainder of this paper is structured in the following order. First, the role of trust, commitment and satisfaction in business relationships are considered, and then these constructs are discussed within an interaction context. Next hypotheses are developed concerning the association of these constructs across the partners. Third, a methodology based on the interactions between university research institutions and commercialising firms is elaborated. Fourth, an empirical study using structural equation modelling is reported. Finally, suggestions for future research and management implications are provided.

LITERATURE REVIEW

In this section we discuss the role of trust and commitment in the development of relationship satisfaction. We also consider the across dyad development of these three constructs that results from perceptions of the other party's trust and commitment.

Trust

Over the last two decades a large range of relationship characteristics have emerged as relevant to Relationship Marketing (RM) theory, however trust has achieved an outstanding level of attention and significance in a large range of studies and contexts. Cross-disciplinary research by Rousseau, Sitkin, Burt and Camerer (1998) has outlined trust not as behaviour, but as an underlying psychological condition based on the overall relationship. This understanding is adopted, with trust defined in line with other authors as "a willingness to rely on an exchange partner in whom one has confidence" (Moorman et al., 1992, p. 315).

The RM literature has provided ample evidence for the effect of trust on relationship outcomes, including satisfaction (Farrelly, 2002), perceived task performance (Smith and Barclay, 1997) and relationship performance (Medlin, Aurifeille and Quester, 2005). It is important to note though that trust is related to risk and uncertainty (Young and Wilkinson, 1989), as expressed by Grönroos (1994, p. 9): "If there is no vulnerability .... uncertainty trust is unnecessary". Hence, the impact of trust on relationship outcomes should be tested in a context characterised by risk and uncertainty, such as a research-industry relationship.

Commitment

Following Morgan and Hunt's (1994) commitment-trust theory, the commitment construct has been examined alongside trust. Two perspectives or components of commitment have dominated research in marketing and management. First, behavioural or instrumental commitment involves a contribution to the relationship (Plewa and Quester, 2006) and thus the presence of inputs or costs that are specific to the situation and relationship (Gundlach, Achrol and Mentzer, 1995). With high sacrifices related to relationship termination or switching, relationship-specific investments might lock a party into a relationship (Perry, Cavaye and Coote, 2002). As these commitments are to a varying degree "difficult or impossible to redeploy in another channel relationship" (Anderson and Weitz, 1992, p. 20) they are therefore often employed under uncertainty of future benefit (Stewart and Durkin, 1999) and so rely on an act of trust by managers.

Second, affective or social commitment is typified by emotional and psychological ties between relationship actors (Young and Denize, 1995). Characterised by cooperative understanding (Perry et al., 2002), mutual friendship and liking (Hocutt, 1998) and positive emotional attachment (Gruen, Summers and Acito, 2000), affective commitment relates closely to other behavioural variables such as motivation, loyalty and involvement (Gundlach et al., 1995). This chapter adopts a comprehensive definition of commitment as "a desire to develop a stable relationship, a willingness to make short-term sacrifices to maintain the relationship, and a confidence in the stability of the relationship" (Anderson and Weitz,1992, p. 19). In this view commitment is to the relationship, with expectations of future outcomes structuring the activities of the relationship.

Satisfaction

Satisfaction can be understood as an affective construct (Lam, Sharkar, Erramilli, and Murthy, 2004, Patterson and Spreng, 1997), capturing an overall post-purchase evaluation based on outcomes and past experiences (Shamdasani and Sheth, 1995) and restricting it to the current customers' assessment of the supplier's offering (Eggert and Ulaga, 2002). Most prominently, satisfaction has been conceptualised as an affective measure based on the disconfirmation paradigm, as a feeling based on a comparison between expectations and perceived performance (Churchill and Suprenant, 1982, Parasuraman, Zeithaml and Berry, 1988). Based on previous literature (Bucklin and Sengupta, 1993, Hennig-Thurau et al., 2002, Li and Dant, 1997), this chapter defines the concept of satisfaction as an affective outcome measure resulting from the evaluation of all aspects of a relationship. When partners attribute a sense of satisfaction to a relationship one can assume that the economic outcomes, on which the relationship is presupposed, must have a high chance of occurring.

Interaction

The Interaction Framework of the Industrial Marketing and Purchasing (IMP) Group (Gemünden et al. 1997; Håkansson 1982; Håkansson and Snehota 1995; Hallén et al. 1989; Möller and Wilson 1995; Naudé and Turnbull 1998) suggests that understanding business relationships requires examining the way firms adapt to each other over time (Hallén et al. 1991). Further, one can not understand a relationship by examining only one party's perceptions of the relationship. As firms interact an 'atmosphere' develops between them (Håkansson 1982) and in particular the activities and resources of the firms are coordinated by managers to achieve outcomes in the interest of each entity (Medlin 2006).

In effect the business relationship develops as a construct in the managers' minds, and is an outcome of the physical interactions and communication between the firms. The managers of one firm develop trust and commitment towards the relationship. Evidence of this development is clear to the managers of the other firm in the ways activities and resources are applied through time. The evidence of trust and commitment by the other party is likely to have an affect on the beliefs about trust, commitment and satisfaction in the relationship by that other party. In this way the physical interaction between the firms leads to attributions of trust, commitment and satisfaction concerning the other firm and the business relationship.

HYPOTHESES

The associations between trust, commitment and satisfaction in a relationship have been examined in a number of studies, but not always with regard to satisfaction as a dependant variable, nor with regard to the associations between suppliers and buyers. Trust and commitment were found to be key mediating constructs in the development of cooperation and functional conflict in the tyre re-seller industry (Morgan and Hunt 1994). The affect of trust on cooperation was found to be mediated through commitment, with the association between trust and commitment being 0.507 ($p<0.001$) and between commitment and cooperation the association was 0.338 ($p<0.001$), while the direct path between trust and cooperation was not significant. This suggests, assuming that cooperation and satisfaction are likely to be correlated, that commitment will mediate the association between trust and satisfaction with a relationship. We propose, therefore, for each party to a relationship that commitment will mediate the association between trust and satisfaction.

H1   Trust in the relationship is associated with commitment to the relationship for both supplier and buyer.

H2   Commitment to the relationship is associated with satisfaction in the relationship for both supplier and buyer.

The interaction between the parties in a supplier-buyer relationship is likely to result in a number of possible associations between the variables across the two parties in a relationship. The level of trust in the other party is likely to be evident to the other party and this should lead to increases in that partner's level of commitment.

H3a   The level of trust of a supplier is associated positively with the commitment of the buyer in the relationship.

H3b   The level of trust of a buyer is associated positively with the commitment of the supplier in the relationship.

With regard to commitment and levels of satisfaction across the partners in a relationship, we expect there to be a number of positive associations. When one party perceives commitment by the other party we expect that party to reciprocate with further commitment. This follows Van de Ven's (1984) principle that relationships have a spiral path where one side feeds on the other in rounds of development. Further, we propose that that commitment by one party should lead to increasing levels of satisfaction in the relationship by the other party.

H4a   The level of commitment of a supplier is associated positively with the commitment of the buyer in the relationship.

H4b   The level of commitment of a buyer is associated positively with the commitment of the supplier in the relationship.

H5a   The level of commitment of a supplier is associated positively with the level of satisfaction of the buyer in the relationship.

H5b   The level of commitment of a buyer is associated positively with the level of satisfaction of the supplier in the relationship.

METHODOLOGY

A two step data collection process was adopted to gather data from both sides of each relationship. First, a questionnaire was mailed to an effective sample of 847 researchers and 54 business people known to be engaged in research-industry relationships. Response rates of 16.5% (researchers) and 31.5% (industry) were achieved. After an explanation of the aim and a description of the two-step nature of the research, respondents were asked to name their relationship partner and a specific contact person. After deleting those responses that did not indicate a partner, 138 questionnaires were sent out in the second data collection phase, including 123 mailings to industry and 15 to university staff. As expected, response rates were significantly higher than in the first mail-out due to the respondents' knowledge that their respective partner had already participated in the survey. With 61 and 4 responses, response rates of 49.6% (industry) and 26.7% (researchers) were achieved, leading to final sample of 62 relationships.

The final sample exhibits several characteristics. For example, while reported relationship lengths varied greatly between 9 months and 23 years, with an average of 55.6 months, more than half of the respondents reported their relationship to have lasted longer than 3 years. The five main industry types represented in the sample are agriculture, forestry and fishing (17.7%), mining (11.3%), as well as cultural and recreation services, health and community services and government administration and defence (each 9.7%). While all Australian States and Territories were represented in the sample, only 30% of the relationships cross State boarders, indicating a relatively close proximity between relationship partners. Finally, considering staff numbers, business units and research groups were found to have an average of 81 and 25 staff members respectively.

Measurement items validated in the literature were adapted based on preliminary interviews and a questionnaire pre-test. Trust is a well-researched construct and was thus measured based on proven items used by Ganesan (1994), Doney and Cannon (1997) and Morgan and Hunt (1994). Given the comprehensive definition and conceptualisation of commitment, this construct was evaluated based on measurements applied by Anderson and Weitz (1992) and Morgan and Hunt (1994). Satisfaction was operationalised in non-economic terms as the perceived effectiveness of the overall relationship (Bucklin and Sengupta, 1993; Li and Dant, 1997).

MEASURE VALIDITY AND HYPOTHESES TESTS

Following the two-step approach of Anderson and Gerbing (1988), construct measures were prepared by conducting factor analysis using the Maximum Likelihood method. The measurement model for the six theoretical constructs is contained in Appendix I. The correlation matrix for the indicators is in Appendix II. As the factors are independent, rotation was not required (Iacobucci 1994). The Kaiser-Meyer-Olkin Measures of Sampling Adequacy were all greater than 0.7. Although, the chi-square of the measurement model was unreliable for this sample size (87.53 with 62 degrees of freedom p=0.01808), Steiger's (1989) Root Mean Square Error of Approximation (RMSEA) was acceptable at 0.082. Steiger considers any value less than 0.1 as a "good" fit and less than 0.05 as "very good". Steiger's (1989) RMSEA is an appropriate measure of goodness-of-fit in this research because, as a population-based index, it is relatively insensitive to small sample size (Loehlin 1992).

Next, analysis was undertaken using Lisrel 8.88 (see Figure 1). The structural equation model has a non-significant Chi-Square of 103.89 (p = 0.00531) and a RMSEA of 0.089. Steiger (1989) considers any value less than 0.1 as a "good" fit. However, a better indication of model fit is the Adjusted Goodness of Fit Index (AGFI). The AGFI at 0.71 is under the recommended level of 0.9, however given that the model is across supplier-buyer relationships the fit is considered reasonable. The t values of the parameters are all significant statistically.

Support was found for the within buyer and within supplier hypotheses (ie H1 and H2). The role of trust in developing satisfaction with a relationship was mediated by the level of commitment that a party has to the relationship and other party. This result supports the results found by Morgan and Hunt (1994), and extends them to an association to satisfaction in a relationship.

No support was found for hypotheses H3b, although there was support for hypothesis H3a. The level of supplier trust in the relationship was significantly associated with the level of buyer commitment. It appears that perceptions of trust, by a buyer of their supplier, leads to the development of buyer commitment to the relationship. Hypothesis H3b was not supported.

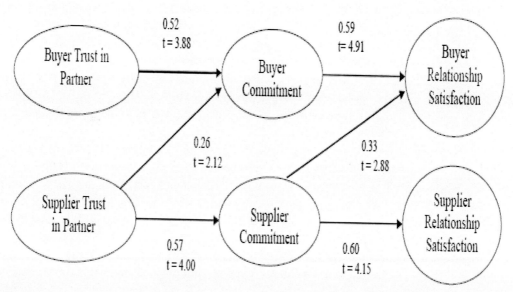

Figure 1. Interaction Model of Trust and Commitment in Research-Industry Relationships.

A similar pattern is evident with regard to across dyad affects concerning commitment and satisfaction. The reciprocal association between buyer and supplier commitment is not found (H4a, H4b), and no support was found for hypothesis H5b, although there was support for hypothesis H5a. The level of supplier commitment in the relationship was significantly associated with the level of buyer satisfaction. It appears that perceptions of commitment, by a buyer of their supplier, leads to the development of buyer satisfaction in the relationship. Given that hypotheses H4a, H4b and H5b were not supported, the support for hypothesis H5a is of note.

Apart from within buyer and within supplier effects, the pattern of supplier-buyer effects exists towards buyer from supplier. Buyer perceptions of supplier trust in the relationship lead to an increase in buyer commitment to the relationship. Similarly, buyer perceptions of supplier commitment lead the buyer to be more satisfied with the relationship. There are at least two possible explanations. The first is that supplier and buyer are connected through time so that, in general, supplier actions precede buyer attributions. This pattern, between buyers and suppliers, is interesting as there is a match with the direction of intellectual property flow, which is the main resource being exchanged in this channel example.

However, further research is required, as the scale questionnaire method does not allow examination of interaction over periods of time. Thus, the associations found may be phenomena of the method. Still the result is interesting in that it highlights the distinct perspectives of the buyers and suppliers.

Conclusion, Future Research and Management Implications

To-date there has been very few quantitative studies that have examined interaction between buyers and suppliers across relationships. The focus of past studies on only one side of business relationships represents a weakness in theoretical development (cf Svensson 2007). Supplier-buyer business relationships are necessarily developed through interaction between the parties. The IMP Group interaction framework offers ways to reconcile similarities and differences across buyers and suppliers in business relationships. In this paper we see how the manager's perceptions of the other firm affect their development of commitment and satisfaction in the relationship.

Our argument is based on the assumption that managers can judge the level of trust and commitment displayed by the other firm. Given the levels of significance found and the way the effects were only found from supplier to buyer, we conclude that ambiguity in perception and also timing variations play important roles in the way managers perceive interaction and outcomes in a business relationship. Evidently future research can examine the reasons for ambiguity, such as goal disparity and so variation in perceptual context (or framing) leading to differences in interpretation, or the ambiguity that arises from cultural differences.

With regard to management implications, we will limit our comments to the relationships between university entities and firms. Past research had already indicated the roles of trust and commitment in a relationship as mediators of relationship satisfaction. Both firms and research suppliers need to cultivate trust and commitment to ensure that commercialisation is successful.

However, this chapter suggests an important role for managers of university research entities: the relationship satisfaction of the research buyer is increased by perceptions that a research institution trusts the other party and is committed to the relationship. There are many ways to manage perceptions of trust and commitment to a relationship, and these tools should be the standard operating tactics of research entity managers. The first is to be truly trusting and committed; to offer only perceptions will surely fail. This means managers should correct errors in such a way as to display good faith, to show benevolence towards the partner and to be honest and credible in their dealings with the partner. These elements of trust are shown through time and require time to be perceived. As Luhmann (1979) notes, actions are not so ambiguous in meaning. With regard to commitment, managers need to display a willingness to act, to adapt and to suffer expenses and managerial costs so that commitment is unambiguously displayed. Further, managers can not leave these matters to perception alone, but must also communicate the costs of commitment to the partner. Managing perceptions requires managing information flows.

Finally, in a globalising world where new products are commercialised at increasing speed, the human element of managing research relationships between universities and commercialising firms will never be a mundane problem. Too much is at stake to leave the management of the relationship to chance; much can be achieved by building sound working relationships; problems can be resolved in entrepreneurial ways when interactions are supported by sound relationships.

APPENDIX II: CORRELATION MATRIX

	Tr(b)-1	Tr(b)-2	Tr(b)-3	Cm(b)-1	Cm(b)-2	Sat(b)-1	Sat(b)-2	Tr(s)-1	Tr(s)-2	Tr(s)-3	Cm(s)-1	Cm(s)-2	Sat(s)-1	Sat(s)-1
Tr(b)-1	1.00													
Tr(b)-2	0.51	1.00												
Tr(b)-3	0.58	0.80	1.00											
Cm(b)-1	0.51	0.34	0.46	1.00										
Cm(b)-2	0.70	0.37	0.49	0.81	1.00									
Sat(b)-1	0.52	0.46	0.49	0.54	0.55	1.00								
Sat(b)-2	0.61	0.46	0.55	0.52	0.62	0.86	1.00							
Tr(s)-1	0.30	0.17	0.27	0.37	0.34	0.50	0.48	1.00						
Tr(s)-2	0.18	0.10	0.19	0.18	0.14	0.30	0.27	0.71	1.00					
Tr(s)-3	0.24	0.12	0.39	0.38	0.43	0.42	0.39	0.56	0.46	1.00				
Cm(s)-1	0.06	0.10	0.25	0.33	0.26	0.43	0.41	0.42	0.22	0.35	1.00			
Cm(s)-2	0.13	0.10	0.13	0.38	0.31	0.41	0.42	0.44	0.30	0.25	0.75	1.00		
Sat(s)-1	0.11	0.09	0.13	0.23	0.21	0.31	0.25	0.40	0.51	0.30	0.43	0.45	1.00	
Sat(s)-2	0.22	0.25	0.29	0.32	0.29	0.39	0.33	0.48	0.50	0.25	0.44	0.48	0.83	1.00

APPENDIX I: MEASUREMENT MODEL

Construct	Item	Lambda	t-value	R^2
1. Trust (buyer)	1	0.67	5.69	0.45
	2	0.84	7.74	0.71
	3	0.91	8.73	0.83
2. Commitment (buyer)	1	0.86	7.88	0.74
	2	0.94	8.89	0.88
3. Satisfaction (buyer)	1	0.91	8.90	0.83
	2	0.95	9.64	0.90
4. Trust (supplier)	1	0.94	8.67	0.88
	2	0.75	6.50	0.42
	3	0.60	4.94	0.36
5. Commitment (supplier)	1	0.82	7.09	0.67
	2	0.91	8.04.	0.83
6. Satisfaction (supplier)	1	0.84	7.50	0.71
	2	0.98	9.19	0.96

$\Phi_{12} = 0.59$, $\Phi_{13} = 0.64$, $\Phi_{14} = 0.31$, $\Phi_{15} = 0.19$, $\Phi_{16} = 0.30$, $\Phi_{23} = 0.67$, $\Phi_{24} = 0.40$,
$\Phi_{25} = 0.39$, $\Phi_{26} = 0.33$, $\Phi_{34} = 0.54$, $\Phi_{35} = 0.51$, $\Phi_{36} = 0.38$,
$\Phi_{45} = 0.51$, $\Phi_{46} = 0.54$, $\Phi_{56} = 0.54$

REFERENCES

Andaleeb, S. S. (1995). Dependence Relations and the Moderating Role of Trust: Implications for Behavioural Intentions in Marketing Channels. *International Journal of Research in Marketing, 12* (2), 157-172.

Anderson, E. and Weitz, B. (1992). The Use of Pledges to Build and Sustain Commitment in Distribution Channels. *Journal of Marketing Research, 29* (1), 18-34.

Anderson, J. C. and Gerbig, D. W. (1988). Structural Equation Modeling in Practice: A Review and Recommended Two-Step Approach. *Psychological Bulletin, 103,* 411-423.

Bucklin, L. P., and Sengupta, S. (1993). Organizing Successful Co-Marketing Alliances. *Journal of Marketing, 57* (2), 32-46.

Churchill, G. A. Jr., and Suprenant, C. (1982). An Investigation Into the Determinants of Customer Satisfaction. *Journal of Marketing* Research, 19 (4), 491-504.

Doney, P. M., and Cannon, J. P. (1997). An Examination of the Nature of Trust in Buyer-Seller Relationships. *Journal of Marketing, 61* (2), 35-51.

Eggert A., and Ulaga, W. (2002). Customer Perceived Value: A Substitute for Satisfaction in Business Markets? *Journal of Business and Industrial Marketing, 17* (2/3), 107-118.

Farrelly, F. J. (2002). *A Predictive Model of Sport Sponsorship Renewal in Australia, Unpublished doctoral dissertation*, University of Adelaide, Adelaide.

Ganesan, S. (1994). Determinants of Long-Term Orientation in Buyer-Seller Relationships. *Journal of Marketing, 58* (2), 1-19.

Gemünden, H. G., Ritter, T., and Walter, A., Eds. (1997). *Relationships and Networks in International Markets. in Relationships and Networks in International Markets*, London: Pergamon.

Grönroos, C. (1994). From Marketing Mix to Relationship Marketing: Towards a Paradigm Shift in Marketing. *Management Decision, 32* (2), 4-20.

Grönroos, C. (1990). *Service Management and Marketing*, Lexington, MA.: Lexington Books.

Gruen, T., Summers, J.O., and Acito, F. (2000). Relationship Marketing Activities, Commitment, and Membership Behaviours in Professional Associations. *Journal of Marketing, 64* (3), 34-49.

Gundlach, G.T., Achrol, R.S., and Mentzer, J.T. (1995). The Structure of Commitment in Exchange. *Journal of Marketing, 59* (1), 78-92.

Håkansson, H., Ed. (1982). *International Marketing and Purchasing of Industrial Goods. in International Marketing and Purchasing of Industrial Goods*, Chichester: Wiley.

Håkansson, H. and Snehota, I. (1995). *Developing Relationships in Business Networks*, London: International Thomson Business Press.

Halinen, A. (1998). Time and Temporality in Research Design: A Review of Buyer-seller Relationship Models. In P. Naudé and P. W. Turnbull editors. *Network Dynamics in International Marketing* (112-139). Oxford: Elsevier Science,.

Hallén, L., Johanson, J. and Seyed-Mohamed, N. (1991). Interfirm Adaptation in Business Relationships. *Journal of Marketing, 55* (2), 29-37.

Hallén, L., Seyed-Mohamed, N. and Johanson, J. (1989). Relationships and Exchange in International Business. in Networks of Relationships. In L. Hallén and J. Johanson editors. *International Industrial Marketing* (3, 7-23). London: JAI Press.

Hennig-Thurau, T., Gwinner, K. P., and Gremler, D. D. (2002). Understanding Relationship Marketing Outcomes: An Integration of Relational Benefits and Relationship Quality. *Journal of Service Research, 4* (3), 230-247.

Hocutt, M. A. (1998). Relationship Dissolution Model: Antecedents of Relationship Commitment and the Likelihood of Dissolving a Relationship. *International Journal of Service Industry Management, 9* (2), 189-200.

Iacobucci, D. (1994). Classic Factor Analysis. In R. P. Bagozzi editor. *Principles of Marketing Research* (279-316), Oxford: Blackwell.

Lam, S. Y., Shankar, V., Erramilli, M. K., and Murthy, B. (2004). Customer Value, Satisfaction, Loyalty, and Switching Costs: An Illustration From a Business-to-Business Service Context. *Journal of the Academy of Marketing Science*, 32 (3), 293-311.

Li, Z. G., and Dant, R. P. (1997). An Exploratory Study of Exclusive Dealing in Channel Relationships. *Journal of the Academy of Marketing Science, 25* (3), 201-213.

Loehlin, J. C. (1992). *Latent Variable Models: An Introduction to Factor, Path and Structural Analysis*, Hillsdale, New Jersey: Erlbaum.

Luhmann, N. (1979). *Trust and Power*, New York: John Wiley.

Medlin, C. J. (2006). Self and Collective Interest in Business Relationships. *Journal of Business Research, 59* (7), 858-865.

Medlin, C.J., Aurifeille, J.-M., and Quester, P.G. (2005). A Collaborative Interest Model of Relational Coordination and Empirical Results. *Journal of Business Research, 58* (2), 214-222.

Möller, K. and Wilson, D. (1995). *Business Marketing: An Interaction and Network Perspective*, Boston, Dordrecht and London: Kluwer Academic Publishers.

Moorman, C., Zaltman, G., and Deshpande, R. (1992). Relationships between Providers and Users of Market Research: The Dynamics of Trust within and between Organisations. *Journal of Marketing Research, 24* (3), 314-328.

Morgan, R. M. and Hunt, S. D. (1994). The Commitment-Trust Theory of Relationship Marketing. *Journal of Marketing, 58* (3), 20-38.

Naudé, P. and P. W. Turnbull (1998). *International Marketing.* Oxford: Elsevier.

Parasuraman, A., Zeithaml, V.A., and Berry, L.L. (1988). SERVQUAL: Multiple-Item Scale for Measuring Consumer Perceptions of Service Quality. *Journal of Retailing, 64* (1), 12-40.

Patterson, P.G., and Spreng, R.A. (1997). Modelling the Relationship between Perceived Value, Satisfaction and Repurchase Intentions in a Business-to-Business, Services Context: An Empirical Examination. *International Journal of Service Industry Management, 8* (5), 414-434.

Perry, C., Cavaye, A., and Coote, L. (2002). Technical and Social Bonds within Business-to-Business Relationships. *Journal of Business and Industrial Marketing, 17* (1), 75-88.

Plewa, C. and Quester, P. (2006). Satisfaction with University-Industry Relationships: The Impact of Commitment, Trust and Championship. *International Journal of Technology Transfer and Commercialisation, 5* (1/2), 79-101.

Rousseau, D. M., Sitkin, S. B., Burt, R. S., and Camerer, C. (1998). Not so Different after all: A Cross-Discipline View of Trust. *Academy of Management Review*, 23 (3), 393-404.

Shamdasani, P. N., and Sheth, J. N. (1995). An Experimental Approach to Investigating Satisfaction and Continuity in Marketing Alliances. *European Journal of Marketing, 29* (4), 6-23.

Smith, J. B., and Barclay, D. W. (1997). The Effects of Organisational Differences and Trust on the Effectiveness of Selling Partner Relationships. *Journal of Marketing, 61* (1), 3-21.

Steiger, J. H. (1989). EzPATH: Causal Modeling, Evanston, IL: SYSTAT Inc.

Stewart, K., and Durkin, M. (1999). Bank Relationships with Students. *Irish Marketing Review, 12* (2), 17-28.

Svensson, G. (2007). A Formula of Consensus in Theoretical Descriptions of the Reality Spectrum: The Unification of Conceptual "Halves". *European Business Review, 19* (3), 248-256.

Van de Ven, A. H. and Walker, G. (1984). The Dynamics of Interorganizational Coordination. *Administrative Science Quarterly, 29*, 598-621.

Young, C. L., and Denize, S. (1995). A Concept of Commitment: Alternative Views of Relational Continuity in Business Service Relationships. *Journal of Business and Industrial Marketing, 10* (5), 22-37.

Young, C. L., and Wilkinson, I. F. (1989). The Role of Trust and Co-operation in Marketing Channels: A Preliminary Study. *European Journal of Marketing, 23* (2), 109-122.

In: Trust, Globalisation and Market Expansion
Editors: J-M. Aurifeille, C. Medlin and C. Tisdell

ISBN 978-1-60741-812-2
© 2009 Nova Science Publishers, Inc.

Chapter 10

TRUST AND CONTROL: INSIDE SOME MAURITIUS CALL CENTERS

Christine Jaeger

FACIREM Researcher,
University of La Réunion, France

ABSTRACT

Some call centers are configured to serve only a local clientele, on the other hand others handle calls from anywhere in the world. This chapter is based on four case studies in Mauritius. After outlining what is generally understood as Trust and Control in Social Sciences, we will explore the various management devices used for incoming call centers and show that they have various "mixes" of the characteristics associated with "Trust" and/or "Control". We then analyze whether these "mixes" vary depending on how the call center is configured - for a local or worldwide clientele - and lastly attempt to propose an outline in response to this question.

Keywords: Call Centers, IT, Trust, Globalization, Control Devices, Human Resources Management.

1. INTRODUCTION

Customers Relationship Management (CRM) epitomizes a remote service typical of the globalized economy. For multinational companies, the matter is to secure loyalty—therefore trust—of their customers by offering constantly and everywhere the opportunity to join agents able of solving their problems in real time.[1] It is well known that the explosion of CRM in the

---

[1] Here we focus on CRCs handling incoming calls because they are precisely the places where problems of customers are managed in real time. CRCs handling outgoing calls have other purposes: most of the time they are aimed at gaining new customers, but that is another story.

last ten years goes hand in hand with rising globalized competition. Quite often, however, CRM is also used by community customers: such as the call centers of local authorities, various administrative services or departments of companies with a limited local market radius. Call centers may be integrated or, more often now, outsourced. We showed in a previous paper[2] that outsourcing generally relates to simple services such as telephone reception (intelligent call routing). When the service is more complex, outsourcing requires partnership relations based on trust, failing which the call center is reintegrated.[3] Indeed, it seems necessary to set up a number of various and subtle devices to manage the work of employees so that they solve customers' problems remotely and in real time and thus secure customers' trust in the company.

One can then wonder whether the closeness—or, on the contrary, worldwide dissemination—of customers generate different sorts of devices to manage the work of call center agents, with various ratios between trust and control.

In this chapter we will first clarify what is generally understood as "trust" in business relationships and its relation with control devices: what is the place of trust in the relations between a company and its operators who answer customers' queries from an often distant platform? We will show that the means used to manage operators' work include a subtle combination of trust and control, even if a very high number of studies on the working conditions in call centers show that control there can take extreme forms, so that the trust/control ratio is generally in favor of control rather than trust. Lastly, on the basis of findings from some customer relations centers (CRCs) observed in Mauritius, we will wonder if this ratio varies according to whether the CRC is used for local or worldwide customers.

2. THE QUESTION OF TRUST AND CONTROL DEVICES

The recent literature dealing with trust in economics, management sciences and sociology is particularly rich and we will obviously not make a general survey of it here. But what is "Trust"? A fast answer consists in saying: "it is the core mechanism of coordination of economic exchanges in a situation of ignorance or uncertainty…"[4] Trust then concerns actors eager to cooperate in a context of uncertainty: they want to take the risk to engage in a relation.

Following Luhman (1979), one can distinguish several kinds of confidence: *assured confidence* on one hand, which he calls "Confidence." It results from our routines: we leave our premises without taking our rifle... On the other hand: *decided confidence,* which he calls "Trust," when one agrees to take the risk of confiding in another person. In business relationships, we refer precisely to Trust: Trust is "the implicit probability that he will carry

---

[2] Jaeger, C. & Peaucelle, J.-L. (2007). Partnerships in Remote Services: The Case of Call Centers in Réunion Island. In Aurifeille, J.-M. & Svizzero, S., (Eds.), *Globalization and Partnerships: Features of Businesses.* Hauppauge, NY: Nova Science Publishers.

[3] Thus the CRC of "Taxis bleus" was repatriated from Morocco to mainland France in 2002; Air Austral's was repatriated from Paris to Réunion Island in 2004; Mondial Assistance Océan Indien's was repatriated from Mauritius to Réunion Island in 2004, etc. Cf. Groote, K. (2005). 80% of the Projects of Outsourcing CRM in failure. *News,*dated 8 March. . *In Data News*, 8 Mars, http://www.relationclient.net/

[4] Louis Quéré (2001), in his introduction to the journal *Réseaux 108,* La confiance, 9-12. He presents, for instance, the works of Georg Simmel, in Möllering, G. (2001). The Nature of Trust from Georg Simmel to a Theory of Expectation, Interpretation and Suspension. *Sociology 35* (2), 403-20.

out a profit action—or at least not harmful to us—sufficiently high so that we engage in an action of co-operation with him" (Gambetta, 1989).

Trust indeed seems necessary to the relationships between and within companies when uncertainty exists. Inter and intra firm relations are the places of incomplete contracts. Incomplete because all the circumstances which the partners of these relations will meet cannot be entirely envisaged in advance, among other reasons because relations are actually spread out in time.[5] Contractual relations are therefore ambiguous: admittedly, the contract exists only between partners who "choose one another" (and trust each other: one does not contract with anybody...). However, trust is not total: if it were, it wouldn't be necessary to draw up a contract providing for sanctions in the event of violation of a clause... How to mitigate the uncertainty of behaviors? How can trust transform the fragile contracts into credible commitments?

Here we can refer to E. Lorenz (1994; 2001): trust is a process, it is built gradually while being shored up by precautions (hence control devices[6]), at least in the beginning of the relations between partners. Lorenz enumerates three characteristics essential to build trust relationships:

1) It is a "tripartite" relation:[7] 'A' trusts 'B' so that he makes 'C'.
   In the case of CRCs, the relation is a little more complex: Company 'A' requires Customer 'B' to trust him to make 'C', e.g. buy from 'A'. Inside the CRC, Executives 'A' have to trust Operators 'B' so that they obtain the trust of Customer 'C'. So this is more than a Principal/Agent relation: it must be reciprocal because trust works two ways only: 'B' must also trust 'A' to engage in this risky relation. This may reduce the cost of too heavy control devices.

2) 'A' is vulnerable, because 'B' is a free actor... and I would add: reciprocally, 'A' is a free actor who could also be an opportunistic being, and then 'B' is also vulnerable. Mutual confidence is useful only in situations of uncertainty and exists only if each of the partners takes risks (even unequal) to engage in such relations.

3) 'A' feels a "justified trust." There again it should be added that 'A' requires 'B' to act in the same way. Such "justified trust" necessary for co-operation is built progressively via a multi-stage training process during which trust can be reinforced (so that there are several degrees of trust).

Initially, trust (like a contract) is established because one chooses a partner who agrees: it is "inductive trust," based on the extrapolation of last behaviors or of the reputation (Hardin, 2002). To engage a process of co-operation, it is necessary to choose a trusted partner. Trust is then reinforced because each participant has an interest in it; this is "calculated trust." Thereafter, if all goes well, trust is reinforced because behaviors (experience) show that all

---

[5] But also because in our complex societies, every person has several roles to play (Seligman, 2001): "The complexity of the system makes it impossible to predict what the other will do to carry out his role because we are involved in a multiplicity of weak ties (cf. Granovetter, 1973, *The Strength of Weak Ties*) and in a multiplicity of roles at the same time... The risk, as a dimension of social relationships... has emerged as a constitutional aspect of life in modern society and trust, as a solution to this kind of risk, has similarly become a component of its definition," 58.

[6] We will use the word "device" for "system" or "apparatus" as Williamson (1985) does when writing on management devices and "control apparatuses" or "control devices."

[7] Cf. the service relation described by Gadrey and Zarifian (2001).

partners fill their sets of conditions: it is Hardin's "encapsulated trust,"[8] which Lorenz calls "justified trust." Obviously, there can be accidents since partners are in a situation of uncertainty and that each actor, being more or less autonomous, can adopt an opportunistic behavior.[9] Consequently, in business relationships (between client and subcontractor or between employer and employee), co-operation implies a certain degree of trust in a way impossible to circumvent, but also a certain degree of control between partners.[10]

What are the relations between trust and control? Does trust make it possible to be freed from more or less expensive control devices? We can provide three types of answers to this question.

1) Trust and control are complementary like communicating vases (Seligman, Karpik, Schuller, etc.): the stronger reciprocal trust is, the fewer control devices are needed.[11] Conversely, the multiplicity of control devices testifies to a small degree of trust between the partners. Thus, Philippe Zarifian (2002) writing about call centers: "either the hierarchy enters a never-ending race between the crafty intelligence of the agents and the sophistication of controls, or it plays the game of trust, with the measurement of the responsibility actually exerted by the agents."

2) Trust is nothing else than a mechanism of informal control: "Trust is a mechanism of control more general than prices and authorities" (Bradach and Eccles, 1996). This position is shared by Granovetter (1973), referring to "the strength of weak ties", Uzzi (1997) when studying clusters, or Axelrod (1984) when he shows that co-operation is established and endures through social and businesses networks that avoid (or moderate) the opportunism of partners. Trust prevails because opportunistic behaviors are discouraged by the danger of being excluded from the co-operation scheme, or even from the social network... But can one then speak about trust?

3) Trust reduces the need for control but does not exclude it. Trust, in principle more efficient than control, cannot exist without control in co-operation, says Neuville (1998): "opportunism is in no way inconsistent with co-operation, it is a leaven of co-operation via trust: the opportunity to enjoy moderate trust of the other compensates, on the one hand, trusting the other and being vulnerable to his possible opportunism, and, on the other hand, relinquishing a potentially higher, immediate profit for the sake of cooperation... Cooperating effectively in this context amounts to

---

[8] In this context, trust is therefore a "device for promise" more than a "device for judgments," Karpik, (1996).

[9] Guy Schuller (2004) lists 3 conditions for the possibility of trust: risk, interdependence and vulnerability.

[10] Cf. Coriat & Guennif (2000), Sako (1993). They distinguish 3 degrees of trust:

  – Contractual Trust: partners keep their promises, they adhere to written or oral agreements. It is essential to any transaction.

  – Competence Trust: partners are expected to fulfil their roles competently.

  – Goodwill Trust: willingness to do more than is expected (involvement). It is essential to rule complex cooperation in situations of uncertainty.

Institutions (including contracts) are the conditions for agents to assume the risk of giving up opportunism: "It is only with the guarantee (always relative) of institutions tempering the risk that involving in pure trust (goodwill trust) is possible." Lorenz (2001).

[11] Hence the contradiction mentioned by Noteboom (1996): "If trust is a matter of risk-taking, a matter of subjective probability expected, it leads to a contradiction: the highest degree of trust fits with a probability of 1, i.e. a lack of risk." Of course, we can argue that since partners are autonomous, there is always the possibility that one or the other may default.

simultaneously and reciprocally building limited trust and practicing moderate opportunism."[12]

This vision is also that of Fenneteau and Naro (2005): trust and control are articulated during the complex relations of co-operation. Which is the case of the CRC handling remote and tripartite (firm/operators/customers) or quadripartite (company/outsourcer/operators/customers) service relations.

On the basis of Tomkins's work (2001), they point out two dimensions of control devices: (1) devices aimed at supervising employees and (2) devices aiming at managing co-operation or controlling events. Each of these dimensions is articulated with trust in a distinct way:

- Control devices to monitor employees consist in setting up information systems and sanctions to guarantee co-operative behaviors. The stronger trust is, the less one needs those devices (and vice versa): in fact those devices correspond to the first vision of the relations between trust and control. Here, trust saves the cost of control (and vice versa).
- Control devices to cooperate are "technical shutters" necessary for risk management in a collective context: to cooperate effectively, everyone has to know what to do (goals), how to do it (procedures) and when (planning). The more complex co-operation, the more necessary these devices, whatever the degree of trust between partners.

When trust increases, control devices can decrease and trust can replace control efficiently. But the technical control systems that make co-operation possible are compatible with strong trust relations. In CRCs, a number of control devices obviously exist and yet, as Zarifian (2002) notes, it is necessary to trust the operators who solve the problems of the calling customers.

3. CONTROL DEVICES AND TRUST RELATIONS IN CRC'S

Methodological framework: Four Mauritius CRCs are observed in this qualitative study aimed at comparing—other things being equal, i.e. without taking into account Réunion Island CRCs, operating differently—two CRCs with local customers (called "Local 1" and "Local 2") and two CRCs with worldwide customers ("Worldwide 1" and "Worldwide 2"). These four CRCs handle incoming calls. The local CRCs are integrated, the global ones are outsourced. Their main features are summarized in the table below:

In the CRCs we observe three types of devices used to supervise the work of operators: (1) technical (software); (2) management that is based on software but largely going beyond that (for example a wage bonus), and (3) practical, set up progressively as risks occur. The

---

[12] Neuville (1998, p. 100) mentions the game (inspired by J. J. Rousseau) between actors who must cooperate to catch a deer if they want more than the rabbit they would catch separately. However, nothing prevents an actor from catching a rabbit for himself while waiting for the deer, especially if the others do not see him..

three types can easily combine with control devices, whatever the degree of trust granted to operators. However, the ratio between control and trust is different in each of the three types.

Table 1. The Four Call Centers Compared

	Local 1	Local 2	Worldwide 1	Worldwide 2
Founded in	2000	1999	2001	2003
Type	In-house	In-house and outsourcer	Outsourcer	Outsourcer
Number of employees	20	170	240	300
Nb of positions	16	100	180	200
Nb of ETP*	8	100	240	300
Activities	50% invoice problems Hotline, Sales	50% Information Hotline, Head Desk	50% help Hotline Head desk, Overflow Reservation	70% complex customized information Hotline
Nb of incoming calls/day	400	20,000	15,000	10,000
Nb of outgoing calls/day	Fluctuates About 100/week	2,000	BPO	E-mails
Time open	8.30 – 5.30 5 days 1/2	24/7	24/7	24/7

*Nb of operators in equivalent full-time employees.

Technical Devices

The four CRCs use the same software to monitor operator performance: Symposium with Hermes pro (Vocalcom).[13]

In all four platforms, as in many others, screen-boards give real time, color (green, yellow or red, according to the urgency) indication of the number of calls on standby, hung up calls, operators online, operators temporarily occupied elsewhere (file processing) and operators available (see figure 1).

---

[13] "The software Hermes Pro (Vocalcom) is an integrated solution for telephony coupled with computers. It includes making and receiving calls, monitoring, listening online. It is made up of modules, all systematically included in the package. Hermes ACD manages incoming calls, Hermes Boost generates predictive numbering, Galileo generates vocal scenarios for receiving calls. Hermes Free processes data and Hermes Connect can interface with any existing PABX, Hermes Statis compiles statistics in real time with simple and cross charts. Hermes Pro is "user-oriented" according to Vocalcom. For example, the Call Blending function allows to manage the flow of incoming calls on a position of outbound calls. Depending on the flow, the software moves the position from outgoing to reception. The software can also handle hot lines and customer care." *Call Centers* 5, January 1999.

Observation of a platform

At the back of the room, hanging from the ceiling, is the "barometer," a rectangular screen visible by all. A = nb of incoming calls, DA = nb of operators answering, NA = nb of outgoing calls, AT = nb of operators free and ready to answer, PL = nb of operators not available (outgoing calls or file processing), EF = efficiency = % of calls not answered (hung up); 00.00 = waiting time of incoming calls (posted in green if waiting lasts less than 60'', then in orange, and then in flickering red for more than 90 second's waiting).

After a few minutes after our arrival (it was not a peak hour), the screen showed the following indications:

A: 0	DA: 10	NA: 1	PL: 4
AT: 7	EF: 100%	00.00	

There were at this time 21 "logged" operators ready on the platform. They had to answer not later than at the 3rd ringing, the waiting time of incoming calls had to be under 15''.

Figure 1. Example of a Screen Board and Explanation.

All these indications appear on the screens of supervisors who can also see each operator's time spent to such or such communication, pause, file processing and so on: "It's Big Brother!" says the manager of Worldwide 1.

These technical devices are here to organize co-operation, while making it possible to supervise the agents. The balance between trust and control inside the CRC depends on the two other types of devices, in particular management devices.

Management Devices

In addition to the wage system and objective bonuses (wages are rather low, agents are recruited at Baccalaureate or undergraduate level), the main and most universal performance indicator (whether the CRC is outsourced or not) is "Quality of Service" or "Efficiency Rate," i.e. the ratio of answered calls within a short period: at Worldwide 1 for instance, 80% of calls must be handled by an operator in less than 20 seconds and hung up calls cannot exceed 5% of incoming calls. Quality of Service is also measured by the number of calls answered out of the number of incoming calls: 90% at Local 1 and Local 2. Like everywhere else, technical devices display incoming flows in real time, agent monitoring and waiting time for callers.[14]

Training is relayed by "coaching," then by "double listening" and is also a core dimension in making operators' behaviors and answers standard compliant. In outsourced CRCs, operators are often dedicated to each client company. Thus, at Worldwide 1, 150 operators take the calls to an American travel agency at peak hours (10 pm to 6 am), 20 are dedicated to a computer company hotline, 30 handle calls for a pharmaceutical firm and 40 other agents take the other customers' calls. At Worldwide 2, 130 operators deal with assistance for an insurance company, 32 operators are in charge of the overflow of a mobile phone company, etc. At Local 2, the least qualified operators answer information calls

---

[14] The Efficiency Rate or SLA (Service Level Agreement) at Local 2 for example, (answered calls/ received calls) must be at least 90% for fixed phone, Internet and at least of 95% for mobile phone.

[14] Local 1: 2' to 2' 30" – Local 2: 40" to 1' for information, 3' for the others calls (on average!) – Worldwide 1 and 2: variable regulations according to types of customers.

(paying calls, 14,000/day) and the more qualified answer other calls. The same sort of specialization exists at Local 1, the most modest of the CRCs observed here.

Time constraints depend on the activities of the CRC: At Worldwide 2 for example, there is no time constraint for the 150 operators who take the calls of the travel agency's customers: call duration varies between 5 minutes and 3 hours... But this is quite uncommon: as a general rule, everyone is ordered to comply with the standard (3 minutes on average) and to respect a prescribed number of calls answered per hour or per day.[15] However, standards are activated only when the quality of service decreases (there are calls on standby, the screen starts to flicker in red, etc.): then agents are reminded that they must work more quickly.

Double listening is an essential part of training. Its frequency and methods are extremely variable from one CRC to another and sometimes from one supervisor to another: some signal they are double listening, others do not. Double listening is always followed by an individual and/or collective "debriefing." When there are time constraints like at Worldwide 2 (for the main client), double listening becomes the essential tool for operator performance evaluation. In all cases, the software allows to locate the customers who have called several times (obviously cluttering the CRC). This indicates bad quality of the emitted answer: debriefing is then organized. When these repeated calls concern a specific agent (there again, easy to locate through Symposium), he/she will be subjected to thorough double listening.

Scripts are patterns of answers to standard calls. In all the CRCs, the reasons for calls are recorded and used to build the scripts that the operators have to follow up. Scripts are worked out with the client company if the CRC is outsourced. Double listening is also used to ensure that scripts are followed.

Schedules are prepared 1 to 3 months in advance according to forecast flows. The construction of these schedules is the core of call center trade: this is what makes the center competitive. Schedule construction takes into account several criteria: incoming flows with known fluctuations, comparison with former periods of reference (e.g. for mass distribution customers), number of training days envisaged, former data from the PABX on the quality of service, waiting times of callers, average duration of calls in similar periods, etc. These elements are used to assign operators precise schedules meant to help them handle flows of incoming calls and their variation as best as possible. These forecasts are 95% accurate at Local 1, and 98% at Local 2 and Worldwide 1 (after 6 months of precise experiment) (see figure 2). They are automatically checked in real time by comparing forecast and real flows. Generally schedules are readjusted one week in advance, and sometimes one day. All the managers interviewed say that the main problem with schedules is agents' last-minute absences.

Most of the time, it is theoretically impossible to change schedules for a rather long period of time. At Worldwide 2, monthly premiums depend on agents' punctuality and respect of schedules, plus the results of double listening. At Local 1, deterioration of service quality is generally due to unforeseen absences.

Other management devices concern wages, objectives and premiums, summarized in table 2 (QS = Quality of Service).

---

[15] Local 1: 2' to 2' 30" – Local 2: 40" to 1' for information, 3' for other calls (on average) – Worldwide 1 and 2: rules vary according to customer type.

	CRC opening hours	Schedules of operators	% answering time/real time attendance *
Local 1	8.30-5.30	2 teams: 8.30-4.30 and 9.30-5.30 1 hr lunch break 10 min break per ½ day	70%
Local 2	24/7	5 schedules of 7 hrs each 42 hrs per week 1 hr lunch break 15 min break per ½ day	90%
Worldwide 1	24/7	195 hrs per month in 10-hr shifts 30 min lunch break 15 min break per ½ day	60 to 80% according to agent's specialization
Worldwide 2	24/7	9 hrs during day and 8 hrs at night Full shift = 3.30-10.30 pm 30 min meal break 15 min per ½ day	Variable according to customers They do additional tasks while phoning: file processing, etc.

* % of response time in relation to telephone/attendance time (in normal hours).

Figure 2. Schedules by Center.

Table 2. Wages, Premiums and Objectives

	Wages and premiums	Objectives
Local 1	8,000 Rs at the beginning + 1,000 max 13,000 Rs on average + 3,000 max	Respect QS, Sales, Subscribed returns, Prospects, etc.
Local 2	6,000 Rs at the beginning + 300 max 7,200 on average + ???	No absence, Respect QS, Sales
Worldwide 1	7,000 Rs + 500 to 1,000 max	Respect QS, Sales, Less than 5% hung up calls (collective goal)
Worldwide 2	6,500 Rs during training, then 7,000 Rs + 200 meal allowance Pay rise: 500 after 6 months and 1,000 after 1 year	No-claims, No unforeseen absence, No delay, Double listening, Bonus performance every 4 months (max ½ wage)

For many authors, these technical and management devices leave apparently little room for trustful relations with employees. Indeed, it is clear that control management devices supported by technical systems generate tensions between the fixed goals of "Quality of Service" to calling customers (individualization of answers) and the necessity to follow pre-established speeches (scripts) within an assigned time (Jaeger, 2002; Guery and Mottay, 2003; Linhart, 2001; Zarifian, 2002, etc.).

However, these devices offer latitude for two reasons: on the one hand, they lead to arbitration between quantity and quality of the services to be returned to the customers; on the other hand, it is necessary to manage risks and the specific problems of each customer. Hence the third type of devices which precisely appear to be at the junction of quantity/quality of the service and risk management.

Informal and Practical Devices

Interpretation of the standards and scripts, informal communication, using the collective, drafting notes for collective or individual uses, arbitrations, attempts to put oneself in the place of the customer, etc. constitute the multiple ways for operators (and often, for their close supervisors) to adapt themselves to the paradoxical injunctions of the organization: it is necessary for them to reach their objectives quickly, but also to be convincing and eager to solve the problems of each caller. Therefore they should make customized answers within the standardized framework of the platform (Jaeger and Linhart, 1998). Symposium follows what they say and do permanently and in detail, but constant monitoring necessarily goes with transgressions so that quality of service is actually given to the customer.[16]

This is why indicators such as number of calls per units of time and average answering time were generally reduced between 2000 and 2006. The number of calls per hour, more often per day, has dropped. The average duration of calls has become a forecasting, more than a regulation, tool. Let us repeat that in one case—Worldwide 2—no average duration of answer is prescribed.

However, when operators have sales objectives, and at the same time must solve problems (three call centers out of four here), then a situation of paradoxical injunction is inescapable: it is a question of selling an additional service to customers who have already difficulties in paying their invoices or face technical problems. Operators must then arbitrate between an immediate service for the company (to sell) and an immediate service for the customer (not to sell) while, in all cases, helping to solve the problem which generated the call. In one CRC, the manager changed the strategy by proposing standard steps according to the difficulties of the customers. This arbitration (helped or not) shows the need for a margin of autonomy and thus of trust in the operators' ability to solve the problems they are constantly confronted with.

Other examples of the balance between trust and control are given by Zarifian (2002):

> "Objectively, the customer can become, under this register, an ally for the agents, because, behind the quality of answers, there are indeed the agents' quality and working conditions. For example: the time to give a relevant answer is not reducible, in its logic, to a prescribed time. It may be shorter or longer than the standard, but above all, its principle is fundamentally different. The same goes for the script: it is useful not only as a means of control but as a support for the agent in that it authorizes him/her to memorize what will be used, not in order to respect the script, but to improve the relevance of the answer made to the customer. That at a given moment the agent should move away from the script is normal and a sign of quality: customers appreciate "natural" answers which really take into account what they want to express during the discussion and the specific problems they want to see solved, facing an interlocutor really listening and understanding."

---

[16] Various authors record such tension: Guery & Mottay (2003): "The economic stakes of call centers are productivity and quality of service. But contradictions are often noted in the literature on these two aspects of the performance, even though a hybrid model aims at combining standardization of processes and customization of service. Beyond this tension between productivity and quality, Kinnie *et al.* (2002) emphasize the dichotomy between, on the one hand, the targets given to employees in call centers and, on the other hand, the methods of control that are exercised. Indeed, they observe the coexistence of hierarchical tight controls on quantitative dimensions (number of calls, duration of communications, etc.) and high quality standards, which can lead employees to situations of tension and contradictions when they perform their work."

In the same vein, double listening appears at the same time as a formal control device and as a way of establishing trust. For operators, double listening is felt both as "control" and "help," especially if it is carried out fairly and regularly: it is made to control the behaviors of "free riders" (Jaeger, 2002). The same goes for PABX data: repeated calls of customers, when they are focused on one or two agents, demonstrate that something is amiss.

Lastly, the most revealing practical devices appear when unforeseen events occur—sudden degradation of the quality of service announced by the screens for example. Then mobilization by trust is necessary. Let us summarize this in the table 3.

Table 3. Comparison of the Four Centers Reactions to Problems

	Local 1	Local 2	Worldwide 1	Worldwide 2
Average incoming calls Expected fluct.	400/day 100 to 900	20,000/day	15,000/day	10,000/day
Max observed unexpected flows	1700/day	25,000/hour	25,000/day	500 to 25,000/day
Main reasons	Storms Technical pbs	Cyclones Technical pbs	Terrorism Technical pbs	Terrorism, Air crash, Technical pbs
Reaction	Mobilising other in-house teams	Mobilising other in-house teams Priority lists Everybody gives information	Mobilising other in-house teams Reporting to Clients	Mobilising other in-house teams Reporting to Clients

It is clear that managing unforeseen flows is extremely bulky and, whatever their origin, requires additional manpower: employees normally assigned to other tasks but who have been operators before, or operators at rest. In all cases, whereas in normal times absences constitute one of the major difficulties to build schedules, when a sudden and unforeseen arrival of calls occurs, staff mobilization is the response for risk management. This means that relations of trust are precisely mobilized to confront these situations. It is hard to imagine that this mode of regulation can systematically exist and be used without relationships of trust or with employees entirely under control.

The uncertainty in the volume and nature of flows is the raison d'être of call centers; therefore it is hard to imagine how control and trust cannot be articulated. Technical tools carry information sometimes used as control devices, sometimes as devices to monitor co-operation, according to the distinction by Fenneteau and Naro (2005). Information may also constitute a signal for mobilization. In these cases, one must conclude that if mobilization is successful, then trust is at the basis of regulation.

Can we argue that the devices thus evidenced articulate control and trust differently, according to whether the call center is local or global?

CONCLUSION

Global or local call centers are not different in terms of technical devices: they all have the same equipment. The management also uses the same types of devices: in the cases studied, training, coaching, double listening, indicators of Quality Service (QS), etc. are equally important. Of course, the size of the call center makes control devices more or less permeable to relations of trust: thus, room for on-time maneuver, holidays, last-minute absences, arbitrations, sales targets are more flexible in a small CRC—e.g. Local 1, where operators may be assigned other tasks than telephoning—than in a large one—e.g. Local 2, where operators spend 90% of their time on the telephone. The content of the service offered by the CRC also differentiates centers: thus Worldwide 1, where insurance assistance is handled, may not leave as much room for maneuver to its operators as Worldwide 2, which handles requests for organizing travels. However, when "it's all go," mobilization of the employees is ineluctably based on trust, whatever the scale of the CRC and the localization of customers. On the whole, while technical and managerial devices are generally used rather (but not only) for controls (whether supervising or organizing cooperation), practical devices are rather (but not only) based on trust.

Thus control devices necessarily go hand in hand with trust relationships. What is interesting here is that "Big Brother," a device for constant monitoring, does not exclude trust. One cannot conclude that any particular device excludes trust. Rather, it is precisely because a device works everywhere and for all, that relationships of trust and good co-operation can be established: they ensure equity among employees individualized in their confrontation to each customer. Our observations, limited as they may be, are in the same direction as Neuville's (1998) when he analyses the overlapping between trust and control devices. Trust and control are articulated in a complementary way,[17] even though the control element undeniably dominates in the CRC (unlike the examples of partnerships examined by Neuville).

But there are differences between local and global CRCs. Global CRCs are always outsourced and therefore have several activities and widespread customers: the work of operators is necessarily less routine that in a purely local CRC where calls always refer to the same company and/or problems. A global CRC (outsourced, then) can absorb quantitative risks more easily: the quality of service it provides has been previously negotiated with the client, as well as the number of calls per day or per hour. If flows exceed what has been negotiated, the CRM will "do its best" without stressing the operators: trust between partners of the outsourcing process allows for flexibility of operators in the event of risks of this type. Such is the case at Worldwide 1 and Worldwide 2.

---

[17] As stated by Zarifian (2002), "The 'output' of a call center is not an industrial commodity but a service. While it is perfectly possible to standardize the issuance of a service by standardizing questions and answers, there are two limitations to this attempt, which operators face all day long. First, a call is almost always quite surprising: you cannot standardize the behavior of customers. Their diversity, the variability of their 'cases,' their subjectivity and affects limit the possibility to reduce questions and answers to standards. Secondly, and most importantly, it is impossible to standardize customer satisfaction. The company may believe that the answers were satisfactory, and yet notice a rising dissatisfaction rate without understanding why, because it forgets that the customer 'judges' and 'evaluates,' and that he does not do that mechanically. Such evaluation is often based on subtle criteria that only the 'better operators,' attentive to the tone and concerns of the customers, can perceive. Companies which have already gained some seniority in the practice of call centers know that judgments are crucial and are beginning to reconsider the control criteria of agents."

Conversely, in a local and integrated call center, everyone pays attention to the QS. Therefore QS appears as both a sign of trust and a control device. In case of danger, time pressure rises and the level of performance required can be difficult to bear. However, turnover in local CRCs is much lower than in global CRCs, careers are therefore more attractive and opportunities of internal mobility more frequent.

Outsourced CRC platforms can easily be relocated: they are subsidiaries of global companies and they follow the decisions of clients (e.g. repatriation). Career advancement opportunities are therefore limited and unstable.

Within the limit of the observations made here, we advance the following assumption: in the local CRC, control devices and trust relationships are continuously linked, while in the global CRC this connection is discontinuous. The local CRC's control devices are activated continuously and trust is necessarily constant. In the global CRC the control devices are also activated continuously—even if they seem less cumbersome—but relations of trust only have to be activated in case of contingencies.

However, we assume that the more technical devices are implemented, the more trust relations can be strongly established: hierarchies are well aware that they can give more autonomy to their employees (and thus all the more trust), because any transgressions, any opportunistic behaviors are constantly tracked and immediately spotted through the technical devices. It goes here like the captain in his plane. He is "Master on board," he may decide to embark or disembark passengers, to take this or that route, but each one of his decisions must be "justified": the black boxes are in charge of control. More technical control can thus go with more autonomy and trust.

With globalization, customized relations in remote service can be adjusted all the more smoothly as technical control devices are more sophisticated. Continuous technical control can be articulated with discontinuous trust relations, and trust will necessarily be mobilized to arbitrate between quality and speed, and to manage risk.

REFERENCES

Aurifeille, J.-M. and Svizzero, S., (Eds.) (2007), *Globalization and Partnerships: Features of Businesses.* Hauppauge, NY: Nova Science Publishers

Axelrod, R. (1984). *Evolution of Cooperation.* New York: Basic Books.

Bornarel, F. (2005). Relations de confiance et renforcement du contrôle, résultats d'une étude conduite dans un cabinet de conseil. *XIV° Conférence de Management Stratégique.* Pays de Loire, Angers 2005. http://www.strategic-aims.com

Bradach, J. L. and Eccles, R. G. (1996). Price, Authority and Trust: From Ideal Types to Plural Forms. *Annual Review of Sociology 27,* 1005-32.

Coriat, B. and Guennif, S. (2001). Incertitude, confiance et institution. In Laufer, R. and Orillard, M. (Eds.), *La confiance en question.* Collection Logiques Sociales. Paris: L'Hamattan.

De Groote, K., (2005). 80% des projets d'externalisation CRM en échec. *In Data News,* 8 Mars, http://www.relationclient.net/

Dufau, M. and Stuchlik, J. B. (2002). *L'organisation du travail dans les centres d'appels*, Agence nationale pour l'amélioration des conditions de travail (ANACT), Coll. Points de Repère.

El Louadi, M. *et al.* (2004). Les corrélats du CRM et du marketing relationnel. Centre d'études et de recherche sur les organisations et la gestion. Toulouse: IAE Université Paul Cézanne.

Ernan, R. (2006). Poor Customer Care Center Experiences Hurt Company Image and Customer Trust. *DMN News*, 21 July, 18-24.

Fenneteau, H. and Naro, G. (2005). Contrôle et confiance dans l'entreprise virtuelle, une illustration logistique. *Revue Française de Gestion 31* (156), 203-19.

Gadrey, J. and Zarifian, P. (2001). *L'émergence d'un modèle du service: enjeux et réalités.* Paris: Editions Liaisons.

Gadrey, J. (1996). *L'économie des services.* Collection Repères, Paris: La Découverte.

Gambetta, D. (1989). *Trust, Making and Breaking Cooperative Relations.* Nuffield Colledge:Oxford Press.

Gleonnec, M. (2004). Confiance et usage des technologies d'information et de communication. *Consommation et Sociétés 4,* 223-235.

Granovetter, M. (1973). The Strength of Weak Ties. *American Journal of Sociology 78* (6), 1360-80.

Granovetter, M. (1985). Economic Action and Social Structure: The Problem of Embeddedness. *American Journal of Sociology 91* (3), 481-510.

Granovetter, M. (1995). *Case Revisited: Business Groups in the Modern Economy.* Oxford University Press.

Green, C. (2007). The Perversity of Measuring Trust. Blog of Trusted Advisors Associates, http://trustedadvisor.com/trustmatters/ 8 January.

Guery, L. and Mottay, D. (2003). Modalités de contrôle et management d'un centre d'appel : une tension productivité/qualité de service accentuée par les outils de contrôle informatisés. *8ème Colloque de l'AIM*, Université Grenoble 2. Grenoble, 22-23 mai.

Hardin, R. (1998). Garbage Out, Garbage In. *Social Research 65* (1), 9-30.

Hardin, R. (2002). *Trust and Trustworthiness.* New York : Russell Sage Foundation.

Hardin, R. (2006). Communautés et réseaux de confiance. In Ogien, A. and Quéré, L. (Eds.), *Les moments de la confiance. Connaissance, affects et engagements* (pp. 90-103). Paris: Economica.

Heintzman, R. and Brian, M. (2005). People, Service and Trust: Is There a Public Service Value Chain? *International Review of Administrative Science 7* (4), 549-75.

Houery, M. (2004). *Rapport du groupe de travail sur l'industrie de la relation clientèle.* Paris: Ministère de l'Industrie.

Jaeger, C. and Linhart, D. (1998). Une Caisse d'allocations familiales en progress : la gestion moderne de la misère. *Réseaux 91,* 31-66.

Jaeger, C. and Caby, L. (1998). La relation fournisseur-client et les technologies de l'information et de la communication. *Réseaux 91,* 95-117.

Jaeger, C. and Peaucelle, J.-L. (2007). Partnerships in Remote Services: The Case of Call Centers in Réunion Island. In Aurifeille, J.-M. and Svizzero, S., (Eds.), *Globalization and Partnerships: Features of Businesses.* (chap7 part III, 22p.). Hauppauge, NY: Nova Science Publishers.

Jaeger, C. (2002). L'impossible évaluation du travail des téléopérateurs : le cas de deux centres d'appels," *Réseaux 114,* 51-90.

Karpik, L. (1996). Dispositifs de confiance et engagements crédibles. *Sociologie du Travail 4* (527), 527-542.

Laufer, R. and Orillard, M., Eds. (2001). *La confiance en question.* Collection Logiques Sociales. Paris: L'Hamattan.

Le Moigne, J.-L. (1991). Confiance et complexité. ITC Compiègne. Proceedings of the Symposium "Du mépris à la confiance, de nouveaux comportements pour faire face à la complexité." Compiègne: Cardinal and Guyonnet.

Lechat, N. and Delaunay, J.-C. (2003). *Les centres d'appels, un secteur en clair-obscur.* Paris: L'Harmattan.

Linhart, D. (2001). La confiance dans les relations de travail. In *La confiance en question.* Collection Logiques Sociales. Paris: L'Hamattan. 72-88.

Lorenz, E. H. (2001). Confiance interorganisationnelle, intermédiaires et communauté de pratiques. *Réseaux 108,* 63-85.

Lorenz, E. H. (1994). Neither Friends nor Strangers: Informal Networks of Subcontracting in French Industry. *Markets, Hierarchies and Networks : The Coordination of social Life.* WISE Publication, London-Thousand Oaks, New Delhi.. *125-139.*

Luhmann, N. (1979). *Vertrauen, Ein Mechanismus der Reduktion sozialer Komplexität.* English translation 1979: *Trust and Power.* Chichester: John Wiley.

Luhmann, N. (2001). Familiarity, Confidence, Trust: Problems and Alternatives. *Réseaux 108,* 13-35. Translated from Gambetta, D. (1989). *Trust, Making and Breaking Cooperative Relations.* Nuffield Colledge, Oxford Press, 94-107.

Luhmann, N. (2006), *La confiance. Un mécanisme de réduction de la complexité sociale,* Paris: Economica.

Mangematin, V. and Thuderoz, C., Eds. (2004). *Des mondes de confiance, un concept à l'épreuve de la réalité sociale.* Paris: CNRS.

Neuville, J.-P. (1998). La tentation opportuniste: Figures et dynamique de la coopération dans le partenariat industriel. *Revue française de sociologie XXXIX-1,* 71-103.

Nooteboom, B. (1996). Trust, Opportunism and Governance: A Process and Control Model. *Organization Studies 17* (6), 985-1010.

Perrier, P. (2002). Centres d'appels. La GRH confrontée à l'industrialisation des services. *Entreprise et Personnel, N° 218.* 35-52

Quéré, L. (2001). La Confiance. *Réseaux 108,* 9-12.

Ramsaran-Fowdar, R. R. and Labiche, M. N. S. (2007). An Assessment on the Role of Trust and Satisfaction in Global Business Partnerships. In Aurifeille, J.-M. and Svizzero, S., (Eds.), *Globalization and Partnerships: Features of Businesses.* (pp. 00-00). Hauppauge, NY: Nova Science Publishers.

Relation client : la crise de confiance ? *Marketing Magazine 103,* Avril 2006.p 60-64 http://www.e-marketing.fr/xml/Magazines/Marketing-Magazine/Avril-2006/MM/103/

Sako, G. (1993). *Prices, Quality and Trust, Inter-Firm Relation in Britain and Japan.* Cambridge: Cambridge University Press.

Schuller, G. (2004). Economie et confiance : La confiance, un facteur indispensable mais complexe. http://www.portstnicolas.org/spip.php?rubrique177.

Seligman, A. B. (2001). Role Complexity, Risk and Emergence of Trust. *Boston University Law Review 81* (3), 619-34, trad. in *Réseaux 108,* 37-61.

Thompson, G., Frances, J., Levacic, R. and Mitchell, J., Eds. (1994). *Markets, Hierarchies and Networks: The Coordination of Social Life.* London-Thousand Oaks-New Delhi: WISE Publications.

Thuderoz, C. and Mangematin, V., Eds. (1999). *La théorie de la confiance, approches économiques et sociologiques.* Levallois-Perret: Gaetan Morin.

Tomkins, C. (2001). Interdependencies, Trust and Information in Relationship, Alliances and Networks, Accounting. *Organizations and Society 26,* 161-91.

Uzzi, B. (1997). Social Structure and Competition in Interfirm Networks: The Paradox of Embeddedness. *Administrative Science Quarterly 42,* 35-67.

Zarifian, P. (2002). Presentation of this issue on Call Centres. *Réseaux 114,* 9-12.

PART IV. THE ROLE OF TRUST IN CONSUMER DECISIONS

In: Trust, Globalisation and Market Expansion
Editors: J-M. Aurifeille, C. Medlin and C. Tisdell

ISBN 978-1-60741-812-2
© 2009 Nova Science Publishers, Inc.

Chapter 11

INTERNATIONAL VOLUNTEERING AND ALTER-GLOBALISATION: A ROAD TO TRUST AND COMMITMENT

Patrick Valeau
University of La Réunion, France

ABSTRACT

"Alter-Globalisation" is a process of increasing the connectivity and interdependency of the world's populations, aiming for more solidarity and more equity. As part of this process, Non-Governmental Organizations from so called "rich countries" regularly send volunteers to so called "poor countries" to manage development projects. Based on interviews with 50 volunteers and 30 people from local populations carried out in 5 countries, this article sets out to identify the obstacles that can often be found in the development of trust between volunteers and local populations. Volunteers arrive with an anticipated commitment including altruism and sometimes prejudices. As a result, the first contact between them and the local population is often confusing and disappointing, sometimes leading to embarrassment, wariness, mistrust or suspicion. This research shows that a period of confusion and doubt is often a necessary step to rebuild a more appropriate commitment that will eventually lead to the trust needed to work together. This research offers a more general insight into working relationships between what were once called "rich" and "poor" countries.

1. INTRODUCTION

Globalisation is often defined as a process of increasing the connectivity and interdependence of the world's markets and businesses (Johnes, 1995). This approach tends to ignore another aspect of globalisation: beyond business, we can define "Alter Globalisation" as a process of increasing the connectivity and interdependency of the world's populations aiming for more solidarity and more equity. Both types of globalisation involve relationships and required trust between people from different cultural background. "A priori", trust may appear easier to achieve in the context of alter-globalisation. However, trust and commitment can never be taken for granted. This chapter analyses trust development through the example of international volunteering and finds a long and difficult process with a lot of misunderstanding, frustration and irritation.

Volunteers overseas are usually energetic western young people with a humanitarian outlook: judging unfair and unacceptable the inequality of wealth between so called "poor" and "rich" countries, they decide to commit themselves to organizations that aim to change this situation. Just getting a small reward, their commitment, using Allen and Meyer's typology (1997), is normative and affective: they only want to give aid and to help.

There are two different ways for Non-Governmental Organizations (NGOs) and their volunteers to help so called "poor" countries: emergency action and development projects. The first occurs in contexts such as war or natural catastrophes and includes providing material supplies such as healthcare and food. In such contexts, there is no need or time for explanation; pragmatism is the keyword. Development projects are slightly different as they take place in a more ordinary context and consist of transferring expertise to allow the local populations, in the long term, to help themselves in reaching a higher standard of wealth. For this, young volunteers come with all kinds of projects proposing technical innovations, such as new ways to cultivate, or new machines to produce, or management tools to become more efficient.

In reality, where volunteers expected trust and gratitude, they often find embarrassment, wariness, mistrust or suspicion. The more they feel these reactions, the more they assert their altruism and may finish up by rejecting these ungrateful people. On the other hand, local populations often do not understand why volunteers have come to help, they think they are quite well paid and often have the feeling that people are not always respectful. Most of all, what makes them feel uncomfortable is that the volunteers keep feeling sorry for them, the volunteers seem to think they know everything and are often domineering. These misunderstandings can turn into anger and often unspoken disagreements about the purpose and meaning of the relationship are problematic, resulting in reduced commitment and inaction. This is how cooperation can end in social disappointment, and material failure.

Based on interviews with 50 volunteers and 30 people from local populations carried out in 5 countries, this article sets out to identify the obstacles that can often be found to developing trust between volunteers and local populations. Beyond cultural misunderstanding, it focuses on the ambiguity of the act of giving and helping. This chapter finally concludes that, in the context of development projects, help and giving are often at risk of being received as a form of condescension, especially if they were not requested. Therefore, the commitment and trust necessary to carry on with these projects relies on a principal of reciprocity that will, in the medium term, guarantees mutual consideration and respect.

The theoretical discussion of the above problems is approached through two sets of concepts: first, performance and management in the non-profit context, and secondly, with an analysis of relationships in terms of commitment and trust, focusing on the process of reciprocal commitment. The data introduces both sides of the story using participants' own words. Confronting these points of view allows us to identify factors that can lead the relationship between volunteers and local populations to success or failure. We can then address different issues about the management of volunteers, including recruitment, training, counselling and eventually control of behaviours at work, making autonomy more conditional.

The results and issues introduced in this article may concern organizations beyond humanitarian action. In fact, globalisation tends to generalize intercultural cooperation to the business context between so called rich and poor countries. Thus, these so called "humanitarian actions" illustrate the difficulties of working together and respecting each others differences. These difficulties clearly occur in the context of business, as well.

2. CONCEPTS AND DEFINITIONS

This conceptual framework is composed of two distinct sets of definitions: the first one describes the context of international volunteering including definitions of non-profit organizations, and exploring performance criteria that can be used to understand and evaluate them. A second set of definitions explores more fundamental issues involved in the building of trust: we connect this concept with commitment, considering among others, the work of Allen and Meyer (1990, 1997).

Non-Governmental Organizations as Non-Profit Organizations Managing Cooperation between "Rich" and "Poor" Countries

The expression Non-Governmental Organization (NGO) emphasizes the independence these organizations would like to achieve from public administrations and power. This issue has often been raised in the context of humanitarian help by Médecins Sans Frontières which has always supported the right to help no matter what local government thinks or allows: this is known as "the right of interference"[1] reference. This issue can be analysed as a "political performance" (Valéau, 2004). But, this is not the only criteria that may be used to understand, evaluate and manage these organizations: beyond the "non-governmental" issue, these organizations remain part of a larger set of organizations belonging to the so called "Non-Profit Sector". The use of this expression opens a larger conception and interpretation of their nature and performance.

From an economic point of view, non-profit organizations (NPO) are often referred as the "third sector". They are analysed as organizations producing goods or, more often, services with the purpose of supplying demands that have been ignored or neglected by the private profit sector and by public services (Salamon, 1992 ; Archambault, 1996). With this in mind, one of the main issues with the economic view of NPOs concerns the added value of this production. For many authors, one of the main difficulties is the separation between those who finance and those who benefit from these activities (Valeau, 2004). Beyond the economic value of the means involved, many authors underline the social, and sometimes indirect, usefulness of these goods and services.

The sociological view of non-profit organizations analyses them as a social network integrating individuals within the society (Laville and Sainsaulieu, 1997). Through having

---

[1] This principal has been developed and supported, among others, by B. Kouchner, historical creator of Médecins sans Frontière and actual French Minister of Foreign Affairs

shared values and belonging to spontaneous collective action, NPOs would reintroduce, within modern society, a primary socialisation as in traditional society. This social integration would include the creation of jobs for people who are usually excluded from the other sectors as well as the sense of belonging provided by volunteering. According to this vision, the performance of these organizations relies, beyond activities, on the way they work. Other sociologists emphasize the part NPOs play as agents of change within the society they find themselves: most of them may be more or less directly and more or less explicitly working for a "better world" (Kanter and Summers, 1987; Cooperrider and Passmore, 1991; Valéau, 2004). Different NPOs may target different levels of change: some are trying to change people's mentality; others want to alter their behaviour. These actions involve very open and sometimes indirect impacts, and as such remain very difficult to measure.

Management Sciences integrate the economic and sociological added values, trying to assess the level of efficiency of these organizations. This approach will often involve a ratio confronting the output produced with the means invested. The management issues still question the value of the services NPOs provide. They are often expected, and would often like, to achieve several goals according to several values. But sooner or later, as demonstrated by Kanter and Summers (1987) and Valéau (2004), these goals and values may follow contradictory paths. The most common example of these contradictions is the eventuality of having to make one or more workers redundant: this option can be economically useful or necessary while it remains socially very negative. Considering this, the managers of NPOs are often concerned with dilemmas and arbitrages.

NPOs often work within the field of international solidarity. This activity can take two forms: short term emergency intervention and long term development. Emergency is the most well known part of NGO activities: it includes providing material supplies such as healthcare and food. It requires a quick and efficient action aimed to save lives. In this context, the goals often justify the means: these actions require a high level of coordination involving very precise rules leaving very little room for initiative. Development projects address more structural problems requiring middle and long terms strategies. The goal is to increase autonomy of the involved community by developing their capacity to overcome their difficulties by themselves. Following this principle, these projects often involve changes in practices and habits that question the economic, the social and even the cultural bases of their society. These changes as such go against traditions. Beyond the conception of the solutions, the definition of the problem addressed can appear very ambiguous as the notion of progress remains very relative (Lévi-Strauss,1955; Godelier, 1984). The history of relations between so called "poor"-"rich" countries is already full of "mistakes" that have been made according to this uncertain principal. Development projects appear more complex, more subtle and, therefore, more ambiguous than emergency action. As examples of development projects we can mention: introduction of processes helping to increase the productivity of agriculture such as the use of animals, introduction of new means of surviving, such as gardening or production of fish, introduction of new manufacturing, for example soaps or clothes, actions aimed at preventing certain illnesses such as Aids; actions to help the creation of small businesses such as micro credit.

NGOs' main human resources are volunteers. The word often refers to part-time unpaid workers, but in the context of NGOs, volunteers often get a little allowance to help them supply their needs during full time work. Most of the time, these volunteers are coordinated by more skilled and experienced paid workers, but nevertheless, they are given lots of responsibilities. In the context of development, this autonomy is even larger as volunteers are often given their own micro-project. Considering the history of international solidarity, from the tyranny of colonialism to the feeling of guilt of « tiermondism »[2], NGOs have understood that, to make their development projects work and last, the local population has to be involved in a way as to eventually take them over. This involvement has become part of the volunteer's job description.

These projects can be seen as work situations involving people from different cultural backgrounds. Culture can be defined as common ways of thinking, talking and behaving shared by the members of a given community but remaining unwritten as well as unspoken (Durkheim, 1915 ; Goffman, 1961). Intercultural encounters induce two types of difficulties:

- difficulties of communication, the message delivered by one may not be totally or correctly understood by the other ;
- Disagreement about the reality and the concepts referred to often stem from differences in values and meanings. Most of all, social norms, in other words, what people ought to think, say or do largely differ between cultures.

The most famous example of this has been given by Hall (1969) through the concept of "proxemy": the physical distance two people ought to keep between them varies between cultures, so that the same distance may seem too close within one culture while appearing too big within another culture. Another important aspect studied by Hofstede (1980) and d'Iribarne (1993) is leadership: they found that what makes a good leader and the style and the attitude expected from him vary from one culture to another. As a result, as shown by Hall (1969) or Carols (1990), intercultural encounters often lead to misunderstanding, awkwardness, hurt feelings, irritation and dislike if not worse.

Considering these different issues and aspects of the context, development projects can be seen as work cooperation between visiting volunteers and the local population, in other words working together and respecting each others differences. The achievement of this cooperation depends on a process of trust and commitment to the shared situation as well as to one another.

Commitment and Trust

We define cooperation as a work relationship between different people aiming to work together in the same direction. This cooperation involves:

- an agreement about the initial situation and/or an understanding and respect of the other parties' perceptions.
- an agreement about the set of actions necessary to change this situation
- a commitment to act in this way
- a belief that the other is also going to act in this way.

---

[2] Tiers-mondism: is vision from the 70's which attributes the responsibility fot poverty in the third world to colonization and further interventions of European countries. According to this theory, the purpose of NGOs is to repair these damages.

We address these issues through commitment and trust.

Commitment is a concept aimed at describing the relationship between an individual and their work environment. To integrate all its possible forms, commitment can be very simply defined as the contrary of indifference: commitment measures the intensity of the relationship to work, whatever its content may be (Valéau, 2004). However, the literature often introduces a distinction between attitudinal and behavioural commitment.

Commitment refers to the individual's representation and attitude to his or her relation to work combining perceptions, meanings and evaluation. Following this perspective, different bases of commitment have been established (Etzioni, 1961; O'Reilly and Chatman, 1986; Becker, 1992; Morrow, 1993). The typology the most often referred to is the one outlined by Allen and Meyer (1997):

Affective commitment is based on emotional attachment, identification and involvement with an organization. Employees with a high level of affective commitment stay in the organization because they want to. This definition from Allen and Meyer accords with the one from Mowday, Porter and Steers (1982) : an identification based on the sharing of organizational goals and values. Similar orientations can be found in numerous other definitions, including old ones such as Cook, Hepworth, Wall and Warr (1981). These authors describe affective commitments in terms of identification, involvement and loyalty. Further examination of these definitions shows that, behind apparently similar words and ideas, lay different interpretations of the phenomena: some talk about conscious subscription, others about deeper internationalizations through deeper socialization.

Normative commitment is based on a feeling of duty and moral obligation. Employees with a high level of normative commitment feel they ought to stay in the organization. This expression used by Allen and Meyer (1990, 1997) refers to some kind of moral duty similar to the one described by Kelman (1959) and Kanter (1968). Wiener (1982) assimilates this base of commitment to the sum of normative pressure internalized by the individual: pressures that would incite him to behave in a way required by the organization. According to this author, this commitment would come, partly, from former socializations that may have given the individual a sense of duty and loyalty, it would also come from his actual identification and subscription to his present organization, its expectations, goals and values would become for him a guide to behavior.

Continuous commitment is defined by Allen and Meyer (1990, 1997) as the attention given to costs involved in an eventual resignation. According to them, an employee with a high continuous commitment is going to stay in the organization mainly for need and necessity. This base of commitment has been conceptualized as an exchange relationship based on different interests (ex. Etzioni, 1961 ; Herbiniak and Alutto, 1972). It has also been defined in terms of investments (Becker, 1960 Allen and Meyer, 1997 ; Powel and Meyer, 2004). As a result, the expression continuous commitment is often preferred to calculative commitment. More recently, Cohen (2007) used the expression investment commitment. A debate, still going, on questions the need to separate the two different subscales that compose this base of commitment : (McGee and Ford, 1987 ; Allen and Meyer, 1997, Powell and Meyer, 2004) : the sacrifices involved in an eventual resignation and the low equivalent alternatives available. According to the results of this study, both dimensions may be connected, as the accumulated investments progressively "trapped" the individual in his or her organization (Staw, 1976 ; Kanter, 1968). Low alternative can be seen as a form of alienative commitment (Etzioni, 1961, Penley and Gould, 1988) : a negative commitment with which individuals carry on in a given relationship because they have not got the choice.

Individuals can feel, at a given time, one or several of these bases of commitment (Allen and Meyer, 1997; Wasti, Tucker,). The bases can also be addressed to different foci (Reicher, 1985; Morrow, 1993; Meyer and Herscovitch, 2001; Stinghamber, 2002) such as the leader, the tasks, the job, the customer, the carrier and co-workers. These attitudes may influence behaviours. In the context of cooperation as analysed, both the volunteers and individuals from the local population develop their own commitment to the common work situation. We will study the compatibility of their respective commitment as well as their mutual commitment (Valéau, 2004). This commitment to one another is part of the psychological contract and can be related to trust. Trust can be defined as a substitute for information or power, ensuring that the other side is going to respect their part of the deal (Deutch, 1973; Gambetta, 1990; Sztompka, 1999; Guinnane, 2005; Golbeck, 2005). Trust in a person is a commitment to an action based on a belief that the future actions of that person will lead to a good outcome. These definitions include two main components: belief and commitment. Belief is not enough to say there is trust, trust really occurs when that belief is used as the foundation for making a commitment leading to particular action (Deutch, 1973; Gambetta, 1990; Sztompka, 1999; Guinnane, 2005; Golbeck, 2005). According to a more psychological approach, trust deals with respect and acceptance (Berne, 1961; Rogers, 1961). This article studies the factors that help or hinder the process of mutual commitment and trust.

3. METHODS AND RESULTS

The phenomena studied in this article are mainly people's experiences. Our methods emphasize semi-directive interviews. The first unit of analysis (Yin, 1989) is the "stories" volunteers and local people tell about the cooperation. From there, the second main unit of analysis (Yin, 1989) is the cooperation itself including and confronting the two sides of the stories. The data gathered during this research shows that, on both sides, anticipated commitment and trust are based on positive and negative prejudices. After a phase of resistance, confrontation with reality often leads to disappointment. The relationships between volunteers and local people often go through embarrassment, wariness, mistrust, suspicion, ungratefulness and frustration. These tensions are often overcome and the relationships return to new trust and commitment based and on a better knowledge of one another.

Methods

For this research, we have selected 80 interviews. To be able to compare data, we have built a sample aiming to maximise diversity (Morse, 1994): we have included volunteers, local people and projects of all kinds (see table 1).

We met volunteers and locals. Our meeting always started or finished with the visit to the project. These observations constituted an important anchor: the project was a common experience of the reality debated within the interview. As such, the interviews always started with a general presentation of the project, this introduction helping the relationship between interviewer and interviewee.

Table 1. Sample Plan

Country / Region	Volunteers	Local people	Project
France – before departure	10		
Benin	10	9	10
Burkina Faso	7	8	7
Guinea	5	5	5
Ivory Coast	5	5	5
Uganda	3	3	3
France – after return	10		
Total	50	30	30

We would ask the volunteer just one single question "Can we look back at your experience: when was the first time you thought about becoming a volunteer?" For the local person, our question was: "When did you first hear about the volunteers and their projects?" Starting from this point, we would follow the story asking them to explain in detail the different aspects of their story. Fairly quickly, the interview would then take on a personal content.

This method obviously involves the risk that the person interviewed rebuilds their experience, after the course of events. We focus on the experience that they felt rather than the objective events, we emphasize the interpretation they make to give them a meaning. Sometimes, interpretation a few months after the event can be more congruent than the immediate interpretation, as time helps people to accept certain things. The congruence of the interpretation by an interviewee can also be improved by the way the interviewer follows the story path (Rogers 1961). The interviewer's attitude can also, in our experience, help the local population express themselves more openly than usual.

Our interpretation of the content of the interviews does not pretend to be an objective truth but a trustworthiness (Guba and Lincoln, 1994; Adler and Adler, 1994). This interpretation operates according to two different levels:

- *first we try to understand what the person interviewed actually meant;*
- *then, from a more critical point of view, we analyse his or her speech as a cognitive activity through which the person interviewed builds the meaning to his or her experience.*

In addition to the interpretation of each speech, we compare them to identify a common process and build general models, such as the three models introduced within the last part of this article.

Qualitative research is often seen as a craft which, compared to quantitative methods, presents certain limits as well as certain advantages. First, built on a sample of 50 volunteers and 30 local people, the models introduced in this article may not be absolutely statistically representative. Nevertheless, grounded in the field (Glaser and Strauss, 1967), these models have been "saturated": they give an account for all the cases encountered and studying new cases did not bring any new information (Guba and Licoln, 1994). In the future, replications will be needed to assess these models within other organizations. Beyond their inner coherence (Guba and Licoln, 1994; Adler and Adler, 1994), the trustworthiness and the relevance of these models has been confirmed by the actors themselves during the restitution (Glaser and Strass, 1978; Morse, 1994). This first set of models also allows us to converse with an other theory (Popper, 1934; Huff, 1999).

The Side of the Volunteers

The common perception often states that volunteers' commitment and conviction always remains high. The data gathered during this research only partially confirms this statement (extract 1, 2 and 4, see table 2), showing that there are times of disappointment during which this commitment becomes more uncertain (extract 3). At that time, trust may be challenged by embarrassment, wariness, mistrust, suspicion and frustration (extract 3). This period of doubt appears to be a step that may eventually lead back to a renewed trust and a new commitment based on a better and more realistic knowledge of the situation and the local people (extract 4).

Table 2. Quotations from the volunteers

N°	Commitment	Contents
1. Before Volunteer's arrival	Anticipated Commitment Affective and Normative Commitment to the Local People	"My mission here? I see it as educative" I want to give them hope"
2. First months after Arrival	Commitment in Action Affective and normative commitment to the local people	"Here, they haven't got the same mentality, they say "yes" and they don't do half of it. I knew it was going to be like this. It is just how I thought it was going to be.» "But I am here for them !"
3. At work for more than six months	Doubts: Low, confused and/or Negative Commitment	"Sometimes I feel totally discouraged, sometimes I feel disappointed. Yes, I feel discouraged and fed up. Sometimes I've got the feeling that all of this is totally useless... that we are wasting our time."
4. At work for more than a year	Adjusted Commitment Diversity and Multiplication of Commitment in terms of Bases and Foci	"I think everyone of us is following his or her own path and all of us don't have the same objectives and wishes." "At first I thought I would never stay two years here and I was sure. But after a few months, things have gone better and I realised that after all, it was not so bad. It has been difficult and I really needed to change my state of mind." "The most important thing is to be there to share. There is always something positive that makes you carry on."

The Side of the Local People

At first, the local population often gives a positive opinion about volunteers (extract 1, see table 3).

Table 3. Quotations from the local people

Steps	Commitment	Contents
1. Before volunteers' arrival	No Anticipated Commitment	*General ideas and prejudices about people from so called "rich" countries*
2. First months after volunteers' Arrival	Commitment in Action Affective and Normative	*"The volunteers, they are really wonderful people and really they give us a lot."* *"The volunteers, they are very good, we are really happy with them."* *"They are working all the time."*
3a. At work for more than six months	Doubts: Low, Confused Commitment	*"The volunteers, we don't really know what they are doing, they do not tell us much"* *"You know, I am not sure that all this is very useful."* *"Yes, they are volunteers, they say they have come to help us …what they are doing, I am not sure."* *"The volunteers, they all have a car, and when we ask them for a lift, they always say they haven't got the time."* *"They drink a lot of coca-cola, and they don't really share."* *"I think they are unfair, they spend all the money people from Europe have given for us."* *"I don't think people here understand that they are volunteers because they've got more than we have: they've got good cars, they drink sodas and beers. They've got money, that is for sure."* *"In my opinion, I think they come to make money! They came because in Europe, there is too much unemployment."*
3b. At work for more than six months	Doubts: Low or negative commitment	*"The volunteer, nobody likes him here. He wants everything his own way, he never listen to anyone."* *"He thinks he is the boss, you know I have more diplomas than him."* *"I think they exaggerate, they behave just as if this was their country."* *"The volunteers do not always behave in a right way, they think they know everything. They're often bossy."* *"They say they have come to help us, but, as far as we are concerned, we haven't asked for anything!"* *"We don't want their help, we are big enough to help ourselves!"*
4. At work for more than a year	Adjusted Commitment Diversity and multiplication of commitment in terms of bases	*"We have learnt to know each other."* *"These volunteers, they've started to make more effort. Now they come to all the events in the village."* *"This volunteer, now he listens a bit more to what we have to say"*

But going deeper into details and authenticity, using semi-directive interview techniques, this research shows mixed feelings similar to volunteers including embarrassment, wariness, mistrust, suspicion, ungratefulness and frustration (extracts 2, 3, see table 3). Nevertheless, individuals from the local populations often come back to trust and commitment too (extracts 4, see table 3). These positive opinions, finally adopted, may be based on the changes observed within the volunteers' behaviours, as well as a better knowledge and understanding of them.

4. DISCUSSION

The main result of this research is to show that building trust and commitment, within the context of development action, between volunteers from so called "rich" countries and individuals from the populations of so called "poor" countries, is a long process that will often include stages such as disappointments, doubts, irritations and tensions and will eventually not always be achieved. The purpose of this discussion is to identify the different factors that may influence this process and to analyse which of them can be managed.

The Problem of Misunderstanding

As far as intercultural misunderstanding is concerned, the main cause seems to be the content of the relationship as much as the communication. More precisely, the relative incompatibility of the volunteers and local population is based on the different realities involved in the relationship. These different realities appear as a main obstacle to their efforts to cooperate. As displayed in table 4, the meaning each party gives to progress, as well as their interpretation of the project differs significantly: volunteers perceive extreme poverty and an urgent need to change things. Being paid under the minimum salary in their countries, they consider themselves as altruistic helpers ; and while local people are used to their situation and are attached to their way of life, the remuneration, called "indemnity", given to the volunteer is equal to the salary of a member of parliament. In view of this, the meaning given to volunteering appears uncertain: the altruism the volunteers try to assert becomes more or less unacceptable for the local people, as it refers to a pejorative interpretation of their situation and themselves. The role of "rescuer" the volunteers seek requires a "victim"; a part that local people are not ready to play (Berne, 1961). As a result, altruism is experienced as a form of condescendence. These intercultural differences (Hofstede, 1980 and d'Iribarne, 1993) are often difficult to identify as they remain «invisible» (Carrols, 1987), «hidden» (Hall, 1969). All these issues remain unspoken, causing irritation within the relationship.

The Process of Commitment

Authors such as Mowday, Porter and Steers (1982) have studied the evolution of commitment over the first months of a new job, discovering that the level of commitment on the first day is influenced by what they called commitment propensity, and that commitment on the first day was a good predictor of the commitment a few months later. Our research confirms this statement: volunteers often anticipate their commitment before their arrival, and this anticipated commitment and the commitment adjusted after a year are often similar in terms of level. Nevertheless, this research shows that many deep and important changes occur in between.

Table 4. Difference in interpretation

Meanings For the volunteer's	Words and Realities	Meanings For the population
Progress	<= change =>	Risk
Development	<= project =>	Money
Poverty	<= Africa =>	Wealth
Minimum salary	<= Indemnity =>	Money given for them
Volunteering	<= 800 dollars =>	Income of an Member of
Altruism	<= volunteering =>	??? – No meaning
Rescuer – victim	<= help =>	Condescendence
Varies / culture	<= Management =>	Superior – inferior
	<= leadership =>	Varies/ Culture

The main contribution of this research, as far as commitment, is concerned is the identification and conceptualisation of the time of doubts and confusion that often occur, as shown in figure 1, in between anticipated and then adjusted commitment. Confusion comes from the cohabitation of the initial anticipated commitment with a new commitment based on the actual experience. Confusion often leads to a general fall in commitment during which doubts overcome the contradictory feelings as well as negative bases, including the impression of "low alternatives" (Allen and Meyer, 1997, Penley and Gould, 1988). During this period, volunteers remain relatively unproductive, unable to focus their mind on their task, all their energy is being invested in wondering if he or she should stay or quit, considering the material but also the affective and normative investments that would be lost.

Freud (1917), Piaget (1926) and Watzlavick (1975) all stated that confusion is a condition for change in one's perception of reality. As far as volunteers are concerned, this time of confusion and doubt appears as normal, or at least a necessary step to adjust representations, feelings and then commitment to the situation actually experienced, to "let go", to mourn unrealistic expectations and prejudices. This reduction in the initial level of commitment effectively sometimes lead volunteers to resign (Bentein and al, 2005), but, for a very large majority, adjusted commitment returns to an intensity comparable with the level of commitment in the beginning. However, using a multidimensional approach such as Allen and Meyer's (1997), this adjusted commitment often appears to be more complex, including different and multiple bases and foci, introducing interactive effects similar to the ones recently studied in the literature (Gellatly and al, 2006; Vandenberghe, 2009). Adjusted commitment is also often more mature and more congruent (Rogers, 1961).

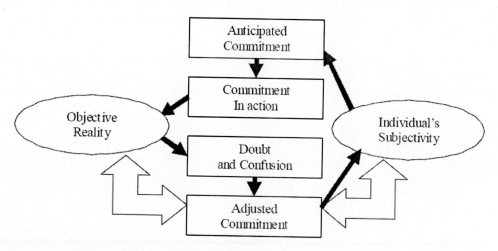

Figure 1. Process of commitment to the work situation.

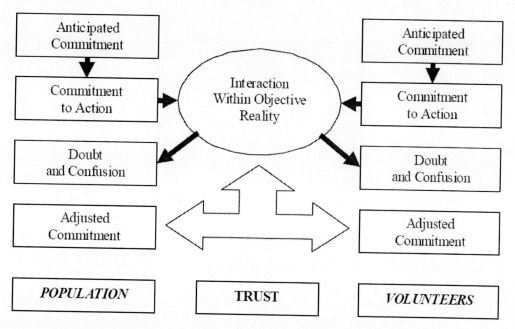

Figure 2. Process of trust and reciprocal commitment within the same work situation.

The Process of Mutual Commitment

In the context of development projects, both sides, volunteers and local people, experience the same commitment process. Most research looks at commitment in relation to the work situation. Some authors integrate commitment to foci such as the hierarchical superior (Stinghambern and al, 2002), but they don't study the other side of the relationship. This research emphasizes commitment as a bilateral relation between volunteers and individuals from the local population. Following this perspective, as displayed in the figure 2, the other's commitment becomes the reality with which he or she is confronted. The difference with figure 1 is that the confrontation with the environment including the "other" is more interactive. Both sides, volunteers and local people, have to build a *"modus vivendi"*. They have to find meanings and parts acceptable for both (Berne, 1961 ; Boltanski and Thevenot, 1991). If, as shown in table 4, the relationship does not match immediately, individuals may end up questioning their certainties as shown in figure 1. Nevertheless, they will eventually succeed in knowing and respecting each other better. As a result, trust may be at the end of the road.

5. MANAGING VOLUNTEERS' PROCESS OF COMMITMENT

The first aspect that could perhaps be managed is the recruitment process: the idea would be to select the individuals who are already more understanding or that present the best potential to open their minds to change (see figure 3). However, this research shows that the possibilities of identifying the right candidates for volunteering are limited as they haven't yet developed the qualities required. The experience of volunteering transforms the individual and it is hard to predict who is going to change and who is going to fail. Interviews show how the volunteers' personal development seems to vary a lot from one individual to another: people that may seem very conservative at first can change dramatically. On the other hand, some that appear more open minded at first will fail to adapt. Quantitative research may help to identify variables explaining these variations. Nevertheless, with regard to the difficulties mentioned above, some NGOs try to eliminate the most fragile profiles, using, for instance, tests of emotional stability. In addition to this pre-selection, Médecins Sans Frontières' strategy consists of sending out the maximum number of new volunteers to see which ones actually adapt.

The second aspect of volunteering that can be managed is pre-departure training. This includes preparing volunteers for cultural misunderstandings and helping them to get rid of their prejudices such as the idea of becoming a "rescuer". Throughout the last decades, NGOs have worked very hard in this area. The training developed often takes place over one or two weeks, where volunteers are generally isolated from the rest of the world. Some NGOs have developed very innovative training, including case studies, testimonies from both former volunteers and individuals from the local population who have worked with them, role play and theatre. The idea is to take volunteers as close as possible to the experience that awaits them. Our observations in the field suggest that volunteers trained in this way evolve better than the ones from NGOs that emphasize integration within the organization, rather than within the population. It could be interesting for volunteers to study the commitment process theorized in this article, showing them how they are going to change and how, in order to achieve this change they may go through doubts and disappointment.

The third level of action is the management of volunteers once they have arrived at their work destination. It is often believed that volunteers benefit from a lot of autonomy. In practice, this is only partially true: volunteers are first given a lot of autonomy, but this remains very conditional. When volunteers behave in a way incompatible with the NGO's values and goals, for instance, it is sometimes the case that volunteers refuse to comply with a decision of the organization, considering that it is contrary to the beneficiaries of their project toward which their commitment is targeted. Faced with such cases, the hierarchy can negotiate behavioural changes by threatening to send them back home. This control helps to deal with obviously inappropriate behaviour, but it can't really help when, as shown in this article, the difficulties lie within the volunteers' condescending attitudes.

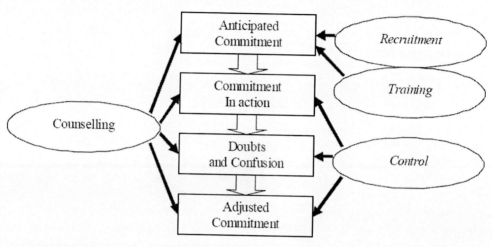

Figure 3. Managing the process of commitment.

CONCLUSION

Volunteers arrive in the field with an anticipated commitment often based on altruism and sometimes on prejudices: they want to give and help. On the other hand, many individuals from the local population experience their intervention as condescending, in fact, they often anticipate and fear it. As a result, the first contact between the two parties m is often confusing and disappointing, sometimes leading to embarrassment, wariness, mistrust or suspicion. This raises many questions about the organization of humanitarian projects: how to share decision making and leadership. Recruitment, training and management can help in many ways to limit the negative effects of the process, but they mainly serve as coaching tools as the commitment adjustment has to run its course. This research suggests that these periods of doubt and confusion are normal and necessary steps to rebuild more appropriate commitment, that will eventually lead to the trust needed to work together.

As in any qualitative research, this study may be complemented by quantitative data, confirming the models explored, and so move from a descriptive and interpretative to a more explanatory approach. However, the qualitative approach offers a specific insight into the commitment process, as it allows us to follow its whole course in detail. Nevertheless, a longitudinal quantitative study may confirm the existence of this period of doubt and negative commitment. Using Allen and Meyer's questionnaire, it could appear as a higher level of the "low alternative" dimension and as a lower level of the three other dimensions. Bentein and al

(2005) have shown that any reduction in the initial level of commitment, no matter how high it is, significantly predicts the turn over of personnel. However, we make the hypothesis that beyond this significant but still limited risk, the majority of individuals experiencing a period of weaker commitment stay in their job and their commitment eventually returns to its initial level.

Further research may also help to find out what, in our proposed model of the co-commitment process, and its passage through doubt, confusion and embarrassment, is specifically related to the Non-Profit Context and its issues it terms of altruism, and what can be extended to intercultural encounters in a business context. Globalisation may be increasing the connectivity and interdependence of the world's markets, but intercultural misunderstandings, and prejudices still affect business transaction and work relationship between so called "poor" and "rich" countries.

REFERENCES

Adler, P. A. and Adler, P. (1994). Observational Techniques, In N.K. Denzin and Lincoln S. Y., *Handbook of Qualitative Research*. London, UK: Sage.

Allen, N. J. and Meyer, J. P. (1997). *Commitment in the workplace: Theory, research, and application*, London, UK: Sage.

Archambault, E. (1996). *Le secteur sans but lucratif*. Paris, France: Economica.

Beauvois J. L., and Joule R. V. (1987) *Petit traité de manipulation à l'usage des honnêtes gens*. Grenoble, France : Presses Universitaires.

Becker, H. S. (1960). Notes on the concept of commitment. *American Journal of Sociology, 66*, 32-40.

Becker, T. E. (1992). Foci and bases of commitment: are they distinctions worth making ?. *Academy of Management Journal, 35(1),* 232-244.

Bentein, K., Vandenberg, R. J., Vandenberghe, C., and Stinglhamber, F. (2005). The role of change in the relationship between commitment and turnover: A latent growth modeling approach. *Journal of Applied Psychology, 90*, 468-482.

Berne, E. (1961). *Transactional analysis in psychotherapy: A systematic individual and social psychiatry*. New York, US: Grove Press.

Black, J.S., Gregersen, H. B., and Mendenhall, M. (1992). *Global Assignments: Successfully Expatriating and Repatriating International Managers*, San Francisco, US: Jossey-Bass.

Boltansly L., and Thevenot L. (1991) *De la justification, les économies des grandeurs*. Gallimard, trad Porter C., *On justification*. Princeton, US: University Press.

Carols, R. (1990). *Cultural Misunderstandings: The French-American Experience*. Chicago, US: University Press.

Cohen A, (2007), Commitment before and after: An evaluation and reconceptualization of organizational commitment, *Human Resource Management Review, 17(3)*, 336-354.

Conway, N., and Briner, R. (2005). *Understanding psychological contracts at work: A critical evaluation of theory and research*. Oxford: University Press.

Cook, J. D., Hepworth, S. J., Wall, T. D., and Warr P. B. (1981). *The Experience of Work*. London, UK: Academic Press.

Cooperrider, D. L., and Passmore, W. A. (1991). The Organization Dimension of Global Change. *Human Relation*, 44(8).

Deutsch, M. (1973). *The Resolution of Conflict*. Yale, UK: University Press.

D'Iribarne, P. (1993). *La logique de l'honneur*. Paris, France: Seuil.

Durkheim, E. (1915). *The Elementary Forms of the Religious Life*, New York, US: Free Press.

Etzioni, A. (1961). *A Comparative Analysis of Complex Organisations on Power, Involvement, and their Correlates*. Glencoe, US: The Free Press

Festinger, L. (1957). *A Theory of Cognitive Dissonance*. Evanston Row Peterson.

Freud, S. (1917). *Mourning and Melancholia. The Standard Edition of the Complete Psychological Works of Sigmund Freud. Standard Edition*.

Gambetta, D. (1990). *Can We Trust?*. London,UK: Blackwell.

Gellatly, I.R., Meyer, J.P., and Luchak, A.A. (2006). Combined effects of the three commitment components on focal and discretionary behaviors: A test of Meyer and Herscovitch's propositions. *Journal of Vocational Behavior, 69*, 331-345.

Glaser, B. and Strauss, A. (1967). *The discovery of grounded theory, strategies of qualitative research*. Chicago, US: Aldine Publishing Company.

Godelier, M. (1986). *Making of Great Men*. Cambridge, UK: University Press.

Goffman, E. (1961). *The presentation of self in everyday life*. New-York: Doubleday Anchor.

Golbeck, J. (2005). *A Definition of Trust for Computing with Social Networks*, University of Maryland, http://www.mindswap.org/papers/TrustDef.doc.

Guba, E. G., and Lincoln, S. Y. (1994). Competing paradigms in Qualitative Research, In Denzin N.K. and Lincoln S.Y., *Handbook of Qualitative Research*, London, UK: Sage.

Guinnane T.W. (2005) *Trust: a concept too many*, Yale University, http://www.econ.yale.edu/growth_pdf/cdp907.pdf

Hall, E. T. (1969). *The Hidden Dimension*. New-York, US: Anchor Books Editions.

Herbiniak, L. G., and Alutto, J. R. (1972). Personal and role-related factors in the development of organizational commitment. *Administrative Science Quarterly, 17*, 555-573.

Hofstede, G. (1980). *Culture's consequences: International differences in work-related values*. Londin, UK: Sage.

Huff, A. S. (1999). *Writing for Scholarly Publication*. London, UK: Sage.

Jones, J. B. (1995). *Globalization and interdependence in the international political economy London*. UK: Pinter.

Kanter, R. M. (1968). Commitment and social organization mechanisms in utopian communities. *American Sociological Review, 33*, 499-517.

Kanter, R. M., and Summers, D.V. (1987). Doing well while doing good, In W.W. Powell, *The Nonprofit Sector. A Research Handbook*. Yale, UK: University Press.

Kelman, H.C. (1959). Compliance, identification and internalization - three processes of attitude change. *Journal of Conflict Resolution, 2* , 51-60.

Laville, J. L., Sainsaulieu, R. (1997). *Sociologie de l'association*, Bruges, Belgium: Desclée de Brouwer.

Levi-Strauss C. (1958)*, Structural Anthropology*, Allen Lane.

MacGee, G.W. and Ford, R.C. (1987). Two (or more ?) dimensions of organizational commitment: re-examination of the affective and continuance commitment scale. *Journal of Applied Psychology, 72*, 638-441.

Meyer, J.P., and Herscovitch L. (2001). Commitment in the workplace: toward a general model. *Human Resource Management Review, 11*, 299-326.

Morrow, P. C. (1993), *The theory and measurement of work commitment*. Greenwich, US: JAI Press Inc.

Morse, J. M. (1994). Designing funded qualitative research. In N. K. Denzin and S. Y.Linclon, *Handbook of Qualitative Research*. Londin, UK: Sage.

Mowday, R. T., Porter, L. W., and Steers R. M. (1982). *Employee-organization linkages : the psychology of commitment , absenteeism and turnover*. London, UK: Academic Press.

O'Reilly, C. A., and Chatman, J. (1986). Organizational commitment and psychological attachement : the effect of compliance, identification and internlization on prosocial behaviour. *Journal of Applied Psychology, 71* , 492-499.

Penley, L. E., and Gould, S. (1988). Etzioni's model of organizational involvement. *Journal of Organizational Behavior, 9* , 43-59.

Pfeffer, J., and Salancick, G. R. (1978). A social information processing approach of job attitude and task design. *Administrative Science Quarterly, 23* , 224-253.

Piaget, J. (1926). *La représentation du monde chez l'enfant*. Paris, France: P.U.F.

Popper, K. (1934). *The Logic of Scientific Discovery*. London, UK: Huchingson

Powell, D. M. and Meyer, J. P., (2004). Side-bet theory and the three component model of organizational commitment. *Journal of Vocational Behavior, 65*, 157-177.

Reicher, A. E. (1985). A review and reconceptualization of organizational commitment. *Academy of Management Journal, 10(3)*, 465-476.

Rogers , C. R. (1961). *On becoming a person*. Houghton, US: Miffin Company.

Rousseau, D. M. (1995). *Psychological contracts in organizations: Understanding written and unwritten agreements*. London, UK: Sage.

Salamon, I. (1992). In search of nonprofit sector II, *Voluntas, 3(2)*, 267-311.

Staw, B. M. (1976). Knee-deep in the big muddy : a study of escalating commitment to a chosen course of action. *Organizational Behavior and Human Performance, 76*, 27-44.

Sztompka P. (1999), *Trust: A Sociological Theory,* Cambridge University Press.

Stinglhamber, F., Bentein, K., and Vandenberghe, C. (2002). *Extension of the three-component model of commitment to five foci: Development of measures and substantive test.* European Journal of Psychological Assessment, 18, *123-138.*

Valéau, P. (2004). *Gérer l'implication dans le respect des différences : des associations L1901 aux autres organisations*, Habilitation à Diriger les Recherches. Lille1. www.valeau.com.

Watzlavick P. J., Weakland, R., and Fisch, H. (1975). *Change, Principles of Problems Formation and Problem Resolution.* New-York, US: Norton.

Vandenberghe, C, and Bentein, K. (2009, In Press). A closer look at the relationship between affective commitment to supervisors and organizations and turnover. *Journal of Occupational and Organizational Psychology.*

Wiener, Y. (1982). Commitment in organization : a normative view. *Academy of Management Review*, 7. 418-428.

Yin, R. K. (1984). *Case study research: Design and methods.* Beverly Hill, US: Sage.

In: Trust, Globalisation and Market Expansion
Editors: J-M. Aurifeille, C. Medlin and C. Tisdell

ISBN 978-1-60741-812-2
© 2009 Nova Science Publishers, Inc.

Chapter 12

Consumers' Global Attitude and Perception of Brand's Globalness

Jacques-Marie Aurifeille[1], Jaime Gil Lafuente[2], Melissa Caid[3] and Stéphane Manin[3]
[1]University of French Polynesia, France
[2]University of Barcelona, Spain
[3]University of La Réunion, France

Abstract

The paper focuses on the relationship between the perceived brand globalness and the consumers' global attitude towards this brand. First, the concept of perceived brand globalness and the hypotheses concerning its relationship with the consumers' global attitude are presented. Next, an experimental study is presented which is based on the attitudes of consumers before and after exposition to an advertisement stressing the globalness of a car brand. Results of this exploratory analysis indicate that consumers are sensitive to the globalness of a brand and that their perceived brand globalness can have an important and a positive effect on their global attitude towards the brand.

Keywords: Globalisation, Attitude, Global Attitude, Brand Globalness, Country of Origin.

1. Introduction

The global attitude of consumers towards a brand, meaning to what degree they appreciate the brand, is currently related to their perception of the brands' features. Since Fishbein's "multi-attribute model of attitude" (Fishbein and Ajzen, 1975) much research has been made to identify the relevant attributes and how they are perceived. One of the most frequently considered attributes is the "country of origin" (COO). It was studied in a large number of papers, thus enabling meta-analyses (Peterson and Jolibert, 1999). However, the importance of the COO attribute remains a source of discussion. Some authors consider that globalisation boosts the importance of the COO (Haubl, 1998, Baker and Ballington, 2002) while other authors point at the success of brands from Asian countries perceived until recently as producing lower quality products (Nakra, 2006). In both cases, globalisation appears to be a key element in the perception of the brands and the global attitude toward theses brands (Roth, 1995a and 1995b).

The impact of globalisation on brand management has been mostly addressed to determine whether a firm should opt for an international or a global strategy, which is choosing between adapting to the specificities of the countries or using a same positioning and segmentation for all the countries (Aurifeille and Quester, 2002). The corresponding works, however, do not raise the question of how consumers perceive the firm's choice of a global strategy and react to it? Indeed, as evidenced by the emergence of a global attitude of people towards globalisation (Manin, 2006), the globalisation phenomena is sufficiently manifest and important to generate perceptions about how much a firm is involved in it. A similitude may be found with other socio-economic variables whose political importance emphasized new dimensions of consumers' brand perception. For instance, for many consumers, ecology has become a dominant factor of the perception of cars and washing powders. Similarly, the perception of some shoes and clothes brands has been tarnished by the use of child labor (World, 2002; Lopez-Calva, 2001). In both cases, globalization was often accused of being the determinant factor of ecological and human right abuses. More generally, the perception of brand globalness should be either positive or negative, depending on the perception of globalisation itself. While some consumers would associate globalness with modernity, openness and power; others could consider that a global brand is a threat for their cultural diversity and freedom of choice, not to mention a generator of unemployment via outsourcing. Therefore, PBG could play a major role in the success of the positioning and segmentation strategies.

The aim of the present paper is to shed some light on the effect of PBG on the consumers' global attitude towards the brand. Being causal, this hypothesis implies an experiment to change the PBG of a brand and to test whether it is correlated with a change in the consumers' global attitude towards the brand. If a significant association is observed, both the hypothesis of the existence of a structured perception of brand globalness (PBG) and the hypothesis that it affects the global attitude will not be rejected. In this experiment, it would be most useful to rely on a measure of the PBG, that is: on a latent factor with valid and reliable indicators of which the consumers are aware. Unfortunately such a measure does not exist. The only measurement proposed concerns brand globalisation (Hsieh, 2002) and consumers' attitude towards globalisation (Manin, 2006). Therefore the experiment had to be designed differently and assess indirectly the effects of PBG.

2. THE EXPERIMENTAL STUDY

As in any empirical study about brands, a category of products must be chosen. Three considerations have guided this choice. First, the brand should belong to a category of products with different apparent levels of globalisation. Second, a stimulus is required to modify experimentally the perception of brands' globalness. Third, as an indication of the external validity of the choice, the product category should have formerly been considered in COO studies. The three criteria led to two possibilities: the car industry and the distribution sector. The car industry was finally chosen because previous research on the COO had indicated that a strong summary effect prevailed in consumers' choice of a car: because cars are complex products, consumers tend to refer to the country of origin as a global indication of the benefits they expect. This choice also means the effect of PBG should less significantly emerge. In addition, more elaborate experimental stimulus were available in the car industry, thus enabling more attitudinal response. A three minute video clip was finally chosen because it promoted explicitly the globalness of a car maker : Renault-Nissan. This advertisement concerned a new car, the Logan, emphasizing that it was conceived for all kinds of passengers all over the world and was built in Rumania by Renault's owned local maker, Dacia,

In addition to the message, the advertisement comprised visuals and sounds that could be perceived in other terms than brand globalness and also influence the watcher's global attitude. To control these effects, a large sampling of the perceptual criteria had to be made. Various lists of criteria were available, for instance in the NCBS (New Car Buyer Surveys) and NVES (New Vehicle Experience Studies) of the main car brands. The meta-analyses derived from the works on the COO could also provide a list of criteria. However, these lists differ, and their relative sampling adequacy was not tested in a global context. Moreover they are not transposable to the study of other product categories. Therefore, it was decided to choose the items proposed by Hsieh (2002) to overcome these shortcomings. First, Hsieh's list of items results from international data. Second, it is aimed at identifying universal perceptual dimensions, thus providing a sampling of variables whose relevance should go beyond the car market. Third, the discriminant and convergent validity of these universal dimensions was successfully tested with the perceptual attributes of cars (table 1)

Table 1. List of the Perceptual Items and Latent Dimensions

Dimension	Items
Sensory	Exciting
	Fun to drive
	Good acceleration
	Stylish
	Sporty
Symbolic	Luxurious
	Prestigious
Utilitarian	Made to last
	Reliable
	Safe in accident
Economic	Fuel saver
	Well serviced

Source: Hsieh (2002).

Hiseh's twelve items were measured using seven point bipolar semantic scales. The global attitude towards Renault was measured in the same way, with a single scale ranging from: "I dislike this brand" to "I like this brand". A convenience sample of 150 respondents was submitted twice to the questionnaire about their perception and their global attitude concerning Renault. Between the two interrogations, the respondents were exposed one time to the advertisement about the Logan.

3. Methodology of the Data Analysis

As a reference, we are using the linear attitude model (Fishbein and Ajzen, 1975. According to this well-known model, the global attitude is predicted by a linear combination of the perceptions of the items. Two models are then to be fit: M_b predicts the global attitude before the advertisement and M_a predicts it after the advertisement.

For the sake of comparability, robustness and generality (cf. Section 2), the predictors are the latent perceptual dimensions. First the common dimensions of the before and after perceptions are identified jointly with a principal component analysis (PCA). Next, each dimension is separated into a predictor before the advertisement and a predictor after the advertisement. This is done by adding the corresponding items after weighting them with their loadings in the common PCA.

If the global attitude is only influenced by Hsieh's perceptual factors, the residuals e_b and e_a of the regression models M_b and M_a should be random. Conversely, if a specific PBG effect exists, the residuals of M_a should translate its influence. Then, the difference $e_b - e_a$ should be significantly correlated with the general attitude after the advertisement: GA_a and its sign would indicate if the impact of the PBG on the global attitude is positive or negative.

Before testing the hypothesis, an additional precaution must be taken to control a bias often met in attitude models. Actually, although modelled as "independent", the consumers' perceptions can be affected by the global attitude through a so-called "halo effect" (Aurifeille, 1991; Beckwith and Lehmann, 1975). In such case, if a change in the PGB influences the global attitude, it also influences the perceptions. Therefore, the residual ea would not translate all of the PBG effect resulting from the advertisement. The many works published on the halo effect are based on the consensus that a very positive global attitude may bias all perceptions upwardly (Holbrook and Huber, 1979). However, there is no clear definition of what is "very positive". Other important issues about the halo are still unclear, eg: is the effect multiplicative or additive, does it affect all perceptions in the same manner? In addition, the outer reference needed to identify the elements of a simultaneous effect was never defined satisfactorily. For example, the average of the perceptions, sometimes proposed as an indicator of the "true" perception scores, is also biased by the halo affecting all scores. As a result many solutions have been proposed to filter the halo with no clear winner (Beckwith and Lehmann, 1976).

The filtering method proposed in this paper relies on Aurifeille's observation that the halo effect should not modify the order in which the perception scores are ranked, whatever the multiplicative or additive effect and whatever the effect is similar or dissimilar for all perceptions (Aurifeille, 1999). This means the coefficients of a rank-order regression of the perceptions on the global attitude should not be biased by a halo effect.

Therefore, according to the test proposed above, the hypothesis of a specific influence of the PBG on the global attitude will be rejected if the difference of the residuals is not significantly correlated with the global attitude after the advertisement: $p(k(e_a - e_b, GA_a) > 0.05$, where e_b and e_a are respectively the residuals of the ordinal regression models M_a and M_b.

4. DATA ANALYSIS

The principal component analysis of the perceptions before and after the advertisement produced four latent dimensions. After a varimax rotation, a structure similar to Hsieh's was identified (table 2).

Table 2. Kendall's Correlation Coefficients of the 4 Perceptual Dimensions

	Sensory	Symbolic	Utilitarian	Economic
Sensory	1			
Symbolic	0.127	1		
Utilitarian	0.166	0.052	1	
Economic	0.36	0.002	0.188	1

The two ordinal regression models Mb and Ma were estimated using Lisrel 8 (Jöreskog and Sörbom, 1996). The Pearson's and Kendall's coefficients of correlation between the difference of the residuals, $d_e = e_b - e_a$, and the global attitude after the advertisement, GA_a, are indicated in table 3.

Table 3. Test of the Hypothesis

Method	Coefficient	Probability of no correlation
Pearson	0,3356	0,000
Kendall	0,2031	0,000

Following the methodology presented in section 3, these result indicate that:

- The hypothesis that a PBG effect was induced by the advertisement cannot be rejected
- The PBG effect appears to be positive: after exposition to an advertisement stressing the brand globalness, the global attitude of the consumers changed independently from the predictors used to model this attitude. This specificity of the PBG differentiates it from a convenience criterion that would be used for summarizing other criteria. Compared to the studies about the COO of the cars, this observation suggests that the PBG should not be considered as just an extension of the "country of origin" criterion
- The PBG effect appears to be important : explaining nearly 10% of the global attitude, as measured by the squared Pearson's correlation coefficient.

CONCLUSION

This preliminary research has been limited by two problems. One was the lack of a scale measuring consumers' perceived brand globalness (PBG). Should this scale exist, the study of a specific PBG effect could be completed by accounting for the interactions between the PBG and the other perceptual criteria. The other problem was the absence of a theoretical model describing how the PBG influences the global attitude. Should this model exist, a structural equation model could be used to test the causality. Thus, the limitations of the experimentation would be overcome. Until then, the positive effect of PBG on the global attitude towards a car brand cannot be generalized to any product category.

Beyond these methodological issues, the results obtained do not only draw attention on the emergence of a specific variable: the perceived globalness of a brand. They also confirm that perceptual variables remotely linked to direct benefits may play a role in consumers' decisions. Hence, globalisation is not just a strategic decision of which consumers are unaware; managers should analyse its influence on the perception of their globalising brands and advertise accordingly.

REFERENCES

Aurifeille, J.M. and Quester, P. (2002). Global vs international involvement-based segmentation: a cross-national exploratory study, *International Marketing Review, vol. 19*, 369-386.

Baker, M.J. and Ballington, L. (2002). Country of Origin as a Source of Competitive Advantage, *Journal of Strategic Marketing* (10), 157-168.

Beckwith, N.E. and Lehmann, O.R. (1975). The importance of Halo Effect in Muti-attribute Attitude Models, *Journal of Marketing Research* (12), 265-275.

Beckwith, N.E. and Lehmann, O.R. (1976). Halo Effects in Multi-Attribute Attitude Models: An Appraisal of Some Unresoved Issues, *Journal of Marketing Research* (13), 418-421.

Fishbein, M. and Ajzen, I. (1975). *Belief, attitude, intention and behaviour: An introduction to theory and research*. Reading, Mass.: Addison-Wesley.

Haubl, G. (1998). Resolving a paradox: why country-of-origin effect may be stronger than ever, *European Advances in Consumer Research, vol. 3,* 147-148.

Holbrook, M.B. and Hubert, J. (1979). Separating Perceptual Dimensions from Affective Overtones, *Journal of Consumer Research* (5), 272-283.

Hsieh, M. (2002). Identifying Brand Image Dimensionality and Measuring the degree of brand Globalisation: A Cross-National Study. *Journal of International Marketing*, 46- 67.

Jöreskog, K.G. and Sörbom, D. (1996). *Lisrel 8*, Chicago, USA: Scientific Software International.

Lopez-Calva, L.F. (2001). *Child labor: myths, theories and facts, Journal of International Affairs*, 22 September 2001.

Manin, S. (2006). A structural model of consumer's sensitivity to globalisation. In: J.M. Aurifeille, C. Tisdell and S. Svizzero (Eds), *Globalization and Partnerships: Features of Business Alliances and International Cooperation* (167-178). New-York, USA: Nova Science Publishers.

Motameni, R. and Shahrokhi, M. (1998). Brand equity valuation : a global perspective, *Journal of Product and Brand Management, vol.7* (4), 275-290.

Nakra P. (2006). Should You Care About Country of Origin Impact? http://www.i-b-t.net/anm/templates/trade_article.asp?articleid=218andzoneid=3.

Peterson, A. and Jolibert, J. (1995). A Meta-Analysis of Country-of-Origin, *Journal of International Business Studies, vol. 26* (4), 883-896.

Roth, M.S. (1995 a). The Effect of Culture and Socio-economics on the Performance of Global Brand Image Strategies, *Journal of Marketing Research, vol.32,* 163-175.

Roth, M.S. (1995 b). Effects of Global Market Conditions on Brand Image Customization and Brand Performance, *Journal of Advertising, Vol.24, N°4.*

World section (2002). *Nike's dilemma: Is doing the right thing wrong? A child labor dispute could eliminate 4,000 Pakistani jobs.* The Christian Science Monitor, 22 December 2002.

In: Trust, Globalisation and Market Expansion
Editors: J-M. Aurifeille, C. Medlin and C. Tisdell
ISBN 978-1-60741-812-2
© 2009 Nova Science Publishers, Inc.

Chapter 13

THE EFFECTS OF PERCEIVED BRAND GLOBALNESS ON BRAND TRUST

Magali Debat[*]

The Franco-Australian Centre for International Research in Management,
University of La Réunion, France

ABSTRACT

The main purpose of our research was to answer this simple but essential question: Does the fact that a brand is perceived as more or less global influence the level of trust consumers have in it? Our second goal was to explain the mechanism: identifying the reasons why perceived brand globalness can generate trust or distrust.

However, we found a total absence of data to test the impact of brand globalness on trust: Despite several research works carried out in the field of global brands, none had clearly defined the concept. To the best of our knowledge, no satisfying (validated) scale of measurement of the degree of globalness has been developed. The first thing we had to do was therefore to clarify the concept of brand globalness and propose a validated scale of measurement. Brand research and managerial practice have nothing to gain from the present stage of conceptual confusion concerning global brands.

Keywords: Global brand, Trust, Perceived brand globalness measurement.

1. INTRODUCTION

These last centuries have witnessed the development of telecommunications and transport, together with the increase and democratization of consumption. This has lead to increasing economic exchanges between countries. In older days people used to consume products manufactured in their surroundings and had to satisfy themselves with the local

---

[*] Doctoral student supervised by Prof. J-M. Aurifeille and Dr. S. Manin

offer. Nowadays, the most isolated populations can have access to products provided by regions from all over the world.

Indeed, to develop their values, brands have spread throughout the globe to become "global brands". The present study aims at understanding if the fact that the consumed brand is a global brand impacts on the behaviour of consumers. More precisely, this study examines whether the degree of globalness of the brand has an effect on the degree to which the brand is trusted by consumers, a key element in the purchase (Romaniuk and Bogomolova, 2005). Hiscock (2001) says that "the ultimate goal of marketing is to generate an intense bond between the consumer and the brand, and the main ingredient of this bond is trust".

Yet, different types of effects of the degree of globalness of a brand have been observed. Holt et al. (2004) demonstrate that, to explain the *preference* for a brand, the impact of the variable "degree of perceived globalness of the brand" is three times more intense than the variable "country of origin". Batra et al. (2000) observe that the degree of perceived brand origin (local or nonlocal) has a significant, positive effect on brand attitudes. This indicates that the more a brand is seen as non-local, the more positive the *attitudes* towards it are.

Kapferer (1992, 2004), Shocker, Srivastava, and Ruekert (1994) find that perceived brand globalness can create consumer perceptions of brand superiority. Since quality is highly related to brand preference, this can explain why consumers prefer brands that they perceive as more global (Holt, Quelch, and Taylor, 2004; Steenkamp, Batra, and Alden, 2003). In addition to quality, global brands are associated to *high prestige or status* (Batra et al., 2000; Kapferer, 1992). Other studies show that prestige is the second factor driving global brand preference (Holt, Quelch and Taylor, 2004; Steenkamp, Batra and Alden, 2003). Nevertheless, contradictory results have been found and it seems that there is no intrinsic consumer preference for global brands (De Mooij, 1998).

To test the impact of brand globalness on trust, we faced a considerable problem: although several studies had been carried out in the field of global brands, no one had clearly defined the concept. No satisfying (validated) scale of measurement of the degree of globalness had been developed. Thus, it appeared necessary to clarify the concept of brand globalness and to propose a validated scale of measurement.

The chapter is structured as follows: In the first section we give an overview of the concepts of "global brand" and "trust". Then we present our hypotheses and our study, carried out in two stages: validation of brand globalness and measurement of the impact of brand globalness on the degree of trust the brand inspires. In the last section, we show our results, the conclusions drawn, the managerial implications and the limits of the present research.

2. THEORETICAL BACKGROUND AND CONCEPTS

Before examining the relationship between Trust and Brand Globalness, the primary concern of marketers will be to better understand these two concepts. We propose to review the literature on the two terms: their definitions, role in consumer behaviour and indicators.

Brand Trust

Although trust has widely been studied in business and social literature, this has not led to a consensus on the way the construct is to be apprehended (Guibert, 1999; Bramall, et al., 2004). To date, no universal definition of trust has been accepted. Thousands of definitions can be found on brand trust—just about one definition by researcher interested in the subject. Despite this lack of agreement, Sitkin and Barclay (1997) identify two main conceptions of the concept in the literature. The first conception is psychological: expectation from the brand. The second is behavioural: risk taking or simply behaving in a certain way. The main gap between these two tenets is that, in the first one, trust is reduced to the only psychological dimension (the behavioural dimension is not considered) whereas the second conception of brand trust is exclusively perceived as behavioural.

Trust seen as a psychological concept refers to presumption (Bidault and Jarillo, 1995; Gurviez and Korchia, 2002), expectation (Sirdeshmukh, Singh and Sabol, 2002) or a belief concernig the brand (Anderson and Weitz, 1989; Anderson and Narus, 1990; Ganesan, 1994; Sirieix and Dubois, 1999). This concept is three-pronged, with a cognitive dimension, an affective dimension and the perceived level of integrity (Ganesan, 1994; Gurviez, 1999).

- The cognitive dimension refers to all the information that has been accumulated on the brand by the consumer. This set of knowledge on the brand would represent the raw materials to construct the belief that the brand is or is not an expert, is or is not credible (capable to fit the expected level of performance). In short, from his/her past experiences with the brand, the consumer evaluates to what extent the brand is trustworthy.
- The second dimension (affective dimension) refers to the belief that the brand is principally involved in the wellbeing of the consumer, that the brand is benevolent and consumer-oriented. Its priority is consumer satisfaction, not its own interests.
- The third, integrity, refers to respect of the brand's promises. In short, it consists in evaluating the level of honesty of the brand.

Trust in the Consumer-Brand Relationship

The level of trust is thought to be one of the key elements of any relationship or exchange between parties (Romaniuk and Bogomolova, 2005). It seems to be a useful construct to explain and predict the quality of the relationship. It has been suggested that brand trust increases brand *loyalty* (Chaudhuri and Holbrook, 2001), has a significant impact on the level of *satisfaction* about retail stores (Chaudhuri and Ray, 2003) and on the level of *value* thought to be possessed by the brand (Sirdeshmukh, Sing and Sabol, 2002).

According to Delgado, et al. (2003), brand trust influences consumer *commitment,* which in turn impacts on the customers' *price tolerance* towards the brand.

Brands enjoying higher levels of trust are more *accessible* to consumers and, thus, will be recalled early. Since brand recall has been found to be positively related to brand choice (Alba, Hutchinson, and Lynch, 1990), the likelihood of brands enjoying higher trust levels—and high recall levels—being chosen by consumers should be higher than that of less trusted competitive brands. However, some authors have questioned this. Ambler (1997) considers the correlation between perceived trustworthiness and a brand's market share to be attributed to the time that a company successfully performed in the market. Trust is considered to be the most important attribute a brand can possess. For example, along with honesty, fairness or excellence, trust has been called one of the fundamental consumer needs in the financial services market (Romaniuk and Bogomolova, 2005).

Finally, trust is an attribute commonly incorporated into brand equity/health measures. Competing brands are then compared on their trust records and assessed in terms of brand performance, based on the level of trust in relation to competitors (Romaniuk and Bogomolova, 2005).

Brand Trust Antecedents

Thanks to the proliferation of studies on the subject, a large number of antecedent variables have been identified. Some are directly related to the partner (the firm), some to the consumer, some to the brand, and some to the relationship between the parties.

Concerning the potential variables directly related to the firm, the following have been identified:

— firm repute (Anderson and Weitz, 1989);
— firm size (Doney and Cannon, 1997). This refers to the firm's physical size and market share;
— the opportunistic character of the firm. Trust and Opportunism are considered as opposite constructs (Morgan and Hunt, 1994). If one partner supposes that the other party could engage in an opportunistic behaviour (behaviour oriented toward its own interests), it will fear that its partner could break its promises. The partner therefore cannot be considered reliable.
— partner's dependence level (Anderson and Narus, 1990; Ganesan, 1994). It can be defined as the need for a firm to maintain the relationship in order to reach its goals (Frazier, 1983).

Potential variables directly related to the consumer:

— The degree of familiarity with the partner (Gurviez, 1999; Sirieix and Dubois, 1999; Gefen, 2000; Kennedy, Ferell and Leclair, 2001). Familiarity refers to the amount of experience with the brand accumulated by the consumer (Alba, Hutchinson and Lynch, 1987).
— The innate tendency to be confident.

Potential variables directly related to the brand:

— Brand image (Sirieix and Dubois, 1999). However, this assumption has not been tested.
— Perceived quality of products (Kennedy, Ferell and Leclair, 2001).

Potential variables directly related to the relationship:

– Duration of relationship (Anderson and Weitz, 1989; Doney and Cannon, 1997). The longer the relationship, the more confident the parties.
– Amount of information shared (level of communication between the parties) (Anderson and Weitz, 1989; Anderson and Narus, 1990; Morgan and Hunt, 1994; Selnes, 1998).
– Amount of values shared (Morgan and Hunt, 1994; Gurviez, 1999).
– Level of satisfaction obtained from the relationship (Crosby, Evans and Crowles, 1990; Sirieix and Dubois, 1999). Being satisfied from past experiences with the brand impacts the degree a consumer trusts the brand. However, other literature suggests that the relationship between the two constructs is opposite. It is because the consumer is satisfied that he/she is trustful to the brand (Anderson and Narus, 1990).
– Amount of investments required for the existence of the relationship (Ganesan 1994). The more costly the birth of the relationship was, the more dependent the parties. The relationship is perceived as more stable. The amount of investment engaged in the relationship is seen as a proof of the desire to engage in the relationship.

What is quite surprising when studying this list of antecedents is our ignorance about the variables related to the characteristics of the brand. Few researchers have tried to explain the level of brand trust in direct consideration of the partner (brand). However, this lacuna could be explained by two main reasons:

(1) Through our personal experiences, we know that some partners inspire more trust than others. We evaluate them on the basis of what they say, how they say it, how they behave (manners, look) and/or what they wear. These indicators are taken into account to give partners credit for their trustworthiness. To us, trust first depends on the evaluation of the partner through indicators that have not yet been identified in the field of brand trust.
(2) These variables directly related to the partner are much more controllable than those related to the firm, the consumer and the relationship.

Degree of Globalness of the Brand

In our market, one characteristic of the brand can appear to the consumer: its degree of perceived globalness. Research has demonstrated that this element is taken into account by consumers when evaluating the brand. It could have a significant impact on *attitude* (three aspects are concerned: beliefs, preference and purchase). Batra, et al. (2000) observe that the degree of perceived brand origin (local or nonlocal) has a significant positive effect on brand attitudes, indicating that the more a brand is seen as nonlocal, the more positive are the attitudes towards that brand.

This can be explained by the fact that perceived brand globalness could create consumer perceptions of *brand superiority* (Kapferer, 1992, 2004; Shocker, Srivastava and Ruekert, 1994). Research also confirms that *quality* is among the most important factors that drive consumer preference for global brands (Holt, Quelch, and Taylor, 2003; Steenkamp, Batra, and Alden, 2003). In addition to quality, international and global brands have been associated with *high prestige or status* (Batra, et al., 2000; Kapferer, 1992). Recent empirical studies have demonstrated that prestige is the second factor driving global brand preference (Holt, Quelch, and Taylor, 2003; Steenkamp, Batra and Alden, 2003). However, some studies have shown that consumers may prefer brands perceived as more local. De Mooij (1998) argues that there is no intrinsic consumer preference for international and global brands.

It is worth noticing that, in the results communicated by Schuiling and Kapferer (2004), what significantly differentiates local brands from international brands is the degree of trustworthiness and reliability credited to the brands (p < .05). Nevertheless, no research has tried to go thoroughly into the understanding of this phenomenon. Understanding the relationship between brand globalness and brand trust in an environment where brands constantly spread throughout the world could help brand managers. Would it be favourable for the brand to highlight the fact that it is local or global?

Since trust constitutes the key element in the purchase (Romaniuk and Bogomolova, 2005), it would be interesting to consider:

(1) Whether the degree of globalness of a brand impacts on the degree of trust the brand inspires;
(2) How this works (if a significant impact is revealed).

The first obstacle we faced in our study was the inexistence of a satisfying and validated scale of the degree of brand globalness. Although the subject was explored by some researchers, "there has been no agreement regarding the way the degree of brand globalization should be measured". (Kapferer, 1991; Hsieh, 2001). According to Johansson and Ronkainen (2005), "the stickiest problem seems to be the difficulty of defining exactly what is 'global' and what is not".

Concerning the existing scales, the main drawbacks were their lack of universality (see the scale of Batra, et al., 2000), their unidimensionality that did not allow us to grasp the elements used to evaluate the level of globalness of a brand (see the scales of Batra, et al., 2000; Johansson et al., 2003). The last flaw of the existing scales was that none had been confirmed. An exploratory study of Holt, Quelch and Taylor (2004) carried out to examine the concept in great depth suggested that the concept had 4 dimensions: Quality signal, Global myth, Social responsability and American values. However, their study presents weaknesses:

− The frequency of the items was used for the determination of the dimensions;
− No scale was proposed (no items were proposed to determine the dimensions).

3. THE PROBLEM

Our main goal was to test if the fact that a brand is seen as more or less global has an impact on the degree of trust it inspires. Our first task was to identify the variables to be integrated into the causal model:

- For brand trust, we adopted a scale developed by Gurviez and Korchia (2002). Brand trust is divided into three dimensions: credibility, integrity and benevolence;
- For brand globalness, no satisfying scale was proposed, so we had to develop one.

Given the scarcity of research on brand globalness, we had to carry out a qualitative study first. This study aimed at identifying the items of the construct and the brand perceptions driven by the concept.

Qualitative Research

A qualitative study through an open-question questionnaire was conducted in order to gain an understanding of the range of items contained in the concept of brand globalness. It also helped our understanding of the perceptions that differenciate a global brand from a local brand. Data were collected from a convenience sample of 32 adults. The most frequent reponses were integrated in the quantitative questionnaire.

4. DATA ANALYSIS AND RESULTS FOR THE DEVELOPMENT OF THE SCALE

Perceived Brand Globalness Scale

In the qualitative questionnaire, we identified the indicators taken into account by the consumers to evaluate the degree of globalness of a brand. Then, we integrated the most frequent ones in a quantitative questionnaire (156 respondents, randomly chosen) to explore the concept (through a principal component analysis). The study focused on one brand only (Nivea). The reason is that it was more convenient to study one sole brand. We chose Nivea because we observed much disagreement on the level of local/globalness when analysing the qualitative questionnaire. To make sure data are not distributed at random and belong to the same semantic field, we carried out two tests on the 12 items: the KMO and Bartlett tests (Table 1).

The results of these tests allowed us to conduct a principal component analysis. For that purpose we used the principal component method (the dimensions found were composed of more homogeneous elements). Before, we made sure that the variables had data distributed normally around their means (see the Skewness and Kurtosis test table in the appendix I).

This PCA extracted three factors, with the first explaining 34.765% of the variance, the second explaining an additional 11.486%, and a third explaining and additional 8.526%. Cronbach's Alpha for the twelve-item perceived brand globalness scale was .8131, above the acceptable value. Then a confirmatory analysis was carried out to confirm the structure of the scale.

Table 1. The KMO and Bartlett tests

Indice KMO et test de Bartlett

Mesure de précision de l'échantillonnage de Kaiser-Meyer-Olkin.		,843
Test de sphéricité de Bartlett	Khi-deux approché	424,954
	ddl	66
	Signification	,000

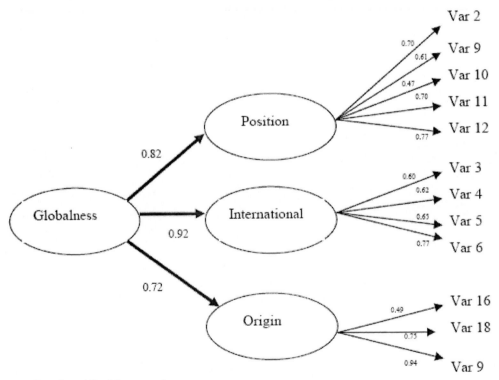

Source: Developed for this research.

Figure 1. Structure of Perceived Brand Globalness (coefficients).

All t-values are above 2. The confirmatory analysis confirms previous results. The dimensions retained are significant in terms of Fit (RMR = 0.094; AGFI = 0.93; CFI = 0.96) and there is valid convergence and discrimination.

The first dimension is represented by five items, viz. the fact that:

Table 2. Factorial Matrix of the First Dimension of Perceived Brand Globalness

No. in Path Diagram	Position
2	- the brand is more or less known throughout the world
9	- the brand's products are more or less consumed
10	- the number of employees is more or less high
11	- the brand's turnover is more or less high
12	- the brand is more or less a leader in its market

The second dimension contains four items, viz. the fact that:

Table 3. Factorial Matrix of the Second Dimension of Perceived Brand Globalness

No. in Path Diagram	International
3	- local/international stars endorse the brand
4	- the brand sponsors local/international events
5	- the languages used in its advertisements are foreign languages
6	- the brand can be found everywhere in the world

The third dimension is represented by three items, viz. the fact that:

Table 4. Factorial Matrix of the third dimension of Perceived Brand Globalness

N° in Path Diagram	Origin
16	- the brand is owned by a firm that is more or less international
18	- the origin of the products is local or not
19	- the origin of brand is local or not

It seems that the first dimension refers to the structural and commercial importance of the brand, the second to the degree of "internationalness" of the brand and the third to its origins (foreign-sourced brand, products and firm). The scale appears in the Appendix II.

Our Hypotheses

The main purpose of our research was to study the influence of the degree of perceived globalness of the brand on the degree of trust the brand inspires.

To reach that goal, we had to insert a scale that made it possible to measure the degree of brand trust. We used the scale developped by Gurviez and Korchia (2002). However, we simplified it by merging its three original dimensions into one and we kept only 4 items (those that significantly explain the degree of trust in the brand through a regression analysis). Cronbach's Alpha for the four-item perceived brand globalness scale was .7140, above the acceptable value. Table 5 presents these items and their betas for the regression explaining the direct question on the degree of trust in the considered brand:

Table 5. Items Determining the Level of Brand Trust

No. in Path Diagram		Standadized betas	Sig
34	Its products present no danger	.243	.000
36	The brand always holds its promises	.264	.000
38	The brand is sincere	.185	.015
40	The brand shows interest for its users	.253	.000
	BETA	.778	.009
R² = 0.491			

The performed regression analysis succeeded in assessing the nomological framework.

Once the Perceived Brand Globaness' dimensions were identified, we used them directly to study how they were related to the concept of Brand Trust.

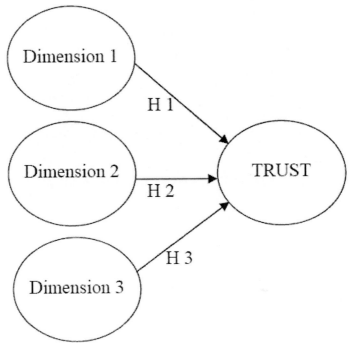

Source: Developed for this research.

Figure 2. The tested causal model.

Our hypotheses were the following:

Given the lack of research that examines brand globalness and our antecedent findings, we propose intuitively-made hypotheses. These are:

H1: The bigger the structure of a brand is perceived, the more trust the brand inspires.

H2: The more international the brand seems, the more trust the brand inspires.

H3: The more non-French a brand is perceived, the less trust the brand inspires.

5. DATA ANALYSIS AND RESULTS FOR THE RELATIONSHIP BETWEEN PERCEIVED BRAND GLOBALNESS AND TRUST

The Causal Analysis

A confirmatory factor analysis was run on the 4 constructs. The fit indexes were acceptable (Chi2 for independance model with 120 ddl = 1278.52; CFI = .93; GFI = .93; root mean square error [RMSEA] = 0.071). Path coefficients for all indicators were significant and above .20. Coefficient alphas for all constructs were above .80 (exept Origin with .4843).

The following figure depicts a conceptual model with the four latent constructs that are based on items shown in the Appendix II.

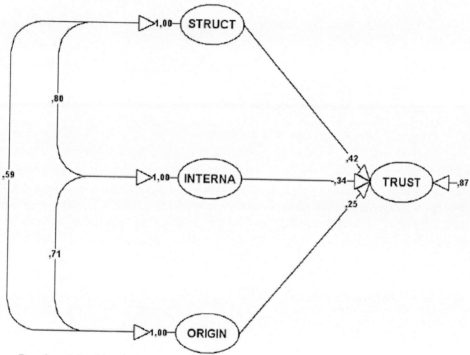

Source: Developed for this research.

Figure 3. The final causal model.

Table 6. Summary of the hypothesis tests

Hypothesis	Unstandardized structural coefficients	T-values
H1: Structural and commercial size to brand trust	.42	3.38
H2: Degree of internationalness of the brand to brand trust	- .34	- 2.09
H3: Degree of foreign source to brand trust	.25	2.35

The results show significant but low relationships between the dimensions of perceived brand globalness and brand trust. It is also noteworthy that the results indicate support for Hypothesis 1 and not for H2 and H3, for which the valence was the opposite of what had been supposed. The degree of internationalness of the brand was negatively related to brand trust whereas the fact of perceiving the brand as foreign was positively related to trust.

Reliability and Validity of the Causal Model

T-values obtained from the LISREL output are significant for all hypothesized structural paths. When the model is estimated, the following goodness-of-fit statistics are obtained: Chi2 (98) = 174.28; RMSEA = 0.071; and RMR = 0.091. The ratio of chi-square per degrees of freedom is less than two (1.77), which indicates an acceptable fit of the model to the data (Hair, et al., 1998). Indicators for global fit were significant: GFI = 0.93; TLI (NNFI) = 0.92; PNFI = 0.71.

6. DISCUSSION AND MANAGERIAL IMPLICATIONS

This study provides several theoretical contributions. As far as we know, no confirmed scale meant to measure the degree of perceived brand globalness has been proposed to date. Researchers interested in studying the role of this perception only had scales generated by exploratory researches. Worse, these scales determined a concept that is objective whereas one precept in marketing is that perception only matters. The goal is to understand whether the more a brand is perceived as global, the more trust it inspires, and not whether the more a brand is objectively global, the more trust it inspires. What influences consumers is what they believe and not what is actually real. Thanks to this proposed scale, we understand how consumers perceive the degree of globalness of a brand. The elements taking a positive part in the evaluation of brand globalness are:

- *the structural and commercial size* of the brand with the belief that the brand has an international notoriety and is widely purchased, that the labour force and the amount of turnover of the firm owning the brand are high and that the brand is a leader in its market;
- the degree of *internationalness* of the brand, with the fact that the brand's communication and market are international;
- the fact that the brand is believed to *come from abroad* or is perceived with *no nationality,* with the following indicators: the brand is owned by a firm that is seen as international, with products manufactured abroad, and the brand is not French (for French consumers).

The results also have important practical implications. This study expands our understanding of consumer trust on a brand. The structural relationships of the concept reinforce the validity of the measurement. Indeed, the more an individual believes that the brand is in a strong position, the more this individual will trust in this brand. H1 cannot be rejected. Managers, when deciding their commercial message, should insist more on the importance of their position with slogans such as "Leader in its market," "No. 1 in its market," "X millions of consumers buy the brand with trust" or more subtle communication.

The second relationship hypothesised in H2 can be rejected: The more international the brand seems, the more the brand inspires trust from the consumers. We observed effective relationship between the two concepts but with the opposite valence. It seems that being perceived as international could generate suspicion. Sponsoring international events, being endorsed by international stars, using another language than the one spoken in the country in advertisements positively participate in the construction of a global brand. However, it could have a negative impact on the degree of trust on this brand. Managers should be aware of this contradiction.

The third relationship hypothesized in H3 can be rejected: The more foreign-sourced a brand is perceived, the less the brand inspires trust in consumers. We observed effective relationship between the two concepts but with the opposite valence. It seems that the distant or fuzzy origin of the brand positively participates into trust. Managers, when deciding their commercial message, should insist more on the origin of the brand and the firm that owns it.

CONCLUSION

This research expands our understanding of consumer preference for global brands. The degree of globalness is likened to success signs that reassure consumers. It seems that consumers adopt this following reasoning: if the brand succeeded in invading the world, it is because of its high skills. So, it can be trusted.

Despite significant relationships between concepts, links remain low: .42 between Commercial and Structural Importance of the brand and Brand Trust, -.34 between Degree of Internationality of the brand and Brand Trust, and .25 between degree of foreignness of the brand and Brand Trust. The direct relationship between Degree of Perceived Brand Globalness (the three dimensions merged all together) and Brand Trust also presents a low unstandardized structural coefficient of .23 (t-values = 2.44). Another limitation to our research is that our study took place in France only (mainland France and Réunion Island). It would have been interesting to carry out a global study to give a universal status to our research, both in terms of scale and observations.

Other limitations that have emerged from the presentation of this chapter during the workshop are that:

- It would have been interesting to study different products and to compare the results. The nature of the product (products presenting a low versus a high degree of risk, products that are more or less ubiquitous) may result to different findings.
- It would also have been worthy to compare results between a brand that is notoriously local and a brand that is considered global.
- And at last but not at least, the dimension "degree of internationality of the brand" in our scale could be critized. A brand when spreading throughout the world faces two main choices that are considered opposite : to adapt its strategy and mix marketing to its different markets (internationality) or to propose the same offer for all its markets

(globalisation). To construct our scale, we asked consumers what was a global brand, and this dimension emerged. To consumers, internationality does not have the same meaning as for marketers and researchers (see the determinants of this dimension). The name of this dimension may lead to misunderstandings.

APPENDIX I

Skewness and Kurtosis Tests of the variables integrated in the scale

Variable	Mean	Skewness	Kurtosis
VAR00002	6.007	-0.790	-0.444
VAR00003	5.050	-0.332	-0.957
VAR00004	4.787	-0.318	-0.806
VAR00005	4.972	-0.322	-1.146
VAR00006	5.447	-0.527	-0.736
VAR00007	3.411	0.217	-0.961
VAR00009	5.801	-0.595	-0.692
VAR00010	5.113	-0.292	-0.661
VAR00011	5.929	-0.654	-0.596
VAR00012	3.617	0.168	-0.828
VAR00016	4.525	-0.145	-0.791
VAR00018	1.248	1.178	-0.621

APPENDIX II

Scale of Measurement of Perceived Brand Globalness

1) To you, the brand is known throughout the world:
   Disagee /__/__/__/__/__/__/__/ Agree

2) The products of the brand are widely purchased:
   Disagee /__/__/__/__/__/__/__/ Agree

3) The firm possessing the brand employs a lot of people:
   Disagee /__/__/__/__/__/__/__/ Agree

4) The turnover of the firm possessing the brand is high:
   Disagee /__/__/__/__/__/__/__/ Agree

5) The brand is leader in its market:
   Disagee /__/__/__/__/__/__/__/ Agree

6) To you, the brand is endorsed by stars that are more:
local /__/__/__/__/__/__/__/ international

7) To you, the brand sponsors events that are more:
local /__/__/__/__/__/__/__/ international

8) The brand uses foreign languages in its advertisements:
Disagee /__/__/__/__/__/__/__/ Agree

9) The brand can be found everywhere in the world:
Disagee /__/__/__/__/__/__/__/ Agree

10) The firm that possesses the brand is international:
Disagee /__/__/__/__/__/__/__/ Agree

11) The brand is: French (for French consumers) /__/ foreign /__/

12) The brand is:
local /__/__/__/__/__/__/__/ international

REFERENCES

Alba J.W., Hutchinson J.W., and Lynch (1990). Memory and Decision Making. *Handbook of Consumer Behavior*. Eds. Thomas S. Robertson and Harold H. 1-49.

Alden, D., Steenkamp, J.B. and Batra, R. (2006). Consumer Attitudes toward Marketplace Globalization: Structure, Antecedents and Consequences. *International Journal of Research in Marketing*. Vol. 23. 227-239.

Ambler, T. (1997). Do Brands Benefit Consumers?. *International Journal of Advertising*. Vol. 16. No. 3.

Anderson, J.C. and Narus, J.A. (1990). A Model of Distributor Firm and Manufacturer Firm Working Partnerships. *Journal of Marketing*. Vol. 54. No. 1. 42-58.

Anderson, J.C. and Weitz B. - Determinants of Continuity in Conventional Industrial Channel Dyads - *Marketing Science* - Vol. 8 - No. 4 - Fall 1989. 310-323.

Atasoy, Y. (2003). *Explaining Globalization*. Atasoy and Carroll eds. Global Shaping.

Aurifeille J-M., Svizerro S. and Tisdell C.A. (2007). Globalization and Partnership. New York: Nova Science.

Batra, R., Ramaswami, V., Alden, D., Steenkamp, J.B. and Ramachander, S. (2000). Effects of Brand Local and Nonlocal Origin on Consumer Attitudes in Developing Countries. *Journal of Consumer Psychology*. Vol. 9. No. 2. 83-95.

Bearden, W. and Etzel, M. (1982). Reference Group Influence on Product and Brand Purchase Decisions. *Journal of Consumer Research*. Vol. 9. 183-194.

Bidault, F. and Jarillo, J. (1995). *La confiance dans les transactions économiques. Confiance entreprise et société*. Eska. Paris.

Bigot, R. and Piau, C. (2003). Les jeunes sont aujourd'hui favorables a la mondialisation. Credoc. No. 168.

Bramall, C., Schoefer, K. and McKechnie, S. (2004). The Determinants and Consequences of Consumer Trust in E-retailing: a Conceptual Framework. *Irish Marketing Review*. Volume 17. No. 1 and 2. 13-22.

Chatterjee, S. and Chaudhuri, A. (2005). Are Trusted Brands Important?. *Marketing Management Journal*. Vol. 15. No. 1. 1-16.

Chaudhuri, A. and Holbrook, M. (2001). The Chain of Effects from Brand Trust to Brand Performance: The Role of Brand Loyalty. *Journal of Marketing*. Vol. 65. No. 2. (April). 81-93.

Chaudhuri, A. and Ray, I. (2003). "Relationships Between Satisfaction, Trust and Commitment in a Retail Environment", presented at the American Marketing Association's Winter Educators' Conference, Orlando, Florida. op. cit. by CHATTERJEE S. and CHAUDHURI A.

Chetochine, G. (2005). Les consommateurs veulent autre chose: Tout, tout de suite, mais pas trop. *Journal du Net*.

Crosby, L.A., Evans, K.R. and Cowles, D. (1990). Relationship Quality in Services Selling: An Interpersonal Influence Perspective. *Journal of Marketing*. Vol. 54. (July). 68-81.

DE Mooij, M. (1998). *Global Marketing and Advertising*. Sage: Thousand Oaks, CA.

Delgado-Ballester, E., Munuera-Aleman, J.L. and Yague-Guillen, M.J. (2003). Development and Validation of a Brand Trust Scale. *International Journal of Market Research*. Vol. 45. No. 1. 35-54.

Doney, P.M. and Cannon, J.P. (1997). An Examination of the Nature of Trust in Buyer-Seller Relationships. *Journal of Marketing*. Vol. 61. No. 2. 35-51.

Dragomer, M. and Kirkland, J. (2001). Global Brands Seeking to Overcome Resistance and Become Bigger Local Players. *PJB.CZ*.

Dumez, H. and Jeunemaitre, A. (2000). Comprendre la globalisation. *La Gazette de la Société et des Techniques. Journal des Mines*. No. 4.

Frazier, G.L. (1983). Interorganizational Exchange Behaviour in Marketing Channels: A Broadened Perspective. *Journal of Marketing*. Vol. 47. No. 4. 68-78.

Ganesan, S. (1994). Determinants of long-term orientation in buyer–seller relationships. *Journal of Marketing*. Vol. 58. 1-19.

Ganesan, S. and Hess, R. (1987). Dimensions and Levels of Trust: Implications for Commitment to a Relationship. *Marketing Letters*. Vol. 8. No. 4.

Guibert, N. (1999). La Confiance en Marketing: Fondements et Applications. *Recherche et Applications en Marketing*. Vol. 14. No. 1.

Gurviez, P. (1999). Gurviez, P. and Korchia, M. (2002).

Gurviez, P. and Korchia, M. (2002). Proposition d'une échelle de mesure multidimensionnelle de la confiance. *Recherche et Applications en Marketing*. Vol. 17. No. 3.

Ha, H.Y. and Perks, H. (2005). Effects of Consumer Perceptions of Brand Experience on the Web: Brand Familiarity, Satisfaction and Brand Trust. *Journal of Consumer Behaviour*. Vol. 4. No. 6. 438-452.

Hair, J.F., Anderson R., Tatham R., and Black, W. (1998).

Henderson, N. (2002). The Many Faces of Qualitative Research. *Marketing Research. 13-17.*

Hiscock, J. (2001). Most Trusted Brands. *Marketing*. Vol. 1.

Holt, D., Quelch, J. and Taylor, E. (2004). How Global Brands Compete. *Harvard Business Review*. Vol. 82. No 9. (September) 68-81.

Hsieh, M. (2002).Identifying Brand Image Dimensionality and Measuring the Degree of Brand Globalization: A Cross-National Study. *Journal of International Marketing*. Vol. 10 .No. 2. 46-67.

Husbands, G. (2004). Is Thinking Global Killing Local?. *Business Management*.

Johansson, J. and Ronkainen, I. (2004). The Brand Challenge. *Marketing Management*.

Johansson, J. and Ronkainen, I. (2005). The Esteem of Global Brands. *Brand Management*. Vol. 12. N° 5. (June). 339-354.

Johansson, J., Steenkamp, J.B. and Batra, R. (2003). How Perceived Brand Globalness Creates Brand Value. *Journal of International Business Studies*. Vol. 34. 53-65.

Kapferer (1992) and Kapferer (2004). op. cit. Schuiling I. and Kapferer J-N. (2004).

Kennedy, M.S., Ferell, L.K., and Leclair, D. (2001). Consumer's Trust of Sales Person and Manufacturer: An Empirical Study. *Journal of Business Research*. Vol. 51.

Levitt, T. (1983). The Globalization of Markets. *Harvard Business Review*. 92-102.

MacReynolds, C., Koch L. and Rumrill, P. (2001). Qualitative Research Strategies in Rehabilitation. 57-65.

Michalowska, A. (2003). Consommateurs et marques globales. *Marketing Magazine*. No. 82.

Morgan, R.M. and Hunt, S.D. (1994). The Commitment-Trust Theory of Relationship Marketing. *Journal of Marketing*. Vol. 58. No. 3. (July). 20-38

Nurko, C. (2004). Global Brands Try Friendly Facelifts. *DesignWeek*.

Onwuegbuzie, A. and Leech, N. (2005). On Becoming a Pragmatic Researcher: The Importance of Combining Quantitative and Qualitative Research Methodologies. *International Journal of Social Research Methodology*. Vol. 8. No. 5. 375-387.

Quelch, J. (1999). Global Brands: Taking Stock. *Business Strategy Review*. Vol. 10. No.1. 1-14.

Riesenberg, H. and Freeling, A. (1991). How Global are Global Brands?. *The McKinsey Quaterly*. No. 4. 3-18.

Romaniuk, J. and Bogomolova, S. (2005). Variation in Brand Trust Scores. *Journal of Targeting, Measurement and Analysis for Marketing*. Vol. 13. No. 4. 363-373.

Roth, M. (1995). The Effects of Culture and Socioeconomics on the Performance of Global Brand Image Strategies. *Journal of Marketing Research*. Vol. 32. (May). 163-175.

Ryder, I. (2005). *Issues and Patterns in Global Branding. Securing the Benefits of Globalisation*. Part IV. Chapter 2.

Schuiling, I. and Kapferer, J-N. (2004). Real Differences Between Local and International Brands: Strategic Implications for International Marketers. *Journal of International Marketing*. Vol. 12. No. 4. 97-112.

Schultz, D. (1995). Moving from Global Brands to Global Bands. *Marketing News*. 30.

Selnes, F. (1998). Antecedents and Consequences of Trust and Satisfaction in Buyer-Seller Relationships. *European Journal of Marketing*. Vol. 32. No. 3 and 4. 305-322.

Shocker, A.D., Srivastava, R.K. and Ruekert, R.W. (1994). Challenges and Opportunities Facing Brand Management: An Introduction to the Special Issue. *Journal of Marketing Research*. No. 31. (May). 149-158.

Sirdeshmukh, D., Singh, J. and Sabol, B. (2002). Consumer Trust, Value and Loyalty in Relational Exchanges. *Journal of Marketing*. Vol. 66. (January). 15-37.

Sirieix, L. and Dubois, P.L. (1999). Vers un modèle Qualité-Satisfaction intégrant la Confiance. *Recherches et Applications en Marketing.* Vol. 14. No. 3.

Sitkin, J.B. and Barclay, D.W. (1997). The Effects of Organizational Differences and Trust on the Effectiveness of Selling Partner Relationships. *Journal of Marketing.* Vol. 61. 3-21.

Steenkamp, J.B., Batra, R. and Alden, D. (2003). How Perceived Brand Globalness Creates Brand Value. *Journal of International Business Studies.* Vol. 34. No 1. 53-65.

VanGelder, S. (2002). *General Strategies for Global Brands.* MetaBrand.

Ward, S., Girardi, A. and Lewandowska, A. (2006). A Cross-National Validation of the Narver and Slater Market Orientation Scale. *Journal of Marketing Theory and Practice.* Vol. 14. No. 2. (Spring). 155-167.

Yu, L. (2003). The Global-Brand Advantage. *MIT Sloan Management Review. 13.*

In: Trust, Globalisation and Market Expansion
Editors: J-M. Aurifeille, C. Medlin and C. Tisdell

ISBN 978-1-60741-812-2
© 2009 Nova Science Publishers, Inc.

Chapter 14

CAN AN INVESTOR TRUST INTERNET STOCK MARKET CONSENSUS?

Stéphane Manin and Robert Trommsdorff
Franco-Australian Centre for International Research in Marketing
University of La Réunion, France

ABSTRACT

This paper studies the validity of the information provided by a Market Consensus on the Boursorama stock market website. When taking a buy or sell position, an investor has overabundant information at his disposal. This information is organized according to the two main methodologies in Financial Market Theory: technical analysis and fundamental analysis. An investor using technical analysis will rely on past stock price and indicators such as the moving average. An investor performing fundamental analysis will base his decision on stock price and indicators such as Price-Earnings Ratio and company profits. Market Consensus is a new approach bypassing traditional methodologies based upon past prices or company value.

Keywords: Financial Market Theory, Market Consensus.

1. INTRODUCTION

Financial Market Theory aims at determining the validity and reliability of information when deciding to buy or sell stock. This has become an even greater issue over the last ten years due to the multiplication of information sources, particularly with the Internet. This trend is very unlikely to reverse any time soon.

The question is whether investors should rely on financial information in such profusion of sources? How useful is such financial information for an investor facing uncertainty?

The connection between financial information, the press or the Internet and financial markets is a recurrent issue in Financial Market Theory (Cutler, Poterba and Summers, 1989;

Coval and Shumway, 2001; Antweiler and Frank, 2004). In dominant patterns, it is generally admitted that financial information influences market players psychologically and sociologically. Nevertheless, how these factors affect expectations of stock market performance remains unclear. For instance, we do not know to what extent financial information influences, reflects or amplifies financial market activities (Tetlock, 2007).

Research on the subject brings to the fore three main questions (Antweiler and Frank, 2004): Do messages help predict returns? Does disagreement among messages generate more trades? Do messages help predict volatility?

These studies produce different findings. Cutler, Poterba and Summers (1989) find that "important qualitative news stories do not seem to help explain large market returns accompanied by quantitative macroeconomic events"; Antweiler and Frank (2004) find relationships between message activity on Internet chat rooms and trading volume and between message activity and return volatility. Glosten, Jagannathan and Runkle (1993) and Engle and Patton (2001) also find evidence supporting the role of trading volume, but they do not find any evidence that the Treasury Bill rate helped forecast volatility. Unlike Antweiler and Frank (2004), Coval and Shumway (2001) do not find relationships between message activity and returns.

Examination of the literature shows that the underlying paradigms differ depending on whether a technical or fundamental approach to Financial Market Theory is adopted.

This chapter does not deal with the validity of an approach in terms of technical analysis or fundamental analysis. This means that we use neither past share price nor accounting information concerning the firm under study to determine the validity of information on a stock market website. There is a wealth of literature testing market efficiency either by studying past security prices (technical analysis) or by studying the value of a firm through accounting and market data (fundamental analysis). We are proposing a new approach which has not been described in the financial literature, and which consists in evaluating the information provided by Market Consensus with regard to a share on a stock market website. In other words, we test market efficiency (Fama, 1970) by means of a previously unstudied indicator, Market Consensus. Furthermore, we present two instances of Market Consensus for a single stock: the market consensus reached by financial analysts and that of ordinary small-time investors. This will enable us to study the informative value of the two market consensuses.

We present a brief review of efficient market theory and the related controversy in Section 2, the financial data used in the study in Section 3, measurements of consensus developed by us in Section 4, management strategies based on our portfolio indicator of differential consensus and alternative strategies in Section 5, findings in terms of forecasting and portfolio management simulation in Section 6. The final section of our chapter is the conclusion.

2. REVIEW OF THE LITERATURE

This chapter tests market efficiency with the market consensus provided respectively by financial analysts and amateur investors. The chapter comes within the scope of the literature on market efficiency, which is briefly presented. A number of articles have challenged the efficient market hypothesis since it was proposed by Fama (1970). A new branch of the literature provides a theoretical basis for market inefficiency in the form of behavioural finance (see Shiller, 2002 for a review of the literature). This chapter's findings challenge the efficient market hypothesis, and can be explained in part by the arguments of behavioural finance. One other section of the financial literature casts some additional theoretical light on this chapter: these are articles on the validity of information supplied by financial analysts. We question the informative value provided by the market consensus of analysts; several studies corroborate our conclusions on the subject.

We will begin by presenting the efficient market hypothesis proposed by Fama (1970), which is a cornerstone of financial theory. Then we will examine behavioural finance as an explanation of market inefficiencies. Articles on financial analysts will be considered only in the empirical section of this chapter.

Except for a small number of studies considering that prices follow a random pattern and thus cannot be predicted (Malkiel, 1973), two theoretical patterns emerge: the Efficient Market Hypothesis (EMH) and behavioural finance, which allows the anomalies of the EMH to be explained.

The EMH (Fama, 1970) states that markets are "informationally efficient,"[1] in other words that prices on traded assets, e.g. stocks, bonds, or property, already reflect all known information. Information or *news* in the EMH is defined as anything that may affect prices that is unknowable in the present and thus appears randomly in the future. The considered information is not limited to financial information but extended to political, economic and social information, whether it be true or false. Such information is considered as non-biased insofar as it reflects investors' collective beliefs.

The EMH states that it is not possible to consistently outperform the market by using any information that the market already knows, except through luck. Stocks always trade at their fair value on stock exchanges, and thus it is impossible for investors to either purchase undervalued stocks or sell stocks for inflated prices. Thus, according to the EMH, no investor has an advantage in predicting a return on a stock price since no one has access to information not already available to everyone else. This basic simplifying assumption of the EMH is clearly incorrect, as information is withheld by cartels and proprietary databases only release information at a cost.

The EMH allows that when faced with new information, some investors may overreact and some may under react. However the EMH is that investors' reactions are random and follow a normal distribution pattern so that the net effect on market prices cannot be reliably exploited to make abnormal profits.

Although it is a cornerstone of modern financial theory, the EMH is highly controversial and often disputed. Followers of the EMH argue it is pointless to search for undervalued stocks or to try to predict trends in the market through either fundamental or technical analysis. While academics point to a large body of evidence in support of EMH, an equal amount of dissension also exists. For example, investors such as Warren Buffett have consistently beaten the market over long periods of time, which, by definition, is impossible according to the EMH.

---

[1] Strong form efficiency (Fama, 1970).

Lehman (1991) concludes that belief in an efficient market pattern is destined to remain a basically philosophical notion. Contrary to conventional financial theory based on the assumption that decision makers are rational and utility maximising, behavioural finance considers that emotion and psychology influence our decisions, causing us to behave in unpredictable or irrational ways. The purpose of behavioural finance is to study how cognitive or emotional biases, be they individual or collective, create anomalies in market prices and returns that may be inexplicable through EMH alone.

One of the central issues in behavioural finance is: Why do investors and managers (and also lenders and borrowers) make systematic errors? Behavioural finance attempts to explain how these errors affect prices and returns (creating market inefficiencies). Behavioural finance also examines what firm managers or other institutions, as well as other financial players, might do to take advantage of market inefficiencies. Inefficiencies like over reactions to information are often cited by behavioral finance as influencing market trends or even causing—if partly—bubbles and crashes. These behaviors can result from poor investor attention, over-confidence or over-optimism, and noise trading. When a series of good news is announced, over reaction can cause a drop in the average return of stock prices, while a series of bad announcements may help stock prices rise. This is because long-term winners are not seen as a wise bet, as their future returns is not potentially high, while stocks that were losers stand a better chance of rebounding. It is important to note that some of the underlying reasons and biases that cause some people to behave irrationally are often against their best interests, as in the recent example of subprimes. Behavioural finance reveals that there are some predictable patterns in the stock market. Investors tend to buy undervalued stock and sell overvalued stock, and, in a market of many participants, the result can be anything but efficient. In fact, many of the anomalies found in conventional theories could be considered short-term chance events that are eventually corrected over time. In his 1998 paper entitled "Market Efficiency, Long-Term Returns and Behavioural Finance," Fama argues that many of the findings in behavioural finance appear to contradict each other, and that all in all, behavioural finance itself appears to be a collection of anomalies that can be explained by market efficiency. As we are studying market consensus provided by financial analysts, we are contributing to existing financial literature on the validity of analyst-based information (see Ramnath, Rock and Shane, 2008 for a review of the literature on financial analysts).

This chapter aims to assess the value of Market Consensus. A consensus may be right, and thus be self-fulfilling in that it guides behaviour, or wrong and lead to collective delusion. Here we are in the research field of behavioural finance: we are testing the explicit assumption that investors' behaviour is driven by market information such as Market Consensus, and showing the value of Market Consensus in terms of forecasting and financial results.

3. FINANCIAL DATA

We have chosen the ten companies listed in the CAC 40[2] stock index with the highest

---

[2] The CAC 40 is a benchmark French stock market index. The index represents a capitalization-weighted measure of the 40 most significant values among the 100 highest market caps on the Paris Bourse (now Euronext Paris). It is one of the main national indices of the pan-European stock exchange group Euronext.

market capitalization at the beginning of this chapter. Market capitalization is a measurement of corporate or economic size equal to the share price multiplied by the number of shares. Hence our stock selection criteria: stocks with the strongest trading volume for each industry sector. Each stock we have chosen can be traded on the SRD (a Deferred Settlement Service concerning only major French and foreign companies negotiated in Paris). On the SRD, buying and selling transactions are settled only at the end of the business month. This allows an investor to buy and sell the same share during the trading month without spending cash, and to bet on the rise of a share and sell just before liquidation date.

The website used to implement our experiment is that of Boursorama,[3] the European financial information leader with 5.2 million visitors a year. The Boursorama website offers a wide range of a free-access or subscriber services such as Stock value with historical quotes, current events, analysts' forecasts (dividend, PER, etc.), a Members' Forum, and a Market Consensus (recommendations by analysts and Boursorama members). The Boursorama Market Consensus used in our experiment is presented in the next section.

This chapter focuses on the following companies:

Total:	Total is one of the leading global oil groups
Electricité de France (EDF):	EDF is France's number one electricity producer and distributor
Vinci:	Vinci is the world leader in the provision of construction, concessions and related services
Société Générale (SocGen):	Société Générale is one of the leading French banking groups
L'Oréal:	L'Oréal is the world leader in cosmetics
Sanofi-Aventis (Sanofi):	Sanofi-Aventis is the first European pharmaceutical group
Carrefour:	Carrefour is Europe's number one and the World's number two in distribution
France Telecom:	France Telecom is the largest French telecommunications operator
BNP Paribas (BNP):	BNP Paribas is the first French banking group
Alcatel-Lucent:	A leader in broadband land networks

All the data series span the period from 3 March 2007 to 29 October 2007, totalling eight trading months.

4. THE MARKET CONSENSUS INDICATOR

We define Market Consensus as the unanimity or quasi unanimity of opinions or knowledge on a topic, a forecast or a planned decision. It has an obvious impact on social behaviour. The consensus on the Boursorama website gives Analysts' and forum members' recommendations on the values of Euronext Paris stocks in terms of purchase or sale (see Figure 1).

---

[3] http://www.boursorama.com.

Opinions: Number	01/04/07	24/03/07	01/03/07	01/02/07	01/01/07
Buy	15	15	15	15	17
▶ Reinforce	8	8	7	10	9
Preserve	7	7	8	7	8
Reduce	0	0	0	0	0
Sell	0	0	0	0	0
Number of analysts	30 =	30	30	32	34

Figure 1. An Example of Consensus from Boursorama.

Thirty analysts provide a recommendation. Half of them (15/30) advise buying the stock, eight advocate position strengthening and seven recommend keeping the stock. No analyst suggests reducing its volume or selling it.

To obtain a comprehensive measure including all analysts' recommendations, we propose to create the following indicator as at date t:

$$C_t^{Pro} = \frac{Buy * N^t{}_{Buy} + Reinforce * N^t{}_{Reinforce} + Preserve * N^t{}_{preserve} + Reduce * N^t{}_{Reduce} + Sell * N^t{}_{Sell}}{N^t{}_{Buy} + N^t{}_{Reinforce} + N^t{}_{Preserve} + N^t{}_{reduce} + N^t{}_{Sell}}$$

with the following buy and sell codes used in this chapter:

	Number of shares
Buy	+2
Reinforce	+1
Preserve	0
Reduce	-1
Sell	-2

Chart 1. Indicator Codes.

Our indicator and codification are structured in such a way that the consensus indicator can be either positive or negative. If the indicator is positive, this means that most recommendations are in favour of buying shares. Conversely, if the indicator is negative, then most recommendations advocate selling the shares.

Let us take the case of the Alactel-Lucent share to illustrate the use and interpretation of our consensus indicator. We present (in Graph 1) the price of the Alcatel-Lucent share in base

100 and the consensus indicator for Analysts ("Professionals") and Boursorama forum members ("Amateurs").

The graph shows rises and decreases of the Alcatel-Lucent share. Yet, the consensus indicator for "Professionals" and "Amateurs" alike is systematically positive. If we refer to our indicator, we should be in a buy position for the whole study period. We can also note that the Professional indicator is definitely lower than the Amateur one, which means Professionals have more doubts about the share than Amateurs. The Amateur indicator seems to follow the Alcatel-Lucent share's evolution; but the Professional indicator is far less obvious in following the Alcatel-Lucent share's movement.

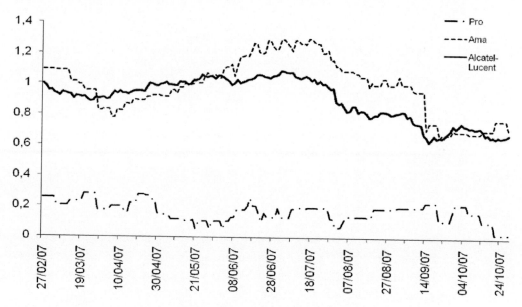

Graph 1. Alcatel Consensus – Analysts' Recommendations on Euronext Paris Values.

The main problem in the use of our consensus indicator is that it remains positive all through this period whereas the Alcatel-Lucent share is clearly decreasing as shown below (Graph 2). The following graph shows the evolution of both the Alcatel-Lucent share and the CAC 40 in base 100.

If we considered the consensus indicator, whether for Professionals or Amateurs, during the study period so as to take a position on the Alcatel-Lucent share, we would systematically be buying it while it undergoes a significant drop. In terms of portfolio management, we would be losers if we followed the consensus indicator.

As the consensus indicator does not seem appropriate for taking a position on the Alcatel-Lucent share over the studied period, another indicator is suggested: the consensus differential for date t:

Confidence difference:
$$\Delta C_t = C_t - C_{t-1}$$

This indicator is no longer an absolute Market Consensus measure, but a relative one. The point is no longer whether buying or selling the share is recommended, but rather whether the consensus synthetic indicator is up or down. The interpretation of this new indicator is simple: a rise of the consensus indicator implies that the concerned share value is trusted to evolve in a favourable way. Conversely, a fall of the consensus indicator generates increased distrust or less trust in the stock's evolution.

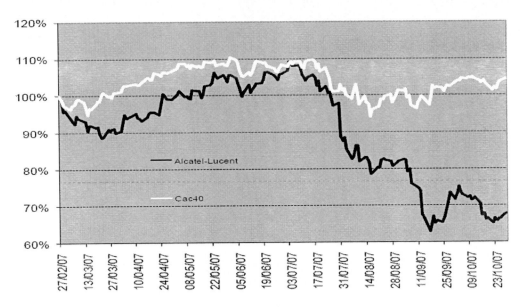

Graph 2. Alcatel-Lucent Share Price Compared to the Cac 40.

In view of the Alcatel-Lucent stock, we shall use the differential consensus indicator to take positions on the market for the simulations of the ten-share portfolio management. Our aim is to check whether our indicator is valuable for an investor. We shall determine if a portfolio management simulation based on our indicator brings "satisfactory" results in terms of share evolution forecasts, and especially risk adjusted returns.

5. TRADING STRATEGIES AND BENCHMARK MODELS

In this section, we shall propose a portfolio management strategy based on consensus differential. As the Boursorama website presents analysts' and Boursorama forum members' consensus, we shall develop two different strategies to study the value of each of these Market Consensuses.

To compare the findings of our two portfolio management strategies, developed from Professional and Amateur consensuses, two other "classic" portfolio management strategies are suggested: respectively the Naive and the Buy and Hold strategies.

We do not directly use market stock price in absolute terms but rather its return rate so as to consider non-dimensional chronological series. We thus examine all shares for the study period in base 100. Our forecasts do not directly focus on prices but on return rates instead.

Therefore there are four portfolio management strategies, which will be briefly presented:

A. Professional Consensus (PC)

The Professionals' forecast concerning share return rate for date t+1 is $\hat{Y}_{t+1}$, which corresponds to the differential Market Consensus of analysts, i.e.:

$$\hat{Y}_{t+1} = C_t^{pro} - C_{t-1}^{Pro}$$

B. Amateur Consensus (AC)

The Amateurs' forecast concerning share return rate for date t+1 is $\hat{Y}_{t+1}$, which corresponds to the differential Market Consensus of Boursorama forum members, i.e.:

$$\hat{Y}_{t+1} = C_t^{Ama} - C_{t-1}^{Ama}$$

It is important to stress that the higher the consensus differential, the more significant position taking is with regard to a stock. A positive differential means that the stock is bought up to the differential, and negative differential means that it is sold at an even higher price as the differential is high.

Stock position taking thus does not only depend on positive or negative consensus differential, but also on differential proportion. Indeed we believe that a major variation in Market Consensus reflects a significant change in confidence level, that is trust in a firm's return rate relative to the market. We assume that stock can be fully divided so that it can be sold or bought in exact proportion to the consensus differential.

C. Naive Strategy

The Naive Strategy simply assumes that the most recent period change is the best predictor of the future. The simplest model is defined by:

$$\hat{Y}_{t+1} = Y_t$$

where Y_t is the actual return rate at period t and $\hat{Y}_{t+1}$ is the forecast return rate for the next period.

If the return rate is rising, we buy the stock whereas if the return rate is falling, we sell it. This strategy implies that autocorrelation is high enough to generate "good" results.

D. Buy and Hold

The Buy and Hold (BH) strategy is a passive investment strategy in which an investor buys stocks and holds them for a long period of time, regardless of fluctuations in the market. An investor who uses a BH strategy actively selects stocks, but once in a position, is not concerned with short-term price movements and technical indicators.

BH strategy is a long-term investment strategy based on the concept that in the long run financial markets provide a good return rate despite periods of volatility or decline. This viewpoint also holds that market timing, i.e. the concept that one can enter the market on the lows and sell on the highs, does not work or does not work for small investors so it is better to simply buy and hold. One of the strongest arguments for the BH strategy is the Efficient Market Hypothesis: if every security is fairly valued at all times, then there is really no point in trading. The first three portfolio management strategies are said to be active since we modify position on the market according to different indicators: consensus differential for the first two strategies and last return rate for the Naive strategy. The Buy and Hold strategy is said to be passive because it recommends holding the stock from beginning to end of the period without making any changes.

6. FORECASTING ACCURACY AND TRADING SIMULATION

In this section we present the findings of the four models in terms of price prevision and financial return obtained through portfolio management simulation. We list the findings for the study's ten shares and for the same period of time (2 March 2007 to 29 October 2007). Naive and BH strategies are benchmarks.

A. Forecasting Accuracy Results

We use only one criterion to make comparisons between the forecasting ability of our indicator with our benchmark strategies. The criterion is the Correct Directional Change (CDC):

$$CDC = \frac{100}{N} \sum_{t=1}^{N} D_t$$

where $D_t = 1$ if $Y_t \hat{Y}_t > 0$ else $D_t = 0$

CDC measures the capacity of a model to correctly predict the subsequent actual change. It is an important issue in a trading strategy that relies on the forecast direction rather than its level.

The statistical performance measure is presented in Chart 2. Findings are presented for all trading days (All), upward movements (Up) and downward movements (Down).

CDC	Pro			Ama			Naive		
	All	Up	Down	All	Up	Down	All	Up	Down
Total	48.2%	46.9%	51.9%	47.6%	55.6%	42.0%	53.0%	53.1%	55.6%
EDF	44.6%	46.1%	45.8%	50.6%	53.9%	50.0%	48.2%	55.1%	43.1%
Vinci	42.8%	56.0%	31.2%	53.6%	53.6%	57.1%	47.6%	50.0%	48.1%
SocGen	51.2%	54.9%	49.4%	48.2%	47.6%	50.6%	51.8%	53.7%	51.9%
L'Oréal	49.4%	52.7%	46.6%	55.4%	53.8%	58.9%	39.8%	46.2%	32.9%
Sanofi	50.0%	69.7%	28.4%	52.4%	59.6%	45.9%	56.6%	61.8%	52.7%
Carrefour	57.2%	60.9%	57.0%	44.0%	56.5%	36.6%	53.6%	49.3%	59.1%
France Telecom	47.0%	52.4%	45.3%	47.0%	52.4%	45.3%	50.6%	54.8%	50.7%
BNP	48.2%	51.2%	46.9%	45.8%	45.1%	48.1%	50.0%	52.4%	49.4%
Alcatel-Lucent	45.8%	50.6%	45.0%	52.4%	49.4%	60.0%	48.8%	50.6%	51.3%
Average	48.4%	54.1%	44.7%	49.7%	52.7%	49.5%	50.0%	52.7%	49.5%

Chart 2. Statistical Performance.

Forecasting accuracy statistics do not provide very conclusive results.

For all stocks during the whole study period, the CDC average is below 50% for Professionals and Amateurs alike, and it reaches exactly 50% for the Naive strategy. So the prediction based on the consensus differential indicator does not seem to meet expectations.

However, if we examine the findings more closely, we come across disturbing results: in all three strategies the CDC is on average above 50% for upward movements and under 50% for downward movements. This could be explained by the rising trend of all stocks over the study period; it is obviously true for the Naive strategy which follows the general trend, and so is likely a positively biased benchmark in this study.

On the contrary, in terms of consensus differential, the results may reflect opinion inertia on the part of market participants (analysts or forum members) who, as stock value increases, improve their confidence level measured by the total consensus indicator. Our theory can be illustrated by the following graph showing the evolution of the Alcatel-Lucent stock as well as the Amateurs' consensus indicator (Graph 3):

Detailed findings for Alcatel-Lucent give an overall CDC of 52.4% for Amateurs with 60% fall and less than 50% rise. As the Alcatel-Lucent stock trend is clearly bearish for the period under study, it is essential to get "good" results down rather than up, as is the case here. In addition, it can be observed that the CDC is generally higher in 5 cases out of 10 for Amateurs, while that of Professionals is higher only 2 times out of 10. It therefore seems that the differential indicator of Amateurs is better in terms of forecast than that of Professionals.

It should be noted that the CDC only indicates whether we are in the right market trend. Actually we are using the Consensus Differential Indicator to determine not only the direction but also the scope of stock change, which is not measured by the CDC. We can therefore have a "relatively" low CDC but good results in terms of portfolio management.

The Consensus Differential Indicator does not seem to be an advanced stock variation forecast indicator, but rather a lagging indicator of a stock's up or downward trend.

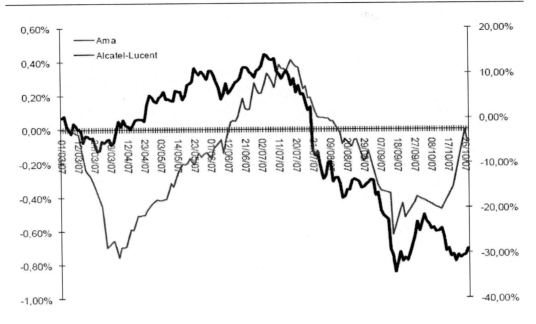

Graph 3. Alcatel-Lucent stock and Amateur Consensus Indicator.

B. Trading Performance Results

True merit evaluation should be based on the performance of a trading strategy rather than the forecasting accuracy, because:

> *"Low forecast errors and trading profits are not synonymous since a large trade forecasted incorrectly... could have accounted for most of the trading system's profits."* *(Kaastra and Boyd, 1996: 229)*

Trading performance measures are commonly used in the fund management industry. The measures are: annualized return, annualized volatility and Sharpe ratio.

- Annualized return (R) is a performance measure of a trading strategy:

$$R_a = 252 \frac{1}{N} \sum_{t=1}^{N} R_t$$

where $\quad R_t = \left(\frac{P_t}{P_{t-1}}\right) - 1 \quad$ and $\quad$ P$_t$ is a net asset value at time t.

- Annualized volatility (Vol) is a measure of risk:

$$\sigma_a = \sqrt{252}\sqrt{\frac{1}{N-1}\sum_{t=1}^{N}\left(R_t - \overline{R}\right)^2}$$

- The Sharpe ratio (SR) is a risk-adjusted measure of return:

$$SR = \frac{R_a - R_f}{\sigma_a}$$

where R_f is a risk-free rate (equal to 4% for our study).

Trading results are presented in Charts 3 and 4:

	PC			AC		
	R	Vol	SR	R	Vol	SR
Total	9.86%	19.30%	0.30	-9.06%	22.38%	-0.58
EDF	-41.15%	24.41%	-1.85	28.85%	25.95%	0.96
Vinci	-59.08%	37.63%	-1.68	25.75%	23.67%	0.92
SocGen	-8.91%	31.25%	-0.41	-39.58%	33.66%	-1.29
L'Oréal	-14.51%	19.50%	-0.95	16.50%	18.47%	0.68
Sanofi	-13.64%	19.04%	-0.93	14.54%	17.66%	0.60
Carrefour	28.34%	19.46%	1.25	-6.22%	25.13%	-0.41
FranceTelecom	-1.14%	21.40%	-0.24	32.59%	21.40%	1.34
BNP	-5.71%	28.06%	-0.35	-5.48%	29.74%	-0.32
Alcatel-Lucent	-29.74%	34.08%	-0.99	65.31%	28.86%	2.12
Average	-13.57%	25.41%	-0.58	12.32%	24.69%	0.40

Chart 3. Trading Results for Professional Consensus (PC) and Amateur Consensus (AC).

A comparison of the trading outcomes shows that Amateur Consensus results are quite impressive. The Amateur Consensus model outperforms benchmark strategies (Naive and Buy and Hold) and the Professional Consensus strategy in terms of annualized return and risk-adjusted performance with a Sharpe ratio of 0.4. The Amateur Consensus model has a positive annualised return rate 4 times out of 10 and its average is 12.32% for an annualised volatility of 24.69%.

It can be noted that the Professional Consensus model achieves the worse results, being negative on the annualised return rate 8 times out of 10 and with an average of -13.57. In comparison, both benchmark strategies are positive on return rates and Sharpe ratios. Thus, on the whole, a strategy based on Market Consensus from Professionals performs worse than benchmark strategies. Conversely, the Amateur Market Consensus-based strategy produces better results than benchmark strategies.

	Naive			Buy and Hold		
	R	Vol	SR	R	Vol	SR
Total	35.03%	21.63%	1.43	18.51%	21.04%	0.69
EDF	-4.36%	30.52%	-0.27	78.49%	22.21%	3.35
Vinci	3.78%	29.41%	-0.01	15.63%	27.16%	0.43
SocGen	13.07%	30.25%	0.30	-13.73%	30.26%	-0.59
L'Oréal	-46.49%	24.47%	-2.06	24.31%	19.13%	1.06
Sanofi	29.92%	16.98%	1.53	-11.86%	18.22%	-0.87
Carrefour	4.89%	23.09%	0.04	-8.21%	22.57%	-0.54
FranceTelecom	11.36%	22.04%	0.33	44.89%	22.67%	1.80
BNP	-5.06%	31.04%	-0.29	-6.12%	26.89%	-0.38
Alcatel-Lucent	2.74%	28.66%	-0.04	-44.58%	31.17%	-1.56
Average	4.49%	25.81%	0.10	9.73%	24.13%	0.34

Chart 4. Trading Results for Naive and Buy and Hold.

This last remark is of the utmost importance, as it seems that Boursorama members' Market Consensus gives real "added value" in terms of portfolio management for an investor, while analysts' Market Consensus does not lead to satisfactory financial outcomes.

These disappointing results from analysts are analogous to those in other studies in the literature of behavioural finance, where analysts underreact to new information (*"most of the research to date has concluded that analysts underreact to information"* [Ramnath, Rock and Shane, 2008]). A recent study by I. Nolte and W. Pohlmeier (2007) shows that experts are unable to outperform the random walk model in forecasting chronological series (*"We do not find convincing evidence that forecasts based on the predictions of experts from specific groups are systematically superior compared to the ones from other groups or the random walk forecasts"*).

Generally investors on financial markets do not invest in one stock but in several simultaneously. If we build an equally balanced ten-stock portfolio over the duration of the study we get the following results shown in Chart 5 and Figure 2.

Results are similar to previous conclusions, but thanks to diversification the results are better still for the Amateur Consensus strategy since risk has been considerably reduced, and the Sharpe ratio is even better. Benchmark strategies not only generate lower return rates but, above all, higher risk.

Individual study of each stock shows that on average results are slightly better in terms of risk-adjusted yield (0.40 for Amateur Consensus against 0.36 for Buy and Hold), but when stocks are combined the result of the Sharpe ratio for Buy and Hold improves by 76% (0.35 with diversification against 0.60 without diversification), while the result of the Sharpe ratio for Amateur Consensus improves sharply from 0.40 to 1.66, an increase of 316%. What is extremely interesting about these results is that diversification operates not solely because stocks are not perfectly correlated but also because market consensuses are only partially correlated.

Portfolio	PC	AC	Naive	BH
R	-13.57%	12.32%	4.49%	9.73%
Vol	8.65%	7.41%	12.96%	16.24%
SR	- 1.57	1.66	0.35	0.60

Chart 5. Portfolio Strategies.

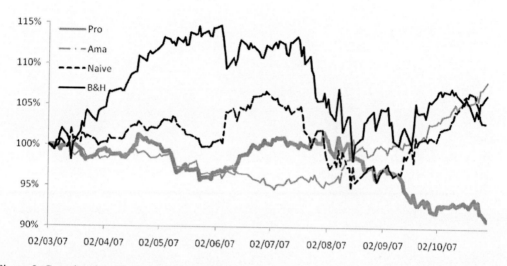

Figure 2. Cumulated Profit Graph for Strategies.

We thus have a counterintuitive result, since using the Professional Market Consensus gives poor results while if the Amateur Consensus is used results are more convincing. How can this be accounted for? Several explanations may be put forward:

1. The number of analysts is much lower than that of Boursorama members (in the case of Alcatel-Lucent the ratio is 1 to 20 on certain days). It should be noted that when the Alcatel-Lucent stock fell, we observed a higher number of Amateurs giving their opinions in Market Consensus while Professionals were not more numerous.
2. Analysts change their opinions less frequently than Amateurs: in the Société Générale's Jérôme Kerviel affair of late January 2008 (Monday 21st), we observed that analysts changed their opinions only a week later (Monday 28 January) while Amateurs changed their opinions on the stock immediately after the record €4.9 billion loss was announced on Thursday 24 January, switching from buyers to sellers following the consensus indicator (see Annexes). Professionals therefore seem to be less reactive than Amateurs.
3. The portfolio management time frame is relatively "short" in our study since we can modify portfolio composition daily; outcomes may be different for longer time frames.
4.

To close our study of financial results, we suggest the following statistical test to check whether AC strategy gives random results or not:

The Z statistic for trading with Ama confidence difference
H0: Trade outcomes occurred in a random sequence
H1: Outcomes were non random

The Z statistic is equal to:

$$z = \frac{r - \left(\dfrac{2n_1 n_2}{n_1 + n_2} + 1 \right)}{\sqrt{\dfrac{2n_1 n_2 (2n_1 n_2 - n_1 - n_2)}{(n_1 + n_2)^2 (n_1 + n_2 - 1)}}}$$

where:
  r = number of runs observed
  n1 = number of winning trades
  n2 = number of losing trades

and Z = 0.35 < theoretical Z value for 5% level of significance (+/- 1.96).

Chart 6 gives the Z statistic for Amateur Consensus strategy.

	Z
Total	-0.78
EDF	0.42
Vinci	0.70
SocGen	-0.23
L'Oréal	2.90
Sanofi	-1.76
Carrefour	-0.83
FranceTelecom	-0.23
BNP	0.45
Alcatel-Lucent	0.35

Chart 6. Z Statistic for AC Strategy.

The Z statistic is significant only for the L'Oréal stock and non significant for other stock. Therefore, apart from the L'Oréal stock, Z statistic produces a random outcome.

There are a certain number of limitations to our study, viz.:

1. We did not include transaction costs in portfolio management simulation; this should bring down the financial result for all active strategies (PC, AC and Naive).

2. We did not take account of stock prices but stock return rates; we must therefore alter portfolio management on the basis of stock price in Professional Consensus and Amateur Consensus strategies.

3. The duration of the study is relatively short: the database spans only eight months, but the management time frame could be much longer. A different time frame and study duration should alter findings.

Conversely we could have improved our Professional Consensus and Amateur Consensus strategies by including portfolio management techniques such as "money management" (position sizing) or making consensus indicator parameters variable and optimising them over a sub-period, etc.

CONCLUSION

This chapter seems to show that there is a certain market inefficiency on the stock market since a strategy based on Amateur Consensus is superior in terms of risk-adjusted yield to the Buy and Hold strategy. Thus Amateur Market Consensus has informative value, which is not the case for Analysts' Market Consensus.

This chapter leads on to a wide range of issues which should be studied in greater detail in the future, serving to make our simulations more realistic, with better understanding and interpretation of results. One line of research would be the study of the stock return momentum effect (see Swinkels, 2004), which could be explained by the opinion inertia we have reported. This opinion inertia is probably due to psychological behaviour, much as overreaction or underreaction cause momentum effects (Daniel, Hirshleider and Subrahmanyam, 1998, and Barberis, Shleifer and Vishny, 1998).

Another possible line of research is to examine whether transaction fees make an Amateur Consensus-based strategy superior to a Buy and Hold strategy, as the market inefficiency obtained by the Amateur Consensus strategy may be insufficient with transaction costs.

The question remains of whether our conclusions on French analysts can be generalized to other analysts in the world. One recent study (Jegadeesh and Kim, 2006) shows that American analysts outperform the analysts of other developed nations. (US analysts are more skilled at identifying mispriced stocks than their foreign counterparts).

REFERENCES

Antweiller W, Frank M (2004). Is All That Talk Just Noise? The Information Content of Internet Stock Message Boards. *The Journal of Finance 59*, 3, June.

Balsara, N. (1992). Money Management Strategies for Futures Traders. *Wiley Finance Editions,* 176-177.

Barberis, N., Shleifer, A. and Vishny, R. (1998). A Model of Investor Sentiment. *Journal of Financial Economics 49*, 307-343.

Coval J, Shumway T (2001Is sound just noise?. The Journal of Finance 56, 5.

Cutler D, Poterba J, Summers L (1989). What Moves Stock Prices?. *NBER Working Paper,* No. W2538.

Daniel, K. D., Hirshleider, D. and Subrahmanyam, A. (1998). Investor Psychology and Security Market Under an Overreaction. *Journal of Finance 53 (6),* 1839-1885.

Engle, R. F., and Patton, A. J. (2001). What Good is a Volatility Model? *Quantitative Finance 1,* 237-245.

Fama, Eugene F. (1970). *Efficient Capital Markets: A Review of Theory and Empirical Work 25, 2.*

Glosten, L. R., Jagannathan, R. and Runkle, D. (1993). On the Relation Between the Expected Value and the Volatility of the Nominal Excess Return on Stocks. *Journal of Finance 48,* 1779-1801.

Jegadeesh, N. and Kim, W. (2006). Value of Analyst Recommendations: International Evidence. *Journal of Financial Markets 9,* 274-309.

Kaastra, I. and Boyd, M. (1996). Designing a Neural Network for Forecasting Financial and Economic Time Series. *Neurocomputing 10,* 215-36.

Kahneman, D. and Tversky, A. (1979). Prospect Theory: An Analysis of Decision-Making under Risk. *Econometrica 47(2),* 263-91.

Lehman, B. (1991). Asset Prices and Intrinsic Value. *Journal of Monetary Economics 28,* 485-500.

Malkiel, Burton G. (1973). *A Random Walk Down Wall Street.* 6th ed. New York: W. W. Norton and Company, Inc.

Mullainathan, S. and Thaler, R. H. (2001). Behavioral Economics. *International Encyclopedia of the Social and Behavioral Sciences,* 1094–1100.

Nolte, I. and Pohlmeier, W. (2007). Using Forecasts of Forecasters to Forecast. *International Journal of Forecasting 23,* 15-82.

Ramnath, S., Rock, S. and Shane, P. (2008). The Financial Analyst Forecasting Literature: A Taxonomy with Suggestions for Further Research. *International Journal of Forecasting 24,* 34-75.

Shiller R (2001). From Efficient Markets Theory to Behavioral Finance, *NBER Working Paper.*

Tetlock, P (2007). Giving Content to Investor Sentiment: The Role of Media in the Stock Market. *The Journal of Finance 62,* 3, 1139-1168.

In: Trust, Globalisation and Market Expansion
Editors: J-M. Aurifeille, C. Medlin and C. Tisdell

ISBN 978-1-60741-812-2
© 2009 Nova Science Publishers, Inc.

Chapter 15

AN EXAMINATION OF TRUST IN CULTURALLY DIVERSE FOOD SUPPLY CHAINS

Peter J. Batt

Curtin University of Technology,
Western Australia, Australia

ABSTRACT

Empirical evidence is presented which suggests that trust is more important in facilitating exchange in the transitional economies. Furthermore, there is evidence to suggest that the various item measures often employed to evaluate trust in Europe, North America and Australia, fail to accurately describe the trust construct in the transitional economies. Further studies are necessary to develop a more robust measure of trust in the context of the transitional economies where social capital is believed to play a much greater role in facilitating exchange.

Keywords: trust, Australia, transitional economies.

1. INTRODUCTION

For some time, trust has been regarded as the critical determinant of a good relationship (Anderson and Narus 1990; Dwyer, Schur and Oh 1987; Morgan and Hunt 1994). Trust reduces the perception of risk associated with opportunistic behaviour, thereby reducing the transaction costs in an exchange relationship (Ganesan 1994). When trust exists, partners in an exchange relationship believe that long-term idiosyncratic investments can be made with limited risk because both parties will refrain from using their power to renege on contracts or to use a change in circumstances to obtain profits in their own favour. Buyer's who trust their suppliers are less likely to use alternative sources of supply and are more likely to accept any short-term inequities that may arise in the exchange relationship in the belief that things will even out in the long-term.

Trust is also the critical determinant of many factors related to performance including the more open exchange of relevant ideas and emotions; greater clarification of goals and problems; more extensive search for alternative courses of action; greater satisfaction with efforts; and greater motivation to implement decisions (Achrol 1997). Trust increases the partner's tolerance for each others behaviour, facilitating the informal resolution of conflict, which in turn, allows the partners to better adapt to the needs and capabilities of their counterpart (Hakansson and Sharma 1996). Trust reduces the need for structural mechanisms of control (Achrol 1997) and, over time, both firms learn to become more interdependent (Kumar 1996).

However, while trust is one of the most extensively researched constructs appearing in the buyer-seller relationship literature, the majority of research and theory development has been undertaken in Europe and North America. To understand trust, Lyon (2000) believes that it is necessary to understand how markets operate in different countries and to be sensitive to local path dependencies, rather than to assume there are universal market forces or conditions that can be transplanted everywhere. Similarly, Moore (1999) suggests that it is dangerous to conflate trust over a wide range of social domains and to assume that one is describing an equivalent phenomenon in all contexts. Trust is not a generic phenomenon nor is it similar in all social domains, for the concept of trust is both emotive and of different emotional significance in different cultures.

While a multitude of trust measures have been employed in the business-to-business literature, there is little empirical evidence to support the extent to which these trust measures may be employed in the transitional economies. To date, the most common measure of trust that has been employed by researchers in the developing world is the question from the World Values Survey that asks, "Generally speaking would you say that most people can be trusted or that you can't be too careful in dealing with people" (Inglehart, Basanez and Moreno 1998). However, such a general question fails to capture the various dimensions of trust that are widely accepted in the business-to-business marketing literature.

In this paper, seven measures of trust developed from the business-to-business marketing literature are employed to explore the extent to which trust is consistent between Australia and three developing countries in South East Asia (Indonesia, the Philippines and Vietnam).

2. THE TRUST CONSTRUCT IN BUSINESS-TO-BUSINESS RELATIONSHIPS

For any potential exchange, trust will be critical if two situational factors are present: risk and incomplete buyer information. Since most potential sales transactions present some degree of risk and uncertainty to the potential buyer, without some degree of trust, the perceived risk may be too great for the transaction to occur (Hawes, Mast and Swan, 1989).

More specifically, trust becomes important in an exchange whenever there is a high level of performance ambiguity and poor product performance will have a significant adverse impact on the value derived by the buyer (Singh and Sirdeshmukh 2000). In such circumstances, trust acts as an information resource that directly reduces the perceived threat of information asymmetry and performance ambiguity.

Anderson and Narus (1990) view trust as a belief that the partner will perform actions that will result in positive outcomes for the firm and will not take unexpected actions that may result in negative outcomes. Moorman, Deshpande and Zaltman (1993) define trust as the willingness to rely on an exchange partner in whom one has confidence.

While both of these definitions view trust as a behavioural intention that reflects reliance on the other partner, both definitions, in part, capture quite different aspects of the construct. Moorman, Deshpande and Zaltman's (1993) definition of trust as a belief, a sentiment or an expectation about an exchange partner, results from the partner's expertise, reliability and intentionality. This component of trust, which Ganesan (1994) describes as credibility, is based on the extent to which the buyer believes that the supplier has the necessary expertise to perform the activity effectively and reliably.

However, trust also relates to the focal firm's intention to rely on their exchange partner. Ganesan (1994) describes this component as benevolence, because it is based on the extent to which the focal firm believes that its partner has intentions and motives beneficial to it. A benevolent partner will subordinate immediate self-interest for the long-term benefit of both parties and will not take actions that may have a negative impact on the firm (Geyskens, Steenkamp and Kumar, 1998).

In building trust in buyer-seller relationships, Sako (1992) finds it necessary to differentiate between trust at three levels. Contractual trust is an expectation that the exchange partner will abide by its written or oral contractual obligations and act according to generally accepted business practice. Competence trust is derived from the assumption that the entrusted firm will carry out the activities competently and reliably. Goodwill trust arises where both parties have developed mutual expectations that the other will do more than what it is formally committed to perform. Here, the firm not only expects the other not to act opportunistically, but that it will, altruistically, go out of its way to help (McCutcheon and Stuart 2000). While history, cumulative interaction and transference may build the lower forms of trust the development of goodwill trust will require not only the absence of exploitation and coercion, but also a history of demonstrated good intentions. Not only must the buying firm demonstrate its trustworthiness, but it must also test the exchange partner's trustworthiness.

While Sako (1992) differentiates between contractual trust, competence trust and goodwill trust, Plank, Reid and Pullins (1999) contest that trust is comprised of three individual components: personal trust, product trust and company trust. Swan, Trawick and Silva (1985) indicate how competence, customer orientation, honesty, dependability and likeability facilitate the development of trust between sales representatives and their customers. Moorman, Deshpande and Zaltman (1993) argue that the interpersonal factors that most affect trust include perceived expertise, sincerity, integrity, tactfulness, timeliness and confidentiality. Crosby, Evans and Cowles (1990) contend that mutual disclosure, a cooperative rather than a competitive intention and the style and intensity of communication between individuals is critical in establishing and maintaining interpersonal relationships.

Similarly, Anderson and Narus (1990), Doney and Cannon (1997) and Smeltzer (1997) find it necessary to differentiate between trust in an individual and trust in an organization. However, since both inter-personal trust and inter-organizational trust are based upon successful exchange experiences with an exchange partner (Sydow 2000), it can become difficult to differentiate between personal trust and organizational trust.

3. METHODOLOGY

The data on which this study is based was drawn from five independent studies; three of which were conducted in South East Asia and two in Western Australia. Data for two of the South East Asian studies was collected from detailed personal interviews with potato farmers in the Philippines (Batt 2002) and Vietnam (Batt 2003a). The third study was undertaken in Bali, Indonesia, where the relationship between vegetable farmers and their preferred trading partner was explored (Batt and Parining 2002).

For the Filipino study, 235 potato farmers in the highlands of Northern Luzon were asked to respond to a comprehensive questionnaire that sought to investigate the nature of the farmer's relationship with their most preferred seed supplier. Farmers were selected from one of five municipalities in proportion to the total area of potatoes planted in Benguet and Mountain Province (Gayao et al. 1997). Given that the majority of potato farmers in Northern Luzon speak English, the survey instrument was written in English and the interviews were conducted in English, although farmers often responded in their native dialect. The interviews were conducted in the farmer's home by a research officer employed by the Highland Agriculture and Resources Research and Development Consortium, Benguet State University, who was fluent in both languages.

For the Vietnamese study, detailed personal interviews were conducted with 60 potato farmers in the Red River Delta that sought to explore the nature of the farmer's relationship with their most preferred potato buyer. Twenty farmers were interviewed from each of the three major potato producing provinces in the Red River Delta (Hai Duong, Thai Binh and Bac Giang). Enumerators interviewed 4 farmers from a minimum of 5 districts, interviewing no more than two farmers from any one village. Interviews were conducted by research staff from the Food Crops Research Institute, Gia Loc. The survey instrument was initially written in English before being translated into Vietnamese by two independent translators. Any discrepancies in translation were resolved in discussion with a third translator.

In Bali, Indonesia, 200 vegetable farmers were asked to respond to a questionnaire that sought to investigate the nature of the farmer's relationship with their most preferred buyer. Equal numbers of farmers (100) were selected from the two major vegetable growing areas of Bedugul and Kitamani, with the only criteria for selection being that the respondent was a full-time vegetable farmer. The survey instrument was again written in English before translation by academic staff at Universitas Udayana to Bahasa Indonesia. Interviews were conducted in the farmer's home by two research assistants from Universitas Udayana.

Data for the two Western Australian studies were taken from the results of mail questionnaires sent to all fresh fruit and vegetable growers which sought to examine the nature of the grower's relationship with their preferred market agent (Batt 2003b) and to all wine grape growers in WA to examine the nature of the growers relationship with their preferred winery (Batt and Wilson 2001).

Using a list provided by the Western Australian Chamber of Fruit and Vegetable Industries, all 1,260 fresh fruit and vegetable growers dealing with market agents in the Perth Metropolitan Market were asked to complete a mail questionnaire. While a response rate of just 16% was considered disappointing (196), responses were received from a broad range of fresh fruit and vegetable growers throughout the state.

From a membership list provided by the Wine Industry Association of Western Australia, all members were provided with a comprehensive questionnaire that sought to explore the nature of the relationship between grape growers and wineries. Two survey instruments were developed. Each of the wineries received a questionnaire asking them about the nature of the relationship they had with their most preferred grape grower. Conversely, each of the grape growers received a questionnaire asking them about the nature of their relationship with their most preferred winery. A total of 32 wineries and 26 grape growers responded to the questionnaire. For the trust construct, as there was no significant difference in the response between grape growers and the wineries with whom they transacted, the results were pooled.

In each of the five studies, trust was evaluated using seven item measures developed from the literature:

1. I trust my most preferred trading partner
   Anderson and Narus (1990), Crosby, Evans and Cowles (1990), Doney and Cannon (1997) Bennett and Gabriel (2001).

2. I have confidence in my preferred trading partner
   Kumar, Scheer and Steenkamp (1995), Campbell (1997)

3. My preferred trading partner has a reputation for being honest
   Doney and Cannon (1997)

4. I believe in the information provided by my preferred trading partner
   Doney and Cannon (1997)

5. My preferred trading partners always keeps their promise
   Crosby, Evans and Cowles (1990), Kumar et al. (1995), Doney and Cannon (1997), Dorsch et al. (1998), Bennett and Gabriel (2001)

6. My preferred trading partner always considers my best interests
   Crosby, Evans and Cowles (1990), Ganesan (1994), Kumar, Scheer and Steenkamp (1995), Doney and Cannon (1997)

7. My preferred trading partner is not always sincere
   Crosby, Evans and Cowles (1990), Kumar, Scheer and Steenkamp (1995), Dorsch, Swanson and Kelly (1998)

For three of the studies (the Philippines, Indonesia and fresh fruit and vegetables), respondents were asked to indicate the extent to which they agreed with the seven item measures on a 7 point Likert scale where 1 was "I disagree a lot" and 7 was "I agree a lot". However, for the two other studies, as only a six point Likert scale had been used, it was necessary to re-code the responses.

To analyse the data, principal component analysis was undertaken using the maximum likelihood estimation procedure with oblique factor rotation, to identify a common trust measure. The goodness-of-fit was ascertained by examining the associated probability and the ratio of the chi-square over the degrees of freedom The contribution that each item made to the resultant latent construct(s) was achieved by applying the reliability coefficient (Cronbach 1951).

4. RESULTS

Principal component analysis initially revealed the presence of two latent constructs. However, one of the item measures (My preferred trading partner is not always sincere) was common to both constructs with loadings of 0.287 and 0.048. When this item was deleted, the subsequent analysis revealed the presence of a single construct, but one item (My preferred trading partner always considers my best interests) was found to have a loading of only 0.502. While the construct had a Cronbach's alpha of 0.703, the diagnostics suggested that if this item was deleted, the Cronbach's alpha could be improved to 0.896. Consequently, this item was also deleted and a third iteration performed. The result was a single construct that collectively explained 64% of the variance, but the chi-square value of 41.5 with 5 degrees of value was considered to be too high and the probability was 0.000. A third variable (I believe the information provided by my preferred trading partner) was deleted on the basis that it contributed the least to the latent construct. The fourth and final iteration revealed a single latent construct that collectively explained 68.9% of the variance. With a probability of 0.002 and a chi-square of 12.3 with 2 degrees of freedom, while considered less than ideal, such was the best solution that could be obtained (Table 1).

Table 1. Principal component analysis

I have confidence in my preferred trading partner	0.895
I trust my most preferred trading partner	0.861
My preferred trading partner has a reputation for being honest	0.845
My preferred trading partner always keeps their promises	0.708
Eigenvalue	2.76
Cronbach's alpha	0.894
Chi-square (df = 2)	12.38
Significance	0.002

From an examination of the summated means and standard deviations, it was apparent that higher levels of trust were present in exchange transactions with preferred trading partners in the transitional economies (Table 2).

For two of the trust measures, "I trust my most preferred trading partner" and "My preferred trading partner always keeps their promises", the mean responses from Vietnam, Indonesia and the Philippines were significantly higher than the means recorded in either of the Australian studies. For the two other item measures, the mean responses from the wine industry were not significantly different from at least one of the South East Asian countries.

In the fresh fruit and vegetable industry study in WA, the mean responses for all four item measures: "I trust my most preferred trading partner", "My preferred trading partner has a reputation for being honest", "I have confidence in my preferred trading partner" and "My preferred trading partner always keeps their promises", were significantly lower than the means recorded in any of the four other studies.

Table 2a. Means of trust measures

	South East Asia			Australia	
	P	I	V	WI	FFV
I trust my most preferred trading partner	6.14[a]	6.16[a]	6.32[a]	5.59[b]	4.77[c]
My preferred trading partner has a reputation for being honest	5.94[ab]	6.22[a]	6.39[a]	5.67[b]	5.03[c]
I have confidence in my preferred trading partner	5.98[bc]	6.17[ab]	6.56[a]	5.64[c]	5.04[d]
My preferred trading partner always keeps their promises	5.59[b]	5.94[b]	6.51[a]	5.05[c]	4.56[d]
Mean	5.91[b]	6.12[ab]	6.44[a]	5.48[c]	4.85[d]

Table 2b. Standard deviation of trust measures

	South East Asia			Australia	
	P	I	V	WI	FFV
I trust my most preferred trading partner	0.596	0.855	1.105	1.352	1.838
My preferred trading partner has a reputation for being honest	0.403	0.877	1.439	1.132	1.679
I have confidence in my preferred trading partner	0.375	0.833	0.772	1.158	1.716
My preferred trading partner always keeps their promises	0.644	0.960	0.878	1.669	1.627
Mean	0.344	0.714	0.757	1.174	1.513

where
  P is the Philippines
  I is Indonesia
  V is Vietnam
  WI is wine industry
  FFV is fresh fruit and vegetable growers
  1 is "I disagree a lot" and 7 is "I agree a lot"
  those items with the same superscript are not significantly different at p = 0.05

CONCLUSION

In the transitional economies, it is abundantly clear that smallholder farmers place much more importance on trust in their economic transactions with preferred trading partners. While Moore (1999) contends that average levels of trust are higher in the world's better governed and more wealthy societies, McMillan and Woodruff (1999) demonstrate that in the transitional economies, where property rights are ill defined and there is no formal legal system to enforce contracts, trust is more important in on-going exchange relationships. Similarly, Lyon (2000) believes that trust is more important in facilitating exchange in the transitional economies. Trust will operate when farmers are more confident that their preferred trading partner will not act opportunistically. Trust comes from the generalized norms of morality (reciprocity), the various sources of information the farmer uses to evaluate a potential partner's reputation and various social sanctions which include the loss of benefits, damage to reputations and social pressure from the community.

Herbig and Milewicz (1995) view reputation as a customer's estimation of the consistency over time of an attribute, based on an evaluation of the supplier's willingness and ability to perform an activity repeatedly in a similar fashion. Similarly, Moorman, Zaltman and Deshpande (1992) regard reputation as an indicator of reliability. Derived primarily from personal experience, perceptions of a supplier's past performance may also be drawn from the various signalling behaviours the supplier undertakes to both develop and maintain its reputation (Fombrun and Shanley 1990). Reputation therefore creates expectations, not only about the key attributes of the supplier, but about how that supplier will behave in the future. Reputation may not only signal a supplier's ability to deliver valued outcomes to its customers in situations of information overload or information inadequacy, but it may also provide an important cue about how its products compare with those from competing firms.

However, in the context of developing long-term buyer-seller relationships in the transitional economies, Fafchamps (1996) describes reputation as a collective coordination and information sharing device which ensures contracts are complied with. In its simplest form, individuals will choose not to interact with those firms who are known not to comply with their contractual obligations. Reputation is a form of social collateral that can guarantee contract performance without prior acquaintance. Concern for ones reputation may be sufficient to ensure compliance and to enable firms to offer credit or take large orders without knowing each other personally. When neither party has any hands-on experience of the others performance, reputation may furnish the partner with a belief system that enables it to organize its behaviour towards a potential partner (Bennett and Gabriel 2001). A good reputation can reduce anxiety and resolve ambiguities.

However, trust is both a dynamic and continuous variable. One can trust and distrust at the same time and thus trust can vary within and between relationships as well as over time (Wicks, Berman and Jones 1999). Smeltzer (1997) considers how trust is influenced by the length of the relationship, the dynamics of the industry, the people involved and the number of times and extent to which trust has been tested in the past. People will generally trust one another until such time as the exchange partner takes various actions to destroy trust and only one instance of opportunistic trading may be enough to destroy trust. Trust is therefore contingent not only upon the stage of development of the relationship (Dwyer, Schur and Oh 1987; Lane 2000), but the cultural norms and values that guide an individual's behaviour and beliefs (Doney and cannon 1997).

In Ghana, Lyon (2000) reports how trust is derived through a common individual, intermediary or guarantor, family linkages and long-term friends, a common ethnic background, attendance at the same church, or the individual's position within the community. Downes, et al. (2002) provide support by describing how language, religious beliefs and educational values impact both on the propensity to trust as well as the process by which trust is developed. La Porta et al. (1997) identify differences in the propensity to trust not only between religious groups but also between the performance of government, civic participation and the economic significance of large firms.

Hewett and Beardon (2001) describe how collectivist societies place greater importance on trust in developing exchange relationships. However, Luff and Kelly (2005) propose that within collectivist societies, there is a sharp distinction between the members of in-groups and out-groups. Collectivist cultures are relatively ineffective with strangers, use avoidance and exploit out-groups more extensively, whereas trust within in-groups is markedly higher. Individualist cultures may be more trusting initially for a wider range of exchange partners than collectivist cultures, but are also more likely to abandon the relationship if it fails to deliver the desired benefits. Collectivists on the other hand take more time and expend more effort in developing trusting relationships, yet once developed, trust may be stronger and more enduring.

Bachmann (2000) reports that the social norm to trust an exchange partner is much stronger in Asia than in Europe or North America. In China, Bjorkman and Kock (1995) describe how trust and the formation of social relationships is a prerequisite for business transactions. Child (2000) describes how trust based relationships within defined family groups protect against opportunism and the very low levels of trust that prevail within Chinese society.

Nevertheless, while it is widely accepted that trust leads to a strong desire to maintain a relationship (Anderson and Narus 1990; Gundlach, Achrol and Mentzer 1995), farmers indicate that the major reason for continuing to trade with their preferred trading partner is the expectation of high returns (Batt 2003b). However, in the fresh produce industry, the sum of the value created tends to be fixed and thin, and thus the issue of dividing it equitably among many channel participants inevitably causes friction and impedes the process of trust building (O'Keffe 1996). Furthermore, in the fresh produce industry, adopting a more relational exchange does not reduce the volatile nature of either supply (quantity and quality) or price which puts more pressure on the relationship.

In examining trust, Luff and Kelly (2005) propose how the size and scope of organizations may influence trust. Sydow (2000) indicates how it is easier for larger firms to trust because they have more power. Fearing retaliation, smaller, less powerful exchange partners are less likely to try to take advantage of them. However, File and Prince (1996) demonstrate that trust is more important within small family firms. Because of the intimate relationship between family interests and needs and those of the business, most small businesses are highly suspicious of unknown suppliers and generally exert much more effort in pre-purchase search and qualifying behaviours when considering new suppliers.

Kool (1994) demonstrates how most farms are small-scale family enterprises. An important aspect of purchasing behaviour on family farms is the interdependence between expenditure on household consumption and farm production inputs. Given a particular income level, a greater expenditure on farm production inputs can only be made at the expense of household consumption and vice versa. As the majority of respondents in this study were small family farms, risk avoidance is likely to result in higher degrees of source loyalty and higher levels of trust in their transactions with preferred trading partners.

REFERENCES

Achrol, R.S. 1997. Changes in the theory of interoganisational relations in marketing: toward a network paradigm, *Journal of the Academy of Marketing Science, 25* (1): 56-71.

Anderson, J.C. and Narus, J.A. 1990. A model of distributor firm and manufacturing firm working relationships, *Journal of Marketing, 54* (1): 42-58.

Bachmann, R. 2000. Conclusion: trust – conceptual aspects of a complex phenomenon, in Lane C. and Bachmann, R. (ed), *Trust Within and Between Organisations*, Oxford University Press: 298-322.

Batt, P.J. and Wilson, H. 2001. Exploring the nature of long-term buyer-seller relationships in the Western Australian wine industry, *Australia New Zealand Wine Industry Journal, 16* (6): 87-96.

Batt, P.J. 2002. Building trust in the Filipino seed potato industry, *Journal of International Food and Agribusiness Marketing, 13* (4): 23-42.

Batt, P.J. and Parining, N. 2002. Trust building behaviour within the Balinese fresh produce industry in Batt, P.J. (ed), *Culture and Collaboration in Distribution Networks.* Proceedings of the inaugural meeting of the IMP Group in Asia, Curtin University [cd]

Batt, P.J. 2003a. Examining the performance of the supply chain for potatoes in the Red River Delta using a pluralistic approach, *Supply Chain Management: an International Journal, 8* (5): 442-454.

Batt, P.J. 2003b. Building trust between growers and market agents, *Supply Chain Management: an International Journal, 8* (1): 65-78.

Bennett, R. and Gabriel, H. 2001. Reputation, trust and supplier commitment: the case of shipping company/seaport relations, *Journal of Business and Industrial Marketing, 16* (6): 424-438.

Bjorkman, I. and Koch, S. 1995. Social relationships and business networks: the case of Western companies in China, *International Business Review, 4* (4): 519-535.

Campbell, A. 1997. Buyer-seller partnerships: flip sides of the same coin? *Journal of Business and Industrial Marketing, 12* (6): 417-434.

Child, J. 2000. Trust and international strategic alliances: the case of Sino-foreign joint ventures, in Lane, C. and Bachmann, R. (ed), *Trust Within and Between Organisations*, Oxford University Press: 241-272.

Cronbach, L.J. (1951). Coefficient alpha and the internal structure of tests. *Psychometrica. 16*: 297-334.

Crosby, L.A., Evans, K.R. and Cowles, D. 1990. Relationship quality in services selling: an interpersonal influence perspective, *Journal of Marketing, 54* (July): 68-81.

Doney, P.M. and Cannon, J.P. 1997. An examination of the nature of trust in buyer-seller relationships, *Journal of Marketing, 61* (April): 35-51.

Dorsch, M.J., Swanson, S.R. and Kelly, S.W. 1998. The role of relationship quality in the stratification of vendors as perceived by customers, *Journal of the Academy of Marketing Science, 26* (2): 128-142.

Downes, M., Hemmasi, M., Graf, L.A., Kelly, L. and Huff, L. 2002. The propensity to trust: a comparative study of United States and Japanese managers, *International Journal of Management, 19* (4): 614-621

Dwyer, F.R., Schurr, P.H. and Oh, S. 1987. Developing buyer-seller relationships, *Journal of Marketing, 51* (April): 11-27.

Fafchamps, M. 1996. The enforcement of commercial contracts in Ghana, *World Development, 24* (3): 427-448.

File, K.M and Prince, R.A. 1996. A psychographic segmentation of industrial family businesses, *Industrial Marketing Management, 25*: 223-234.

Fombrun, C. and Shanley, M. 1990. What's in a name? Reputation building and corporate strategy, *Academy of Management Journal, 33* (2): 233-258.

Ganesan, S. 1994. Determinants of long-term orientation in buyer-seller relationships, *Journal of Marketing, 58* (April): 1-19.

Gayao, B.T., Botangen, A.T., Dati, J., Quindara, H.L., Meldoz, D.T. and Sim, J.V. 1997. *Farm-level Assessment of Potato Production, Marketing and Utilisation in the Highlands of Northern Philippines*. Northern Philippines Root Crops Research and Training Center. Benguet State University. 23 pp.

Geyskens, I., Steenkamp, J-B.E.M. and Kumar, N. 1998. Generalisations about trust in marketing channel relationships using meta-analysis, *International Journal of Research in Marketing, 15* (3): 223-248.

Gundlach, G.T., Achrol, R.S. and Mentzer, J.T. 1995. The structure of commitment in exchange, *Journal of Marketing, Vol 59* (January): 78-92.

Hakansson, H. and Sharma, D.D. 1996. Strategic alliances in a network perspective, in Iacobucci, D. (ed), *Networks in Marketing*, Sage Publications: 108-124.

Hawes, J.M., Mast, K.E. and Swan, J.E. 1989. Trust earning perceptions of sellers and buyers, *Journal of Personal Selling and Sales Management, Vol 9* (Spring): 1-8.

Herbig, P and Milewicz, J. 1995. To be or not to be…credible that is: A model of reputation and credibility among competing firms, *Marketing Intelligence and Planning, 13* (6): 24-33.

Hewett, K. and Beardon, W.O. 2001. Dependence, trust and relational behavior on the part of foreign subsidiary marketing operations: implications for managing global marketing operations, *Journal of Marketing, 65* (October): 51-66.

Inglehart, R., Basanez, M. and Moreno, A. 1998. World Values Survey. University of Michigan Press. Ann Arbor.

Kool, M. 1994. *Buying Behaviour of Farmers*, Wageningen Pers, Wageningen.

Kumar, N., Scheer, L.K. and Steenkamp, J.B. 1995.The effects of supplier fairness on vulnerable resellers, *Journal of Marketing Research, 32* (February): 54-65.

Kumar, N. 1996. The power of trust in manufacturer-retailer relationships, *Harvard Business Review*, November-December: 92-106.

La Porta, R., Lopez de Salanes, F., Shleifer, A. and Vishny, R. 1997. Trust in large organizations, *American Economic Review Papers and Proceedings, 87*: 333-338.

Lane, C. 2000. Introduction: theories and issues in the study of trust, in Lane, C and Bachmann, R. (ed), *Trust Within and Between Organisations*, Oxford University Press: 1-30.

Luff, L. and Kelley, L. 2005. Is collectivism a liability? The impact of culture on organizational trust and customer orientation: a seven nation study, *Journal of Business Research, 58*: 96-102.

Lyon, F. 2000. *Trust, networks and norms: the creation of social capital in agricultural economies in Ghana*, World Development, 28 (4): 663-681.

McCutcheon, D. and Stuart, F.I. 2000. Issues in the choice of supplier alliance partners, *Journal of Operations Management, 18*: 279-301.

McMillan, J. and Woodruff, C. 1999. Interfirm relationships and informal credit in Vietnam, *The Quarterly Journal of Economics*, November: 1285-1320.

Moore. M. 1999. Truth, trust and market transactions: What do we know? *Journal of Development Studies, 36* (1): 74-88.

Moorman, C., Zaltman, G. and Deshpande, R. 1992. Relationships between providers and users of market research: the dynamics of trust within and between organizations, *Journal of Marketing Research, 29* (3): 314-28.

Moorman, C., Deshpande, R. and Zaltman, G. 1993. Factors affecting trust in market research relationships, *Journal of Marketing, 57* (January): 81-101.

Morgan, R.M. and Hunt, S.D. 1994. The commitment-trust theory of relationship marketing, *Journal of Marketing, 58* (July): 20-38.

O'Keffe, M. 1996. Establishing supply chain partnerships: lessons from Australian agribusiness, *Supply Chain Management: An International Journal, 3* (1): 5-9.

Plank, R.E., Reid, D.A. and Pullins, E.B. 1999. Perceived trust in business-to-business sales: a new measure, *Journal of Personal Selling and Sales Management, 14* (3): 61-71.

Sako, M. 1992. *Prices, quality and trust. Inter-firm relations in Britain and Japan.* Cambridge University Press.

Singh, J. and Sirdeshmukh, D. 2000. Agency and trust mechanisms in consumer satisfaction and loyalty judgements, *Journal of the Academy of Marketing Science, 28* (1): 150-167.

Smeltzer, L.R. 1997. The meaning and origin of trust in buyer-seller relationships, *International Journal of Purchasing and Materials Management*, Winter: 40-48.

Sydow, J. 2000. Understanding the constitution of interorganisational trust, in Lane, C and Bachmann, R. (ed), *Trust Within and Between Organisations*, Oxford University Press: 31-63.

Swan, J.E., Trawick, I.F. and Silva, D.W. 1985. How industrial salespeople gain customer trust, *Industrial Marketing Management, 14* (August): 203-211.

Wicks, A.C., Berman, S.L. and Jones, T.M. 1999. The structure of optimal trust: moral and strategic implications, *Academy of Management Review, 24* (1): 99-116.

INDEX

Y